BIOLOGY
for Christian Schools® SECOND ED.
LABORATORY MANUAL

by William S. Pinkston, Jr.

Bob Jones University Press, Greenville, South Carolina 29614

This textbook was written by members of the faculty and staff of Bob Jones University. Standing for the "old-time religion" and the absolute authority of the Bible since 1927, Bob Jones University is the world's leading Fundamentalist Christian university. The staff of the University is devoted to educating Christian men and women to be servants of Jesus Christ in all walks of life.

Providing unparalleled academic excellence, Bob Jones University prepares its students through its offering of over one hundred majors, while its fervent spiritual emphasis prepares their minds and hearts for service and devotion to the Lord Jesus Christ.

If you would like more information about the spiritual and academic opportunities available at Bob Jones University, please call
1-800-BJ-AND-ME (1-800-252-6363).
www.bju.edu

NOTE:
The fact that materials produced by other publishers may be referred to in this volume does not constitute an endorsement by Bob Jones University Press of the content or theological position of materials produced by such publishers. The position of the Bob Jones University Press, and the University itself, is well known. Any references and ancillary materials are listed as an aid to the student or the teacher and in an attempt to maintain the accepted academic standards of the publishing industry.

Laboratory Manual: BIOLOGY for Christian Schools®
Second Edition

William S. Pinkston Jr.

Produced in cooperation with the Bob Jones University Division of Natural Science of the College of Arts and Science and Bob Jones Academy.

for Christian Schools is a registered trademark of Bob Jones University Press.

© 1991, 1999 Bob Jones University Press
Greenville, South Carolina 29614

Printed in the United States of America
All rights reserved

ISBN 0-89084-592-1

15   14   13   12   11

Contents

Introduction

I learned something while walking in a park with a young, blind friend. I was telling him about some of the differences among various trees and shrubs in the park while he was busily feeling bark, leaves, twigs, and flowers. Suddenly his lips went tight, and he knitted his brow. "What's wrong?" I asked.

"It was a bird, wasn't it?" he answered. We were at the edge of a large plaza, and on the other side of it pigeons were busily gathering their lunch. One straggling bird had swooped down near us and then glided across the plaza to join the others.

"Yes," I answered. "Do birds bother you?" I was thinking of taking him to a friend's home to meet a pet cockatiel. "Have you ever touched a bird?"

"Oh, yes, but they come and go so quickly. I never know where they are when they are flying. They catch me off guard and frighten me a little. I know what a bird is, but since I can't see it fly, I don't really understand it."

Students often face a similar problem. It is one thing to read about an object you are not familiar with, listen to a person talk about it, look at pictures of it, and even memorize facts about it. It is quite another matter to actually look at the object, handle it, or do something with it. Sometimes you do not really understand the object being discussed until you become personally familiar with it. It would not be uncommon for a high school biology student to answer correctly every question on a quiz about *Spirogyra* but be surprised to learn that "the stuff in that dish is real *Spirogyra*." But the student who has learned all about *Spirogyra* and then has looked at it, placed some on a slide, and examined it through a microscope does not easily forget the "green stringy stuff," even though he may forget its name. One of the primary purposes of these laboratory exercises is to provide a framework in which you can increase your understanding by becoming personally acquainted with various biological processes and organisms.

A second purpose is to help you study. By asking you to do certain tasks and to answer particular questions (some requiring merely looking up the answer, others requiring thought, and some requiring experimentation), these exercises should help you learn without having to memorize cold facts. It is a well-known educational principle that working with a piece of information not only aids in learning it but also makes it more usable to the learner. This principle lies behind writing themes in English class and working problems in math class.

Of course, you can learn from your themes and math problems only if you work on them faithfully and carefully. Otherwise, they become a burden and, for some students, a game to see how few they can do yet still pass the course. These students lose the benefit of these exercises because they have the wrong approach to their work. The same is true of laboratory work in a high school science course. If you approach it as "something I don't want to do" or as "something that the teacher requires us to do," you will lose many of its benefits. Your attitude toward the laboratory exercises will greatly influence how much you will benefit from them.

The laboratory exercises in this book are designed to go along with *BIOLOGY for Christian Schools*®. As you cover the material in the textbook (referred to in this manual as the text), your teacher will tell you what laboratory exercises you will be expected to do and when they are to be handed in. A laboratory exercise is an assignment on which any student, if he is faithful and diligent, can earn a good grade. The teacher will be able to judge the effort you have put forth by looking at how well you did the laboratory exercises. Do your best on them.

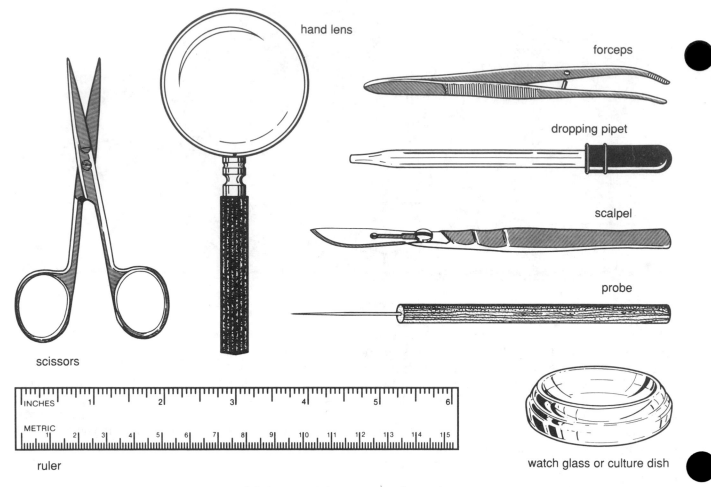

I-1 *Student laboratory equipment*

Equipment

The laboratory equipment necessary for doing these exercises will be provided. Some of the basic tools frequently used in the biology laboratory are illustrated and named in Diagram I-1. Learn the proper names and uses for these tools. Other pieces of equipment (such as the microscope) will be described in the exercises as each piece is needed.

On laboratory days you should be sure to have the following:

❑ *BIOLOGY for Christian Schools*
❑ *Laboratory Manual: BIOLOGY for Christian Schools®*
❑ a large loose-leaf notebook with lined loose-leaf paper for taking class notes and holding returned laboratory exercises
❑ a pencil and an eraser for laboratory drawings

For certain lab days you may also want to bring a protective garment (an old, large shirt to be worn over your school clothes), colored pencils, and hand cream. These pieces of equipment are optional.

Be sure to report all damaged equipment, even if you are not responsible for breaking it. If you are found using a piece of damaged equipment, it may be assumed that you are responsible for breaking the equipment unless you report the damage before you start using it. The policy of your school may be to bill you for such damage or for damage you cause because of carelessness.

Drawings

One of the most common cries echoing through every high school biology laboratory is "But, I can't draw!" This is often more a blessing than a blight. A good scientific drawing does not require artistic ability as much as it requires a good eye, a steady hand, and a lot of eraser.

Let us look at some of the reasons for drawing scientific specimens. Making drawings is one of the best ways to learn some of the complex biological structures and processes. If, however, you feel that a drawing is just bothersome busywork, you will gain little from your drawings. Try a more positive approach. Before attempting a drawing, find out what the text has to say concerning the organism. Look at pictures of the specimen. Then, as you draw the specimen, concentrate on its shape, color, function, name, location, and any other characteristics you can think of. By the time you have finished, you should *know* it.

Some drawings are meant to be a challenge. You will occasionally be asked to draw something that your text does not discuss. In such cases you will need to consult other texts in order to find enough information to make an intelligent drawing. Students commonly try to draw objects they do not understand. Such a drawing will profit little. However, when you have found the necessary information for yourself, you will not quickly forget what you have worked to achieve.

Students often find themselves copying. They do not actually put a sheet of paper over a picture and trace the object, but they sit with a textbook drawing in front of them and reproduce it without really thinking about what they are drawing. This method can produce a beautiful drawing, but drawings made without concentration and thought bring little profit. For guidance, consult drawings of the specimens you are working on but *never copy them*.

Spaces are provided for most of the drawings you will make in these laboratory exercises. Occasionally, if you need to begin a drawing again or you are doing a drawing for which there is not a space, you will need to make a drawing on your own paper. Always use unlined, white paper; typing paper (not the coated, erasable variety) is good.

I-2 *A specimen drawing*

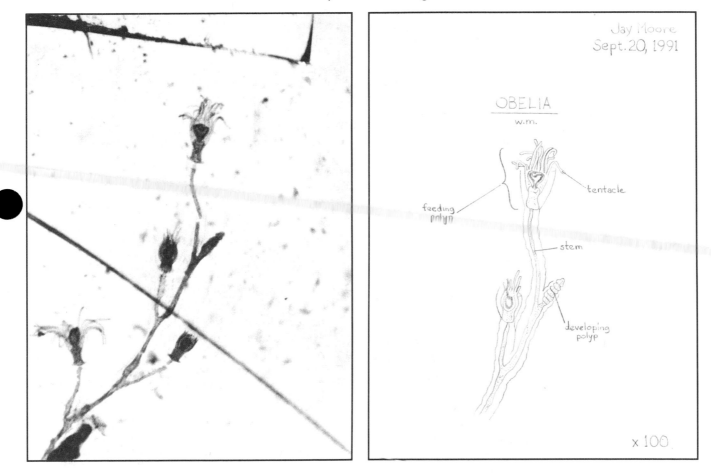

Kinds of Scientific Drawings

Within these laboratory exercises you will be asked to do two different types of drawings:

- **The specimen drawing** is made to show exactly what a specimen looks like. It is drawn from an actual specimen, not from a diagram or a picture in a book. Good specimen drawings can be seen on the bottom of pages 271 and 281 in your text.
- **The schematic drawing** is often a stylized representation to show a process or a relationship, and therefore it often does not look exactly like the specimen. On page 115 of your text is a group of schematic diagrams which do not look like the photographs on the bottom of the page, even though they represent the same process. The schematic drawings explain what is taking place in the process being illustrated.

Requirements for a Good Drawing

- Print all information in the same style. Make all printed material parallel with the bottom edge of the paper.
- Put your name in the upper right-hand corner of the drawing and the date the drawing was made below your name. (If you are making your drawing in spaces provided in this book, your name and the date on the laboratory exercise sheet are sufficient.)
- Center the name of the specimen above the drawing. If the drawing is of a portion of an organism, indicate the portion in the title or under the title. For example, "Fruit fly, leg" indicates that the drawing is of the leg of a fruit fly. The title "Fruit fly" alone indicates a drawing of the entire fly, no matter how much it looks like a leg.
- If the specimen has been prepared in some way before being drawn, indicate this under the name of the specimen. (See Methods of Slide Preparation on the next page.)
- Make the drawing large and center it in the space available.
- Do not use shading and color for specimen drawings. Stippling (holding a pencil in a vertical position and tapping the point on the paper) may be used sparingly. In stippling, the dots are all the same size, and a darkened area is obtained by having many dots. Schematic drawings are often made with colored pencils or pens. A colorful drawing should not be a goal in itself, but color may be used if it *aids understanding*.
- Add labels after the drawing is complete. The label lines should be straight and never cross each other. They should not have arrowheads on them. They should go directly to the object they indicate and touch it or be drawn into it.
- Label everything in the drawing. If you are doing a specimen drawing but do not see some object on your specimen that you know should be there, *do not* take the liberty of drawing it in. In specimen drawings, draw only what you see in the specimen. In schematic drawings, you may take liberties to aid understanding.
- If you used the microscope, indicate the power in the lower right-hand corner. If you used some other type of magnification (such as a hand lens), write "magnified" or "enlarged" in that corner.
- Do not draw the microscope field or the container the specimen is in.

Normal Laboratory Procedure

Normally, the sequence for completing the laboratory exercises is as follows:

1. The lab day and the day the exercise is due will be announced a few days in advance.
2. Before you come to class each lab day, you are expected to **read the assigned laboratory exercise completely** and **do as much of the work as possible.** Sections or questions in the laboratory exercises that are marked with an asterisk (*) can be done without the use of laboratory equipment and can be completed before the lab day.
3. On the lab day, you and your laboratory partner will have enough class time to accomplish the work that requires laboratory equipment if you are prepared and work efficiently. Sometimes answering questions about your work can be done outside of class, allowing you more in-class time to complete the laboratory work.
4. The sections that you do not finish during the classroom laboratory time become part of your homework. If this requires the use of laboratory equipment, you will need to come to the laboratory at announced after-school times or make arrangements with your teacher to finish the work at some other time.

5. Remove your completed laboratory exercise from this book and staple it together with any other materials that the exercise may call for (such as reports or drawings on your own paper) and hand them in on the date they are due. (This date will generally be several days after the lab day.)
6. The laboratory exercise will be graded and handed back in a few days.
7. Place the returned laboratory exercise in a loose-leaf notebook and **keep it.**
8. At the end of the grading period, the loose-leaf notebook, containing all the laboratory exercises you will have done by then, will be turned in for evaluation. Be careful not to lose laboratory exercises.

Required / Extra / Omit

When the teacher gives you the assignment, you will need to mark in your laboratory exercise what parts of the assignment your class will be doing. For each section of the exercise, there are boxes like this:

Methods of Slide Preparation

Term	Abbreviation	Description
Whole mount	w.m.	The entire specimen (e.g., flea) or the entire part of a specimen (e.g., fly leg) is on the slide.
Wet mount	w.m.	A temporarily prepared slide on which the specimen is placed in water.
Preserved slide		A slide on which the specimen is mounted in a medium that permanently keeps the specimen.
Cross section	c.s. or c.x.	The specimen has been cut crosswise
Longitudinal section	l.s. or l.x.	The specimen has been cut lengthwise.
Teased		The specimen has been shredded into pieces.
Smeared		The specimen has been smeared across the slide.
Stained		The specimen has been exposed to dyes in order to color structures.

If your teacher tells you that you are expected to do a particular section of the lab, mark box "R" for "required." If your teacher tells you that you may do a section for extra credit, mark "E" for "extra." If your teacher tells you that you are not to do a section, mark box "O" for "omit."

The extra credit sections will require additional time, and you may have to return to the laboratory after class time. If you are having difficulty with the tests, if your last lab grade was not as good as you had wanted, or if you have been doing poorly on quizzes, you are encouraged to do some of the extra credit sections to gain points. If you are doing well in the course, you should do an extra credit section only if it sounds exceptionally interesting. Extra credit sections must be done *before the laboratory exercise is handed in;* they may not be done at the end of the course to improve your grade.

Late Laboratory Work

Points will be deducted from the score of a laboratory exercise for each day it is late. Normally, laboratory exercises will not be accepted if they are more than 3 days late. If, however, you experience unusual difficulties, talk to your teacher to see if an exception can be made.

The loose-leaf notebook containing all the graded laboratory exercises is due at the end of the grading period; it must be handed in on time, or points will be deducted. If exceptional circumstances cause the notebook to be late, see your teacher.

Frequently, when living organisms are used in a laboratory exercise, you must immediately make up any laboratory exercises that you miss. The organisms may not be available for an extended time.

Tips for Preparing Laboratory Work

- **Mark the drawings you need to make** when you read the laboratory exercise before coming to class. Then check them off as you finish them.
- **Note carefully what you did wrong** when you receive a graded lab, and do not make the same mistakes again. For example, if you are told that your label lines are sloppy on your first drawings, use a ruler to draw the lines on other drawings.
- **Follow carefully the instructions** given in the laboratory exercise. They will usually answer your questions. Most of the points you miss on laboratory exercises will be for either not doing a section or not following directions carefully.
- **The subpoints under a larger point pertain to the larger point.** Since the subpoints usually explain or give more detailed instruction, be sure to read all of the subpoints before you begin work.
- **Do what you can at home** either before you come to class on lab day or after lab day (but before the laboratory exercise is due).
- **Consult your text for material concerning your laboratory work.** If the laboratory exercise tells you to read certain pages in the text, do so. Coming to a lab day unprepared to do a laboratory exercise is a waste of time. Do your best to know what you are doing.

Conduct and Honor System

Some of the materials and tools used in the laboratory are extremely dangerous if they are misused. For this reason, **do not engage in horseplay at any time.** Horseplay is *any use of any piece of laboratory equipment for a purpose for which it was not intended.* Your teacher will impose severe penalties if you commit this offense.

Do *your own work* for this class. Do not obtain answers from other students or their work. This is cheating. Your teacher may allow students to help each other by discussing the material and sharing sources of information, but *you should never tell each other answers or copy each other's work.* Handing in your laboratory exercise is your statement that you have not cheated. If you have difficulties, see your instructor for help. Occasionally, your teacher may give you special permission to use someone else's work as a source when you are making up work.

1A–The Scientific Method

Materials: drawing compass or caliper, ruler

Goals:

To devise a problem that can be solved using the scientific method

To devise an experiment that will supply data to determine an answer to the problem

To collect and interpret data

To analyze and interpret data obtained

To learn the steps of the scientific method

While writing a report on the nervous system, Tom read this information in an encyclopedia:

A nerve is stimulated by touching its endings. One nerve may branch to several nerve endings located in the same area of the skin. If two branches of the same nerve are touched at the same time, only one sensation is felt. The impulses may come from two nerve endings, but since they must travel along the same nerve to the brain, the brain senses only one point. If, however, the nerve endings of two different nerves are touched, the person feels two distinct sensations. This phenomenon, called two-point perception, is easy to demonstrate.

Tom started thinking as he studied the illustration (see Diagram 1A-1). He wondered if nerve endings covered an area of the same size in all the parts of the body. How much area did the nerve endings for each nerve cover? He called his brother and asked him to look at the other side of the room. Tom then took his compass and lightly touched his brother's arm with its two points, holding them in place. He asked his brother how many points he felt. He repeated the action, adjusting the distance between the points. He found that his brother sometimes felt only one point when the back of his hand was touched with the two points of the compass. Tom thought of several problems and experiments that he would like to try.

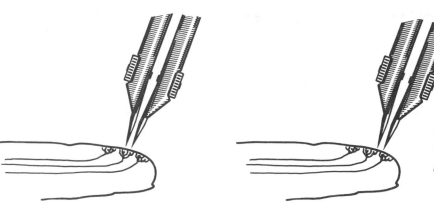

1A-1 *An illustration of two-point perception, using points of a caliper. The person on the left feels one point, while the person on the right feels two.*

*Preliminary Work

Your class will suggest experiments dealing with two-point perception, choose a problem, design and conduct an experiment to supply data that can be used to determine an answer to the problem, and arrive at a conclusion. For this experiment you may use only a drawing compass (or caliper) and a ruler. (Of course, you should also have a pencil, paper, and other classroom materials.) Before you come to class, devise a few problems about two-point perception that you consider interesting and that the class could experiment with. Complete the material below before you come to class so that you can suggest a possible experiment.

I. List several problems dealing with two-point perception which could be used in class.
- Be sure your problems are worded as questions that have limitations and can be answered with yes, no, or a number.
- Avoid problems that might involve danger (e.g., placing compass points on the face) or those you would not be able to test (such as comparing red-haired people with blond-haired people when you have only one red-haired person in your class).

- List possible problems for the experiment. _____
_____
_____
_____
_____

II. Develop the problem you consider the best one by answering the following questions.
- What problem do you consider the best? _____
_____
_____

- What hypothesis would you suggest for this problem? _____
_____

- Describe the steps of an experiment that will supply data either to support or contradict your hypothesis. (Attach additional paper if necessary.) _____
_____
_____
_____
_____
_____
_____

  ❑ What is your experimental variable (single variable)? _____
  _____

  ❑ List the precautions you would take to limit other variables. _____
  _____
  _____
  _____
  _____
  _____
  _____
  _____

  ❑ What is serving as your control group? _____
  _____
  _____

In-Class Procedures

At the beginning of the laboratory period, the class will choose a problem suggested by one of its members. As a group you will then devise an experiment and determine exactly how it will be conducted. The class will then divide into groups and conduct the experiment. Results of the experiment will be recorded on a chart and will be interpreted on the following day. As the class decides which problems to use and devises the experiment to conduct, record this information in the spaces below. (Use additional paper if necessary.)

I. Our problem is– _____

_____

II. Our hypothesis is– _____

_____

III. Our experiment involves– _____

_____

_____

- Our experimental variable is– _____

_____

- Steps taken to limit the variables include the following: _____

_____

_____

_____

_____

_____

_____

- Our procedure for the experiment is as follows: _____

_____

_____

_____

_____

_____

_____

- My observations of problems encountered while conducting the experiment include the following: _____

_____

_____

_____

_____

_____

*Summary

The day following the experiment, the class will interpret the data obtained. After your in-class discussion, answer the following questions.

  I. Regarding the data:
- Do the data tend to support the hypothesis? ☐ yes ☐ no
- What conclusions can be drawn from your data? _____
  _____
  _____
  _____
  _____

  II. Personal observations:
- Were limitations to the problem and controls upon the experiment enough to supply reliable data? ☐ yes ☐ no
- What could you have done to improve the limitations and controls? _____
  _____
  _____
  _____
  _____
  _____
  _____

- Can you think of any additional changes that need to be made? _____
  _____
  _____

- Was the experiment repeated often enough to give reliable data? ☐ yes ☐ no
  How often would be enough to give reliable data? _____
  _____

- Based upon your experience, what other experiments dealing with two-point perception would you like to try? _____
  _____
  _____
  _____

1B–The Microscope

Materials: microscope, hand lens, lens paper, tissue, preserved slides of colored threads and desmids or diatoms, illuminator, immersion oil

Goals:

To learn the basic parts of the microscope
To learn how to operate a microscope properly
To become familiar with the theory of magnification
To make a scientific drawing

> As you study biology, you will need various pieces of equipment to test, measure, or observe living things. The microscope is probably the most useful, as well as one of the most technical, pieces of equipment found in the average high school laboratory. Because of the knowledge that can be obtained by using a modern microscope, today's biology student is frequently better informed in some aspects of biological knowledge than the professional biologist of one hundred years ago.
>
> The microscope is a precision instrument that uses magnification and light refraction to produce an enlarged image. Though durable and easy to handle, the microscope requires proper care. Since repairing or replacing this piece of equipment is expensive, every biology student needs to know how its parts function and how to operate it correctly.

*The Structure of a Microscope

Identify and label the parts of the microscope on Diagram 1B-1. You should be thoroughly familiar with the terms and be able to locate each part on a standard microscope in your classroom.

I. The mechanical parts
- **Body tube:** This long, narrow tube runs half the length of the microscope. The observer looks into one end, and the specimen is placed under the other end. The fixed separation allows the lenses to remain the proper distance apart during viewing.
- **Revolving nosepiece:** A movable disc at the bottom of the body tube allows the interchanging of different sets of lenses (objectives).
- **Coarse adjustment knobs:** There is a large knob on each side of the microscope, usually located directly behind the body tube. These knobs provide great movement of the body tube and quick focusing of the specimen.
- **Fine adjustment knobs:** Usually small, these knobs are found underneath the coarse adjustment knobs or near the inclination joint. By providing slight movement of the body tube, the fine adjustment produces a sharper focus.
- **Arm:** The "backbone" of the microscope; the arm supports the body tube.
- **Base:** The large, usually horseshoe-shaped structure at the bottom of the microscope; the base supports the microscope and keeps it steady.
- **Inclination joint:** Located at the junction between the arm and the base of the microscope, the inclination joint allows the microscope to be tilted.
- **Stage:** A platform positioned directly below the objectives and above the mirror or light source; the stage supports the specimen.
- **Stage clips:** The fastenings on top of the stage hold the slide containing the specimen firmly in place.

II. The optical parts
- **Eyepiece** or **ocular:** Located at the top of the body tube, the eyepiece contains lenses which help increase magnification of the specimen.
- **Objectives:** Two or three metal extensions extend from the bottom of the revolving

nosepiece and contain lenses that produce different magnifications.
- **Diaphragm:** Located between the stage and the mirror, the diaphragm regulates the amount of light that passes through the specimen. (Two types of diaphragms are the *iris diaphragm,* which opens and closes like the iris of an eye, and the *disc diaphragm,* which is a disc with holes of various sizes.)
- **Substage condenser:** Also located between the stage and the mirror, this lens system affects the microscope's resolution by bending and concentrating light before it reaches the specimen. (Some microscopes do not have one.)
- **Mirror:** Found just above the base, the mirror reflects light up toward the stage. (Some microscopes have a built-in electric light source.)

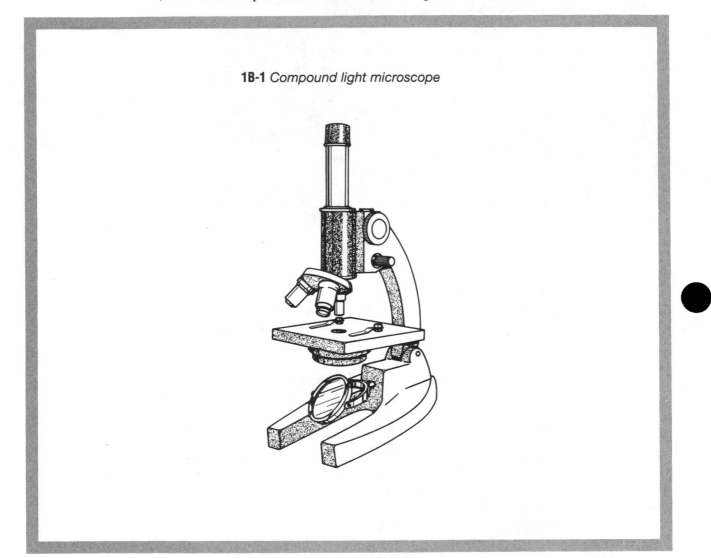

1B-1 *Compound light microscope*

Care of a Microscope

I. Carry the microscope properly. Excessive jars and bumps may knock the lenses out of adjustment.
- When taking a microscope out of the cabinet or cupboard, be careful not to bump the microscope against the sides.
- Carry the microscope with one hand underneath the base and the other on the arm.
- Be sure to keep the microscope close to your body in an upright position so that the ocular does not slip out of the body tube.
- Place the microscope gently on the table about three inches from the edge.

II. Prepare the microscope properly. Your microscope may need to be cleaned before you begin to use it.
   - Use lens paper to clean lens surfaces and the mirror.
     - ❏ Wipe the lenses in one direction across the diameter of the lens.
     - ❏ Dust collected on the lens may be ground in if you use a circular motion and may scratch the lenses.
   - Consult your instructor if any material remains on your objectives. You may need to use a solvent to remove the material. *Never* use your fingernail or another object to chip away hardened material.
   - Under no circumstances should you attempt to take your microscope apart.

III. Return the microscope properly. When returning a microscope after you have used it, be sure to follow this routine:
   - Adjust the inclination joint so that the body tube is straight up and down.
   - Remove the slide from the stage.
   - Put the low-power objective directly under the body tube.
   - Adjust the body tube to its lowest position.
   - Carefully return the microscope to the place where you obtained it.

R E O Obtaining an Image with a Microscope

In order to observe the specimens clearly and easily, you will need to follow carefully the procedures discussed in this section. After you have done these procedures a few times, they will become second nature, and you will be able to do them quickly. Some of the procedures, such as computing the power of your microscope, will need to be done only once; others will need to be done every time you focus on a new specimen. Carefully note all the procedures. If difficulties arise, review these instructions and make sure you have not missed something. Of course, if you have any difficulty, your instructor can help you.

I. Compute the powers available on your microscope.
   - Because of the microscope's magnifying powers, you are able to see organisms many times larger than their actual size. Each increase in power reveals a closer look at the specimen.
   - Written on the parts of the microscope that have magnifying lenses are powers. *Power* in this case refers to the number of times larger the magnified object will appear. Therefore, the total magnification is the product of the magnifying powers of both the ocular and the objective lenses. (Be sure to use only the power of the objective that is directly above the specimen when computing the total power of your microscope. The other objectives are not in use until they are placed over the specimen.)
   - Using the information and the powers found on your microscope, fill in the chart below.

Computing the Magnification of a Microscope

Place the power (number of times it magnifies) of each part of your microscope in the proper space, and then compute the total magnification for each objective.

	Ocular		Objective		Total Magnification
Low-power objective	_____ × times		_____ ×	=	_____ ×
High-power objective	_____ × times		_____ ×	=	_____ ×
Oil-immersion objective	_____ × times		_____ ×	=	_____ ×
Other	_____ × times		_____ ×	=	_____ ×

(Some microscopes do not have an oil-immersion objective; if yours does not, omit that line of the chart. If your microscope has other objectives, include them on separate lines.)

---

*• Answer the following:

❏ Why should the substage condenser not be included in computing the magnification? _____

_____

_____

❏ What aspect of the microscope does the substage condenser affect? _____

_____

II. Obtain the proper light in your microscope.

• You must have proper lighting for satisfactory use of your microscope.

❏ Begin by opening the diaphragm so that it admits as much light as possible. Look under the stage to see if the diaphragm is open completely.

○ To adjust the iris diaphragm, move the tiny lever located under the stage forward or backward.

○ To adjust a disc diaphragm, rotate the dial until the largest hole is properly aligned.

❏ If your microscope has a built-in light source, simply plug it in and turn the switch on.

❏ If your microscope has a mirror, adjust it to provide adequate lighting.

○ Natural light (sunlight) is the best, but *not direct* sunlight, which could damage the eye, leaving a permanent afterimage.

○ Make sure no object comes between the mirror of your microscope and the light source.

○ Use the curved rather than the flat side of the mirror to obtain an even, unobscured circle of light which fills your field of vision.

○ Look through the eyepiece and adjust the mirror.

*• Normally we see light that reflects from an object or light that radiates from something such as a candle flame. In a microscope, however, light is reflected from the mirror and passes through the lenses to our eyes. How are we able to see a specimen placed on the stage of the microscope when no light is reflected from the specimen?

_____

_____

©1995 Bob Jones Press. Reproduction prohibited.

Microscope Slides

The specimen is usually mounted on a **glass slide** and covered with a **coverslip.**

• Be sure the slide is clean before you use it. *Prepared* or *preserved slides* (those professionally made) may be cleaned with a tissue or lens paper. Do not scratch the slide.

• Unless already noted on the label of the slide, all cracks or damage should be reported to your instructor.

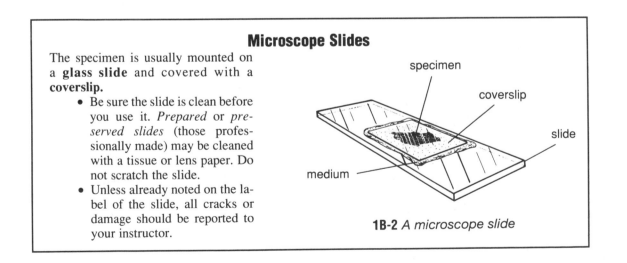

1B-2 *A microscope slide*

III. Position the specimen.
  - Obtain a preserved slide of either diatoms or desmids.
  - Place the slide on the stage, directly over the opening in the stage.
    ❏ Make sure that the coverslip is on top, or you will have trouble focusing.
    ❏ Place the stage clips on both ends of the slide (but not on the coverslip) to hold the slide in place.
  - Position the slide so that the specimen is centered in the opening of the stage.
    ❏ To move the slide on the stage, place your thumbs on opposite corners of the slide and push or pull the slide into position.
    ❏ Use dry slides on the stage of a microscope. If the lower surface of the slide is wet, it tends to form a suction that makes the slide very difficult to move and may cause damage.

IV. Focus the microscope on low power.
  - Focus your microscope, following these steps:
    1. Raise the body tube using the coarse adjustment knob and move the 10× objective clockwise until it fits directly below the body tube. You should hear a click when the objective reaches the correct position.
    2. Looking at your microscope from the side, turn the coarse adjustment knob to move the body tube down toward the stage. Stop when the objective is just above the slide. (Some microscopes have safety devices that will stop the body tube automatically.)
    3. Look into the ocular and carefully move the body tube up slowly until the specimen is brought into view. (The body tube usually moves upward when the coarse adjustment knob is turned toward you; however, look into the ocular while moving it.) (*NOTE:* **Never turn the coarse adjustment knob so that the body tube goes downward while you are looking in the eyepiece.**)
    4. Now use the fine adjustment knob to get sharper images. One turn in either direction is usually enough to focus properly. Do not spin the knob; you could damage the mechanism.
    5. If no image comes into view by the time you have moved the objective one inch from the coverslip, you probably–
       ○ Tried to focus too fast and passed the point of focus. Start at number 2 above and try again.
       ○ Did not have a specimen in your field of view. Check to make sure there is something on the slide directly in the center of the hole in the stage. Then try again.
       ○ Have too much light. Use a slightly smaller opening of your diaphragm and try again.
    6. If you still cannot obtain an image, ask your instructor for help.
  - Note some of the effects of using the light microscope.
    ❏ If you move the slide to the right, how does the position of the material change in your field of view? _____
    ❏ Turn the fine adjustment knob slowly to move the objective up or down. Describe what happens to the image you are viewing. _____
    _____
    _____

V. Prepare a specimen drawing of desmids or diatoms. Follow these instructions:
  - Draw five specimens in Area A. You may obtain all the specimens from one slide. Draw either desmids or diatoms, whichever you are looking at.
  - Make sure you are drawing typical specimens, not just odd globs you find on your slide.
  - These specimens have been preserved and stained; they will not appear green as the ones in your text do.
  - For this set of drawings, draw only the outlines of your specimens. Ignore the internal structures.

R
E
O

Using High Power on Your Microscope

I. Observe a desmid or diatom using high power (400×-450×)
   - Center the desmid or diatom of your choice in your microscope field. Why is it essential to position the specimen in the center? _____

_____

_____

   - Focus your microscope first on low power and then go to high power, following these instructions:
     - On the nosepiece of most microscopes are several objectives. Most modern microscopes are **parfocal:** if a microscope is focused on a specimen using one power, all the objectives will be nearly in focus for that specimen (unless the specimen is exceptionally thick). Most parfocal microscopes can be focused on a higher power with only $\frac{1}{4}$ turn of the fine adjustment knob.
     - All you need to do to change a parfocal microscope to high power (about 400×-450×, but not oil-immersion power, which is about 1,000×) is rotate the nosepiece.
     - While you do so, look at the stage from the side to be sure that the objective does not touch the slide as it clicks into place.

II. Prepare a specimen drawing of a section of a desmid or diatom in Area B. Include the internal structures.

A

B

How to Use the Oil-Immersion Power on Your Microscope

I. Follow these procedures carefully when using oil-immersion objectives.
- Be sure you have a very bright light source. An illuminator is usually necessary.
- Following the procedures given earlier, focus on low power and then change to high power.
- Make sure that what you wish to observe is in the center of the microscope field.
- Raise the tube from the slide.
- Place one small drop of immersion oil on the slide.
  - ❏ The drop should be centered on the coverslip.
  - ❏ Do not get oil on the label of the slide.
- Turn the nosepiece so that the oil-immersion objective (96×-100×) is down.
- Adjust the tube so that the objective touches the drop of oil. Observing from the side, continue adjustment until the objective almost touches the slide.
- Observing through the microscope, adjust the tube very slowly until focus is obtained. The fine adjustment knob is best for this purpose and usually needs to be turned less than one full rotation.
- If the objective is raised so high that the oil separates from the objective, you have passed the point of focus. Repeat the two preceding steps.
- Focus problems often result from too much light. Adjust the diaphragm.
- If the object was centered when you focused using the lower powers, it will be centered under oil-immersion power. If it is not, carefully move the slide to the correct position.
- When you finish, clean the microscope and the slide carefully, following these steps:
  1. Remove excess oil from the slide and objective with a dry tissue.
  2. Clean the slide with a wet tissue, being careful not to wet the label. Dry the slide thoroughly before returning it.
  3. Clean the objective thoroughly with a wet tissue. Pat it dry with a dry tissue.
  4. Polish the objective with lens paper.

II. Using oil-immersion power, observe a desmid or diatom and draw a portion of the specimen in Area C. Include the internal structures.

C

How a Microscope Works

Microscopes work because light bends as it passes through substances of different densities. However, the higher the magnification is, the more difficulties are encountered with resolution and depth of focus. An understanding of these problems is necessary for good microscope use.

I. Reverse image
  - Observe what happens to light rays that are reflected from this paper when they pass through hand lenses by doing the following:
    ❑ Hold two hand lenses, one on top of the other, about four inches from the paper.
    ❑ Hold your head about fourteen inches from the hand lenses.
    ❑ Focus by moving your head.
  - Explain why the image is inverted. You may use diagrams if necessary.

_____

_____

1B-3 *Two hand lenses*

II. Problems with increasing magnification and depth of focus
  - Using low power, focus on a slide of three intersecting threads.

    ❑ Why is the intersection of the three threads black? _____

    _____

    _____

    ❑ By adjusting the focus, you should be able to see all of a thread clearly.
  - Observe the intersection of the three threads on high power, following these steps:
    ❑ With the microscope on low power, move the slide so that the intersection of the three threads is in the exact center of your field of view.
    ❑ Focus your microscope on high power. Now that you have changed powers, note the different size of the black spot in the center of the junction of the three threads.
      ○ Adjust the position of your slide until all three threads are visible.
      ○ You probably will not be able to see all three threads at once because they are stacked and you have limited depth of focus while using high power.
      ○ Using the fine adjustment knob, determine the sequence of threads at the

        intersection. From top to bottom, they are _____

        _____ .

    ❑ Although higher powers of the light microscope allow you to see more detail,

      they present other difficulties. What are they? _____

      _____

      _____

2–Osmosis and Digestion

Materials: osmometer (a semipermeable membrane, a thistle-shaped bulb, a tube, and a beaker), wax marking pencil, distilled water, sucrose solutions, sucrose solutions with invertase, plastic squeeze bottles, dropping pipets, reagent test strips for glucose in urine, metric ruler

Goals:

> To observe a demonstration of osmosis
> To observe various factors affecting the rate of osmosis
> To learn about the action of an enzyme

> An osmometer is a device used to measure the rate of osmosis. A semipermeable membrane is stretched across the large open end of a bulb and filled with a solution. When the bulb is suspended in another solution, the osmosis that occurs can be measured by observing the rise or fall of the solution in the tube above the bulb. (See Diagram 2-1.) In this exercise several osmometers, containing different solutions, will be set up. The rates of osmosis for these solutions will be compared. The data will be collected, and each student will then form a conclusion about osmosis and digestion.

A Demonstration of Osmosis and Digestion

I. Set up the osmometer properly.
- Assemble the bulb and tube.
  - ❑ The osmometer bulbs will be soaking in water before you come to class so that the membranes will be ready to use.
  - ❑ Remove all water from the osmometer bulb by shaking it.
  - ❑ Using a plastic squeeze bottle with a narrow spout, completely fill the osmometer bulb with the proper solution. Set the bulb on a wet paper towel.
  - ❑ Remove the cap from a plastic squeeze bottle of the same solution you used to fill the osmometer bulb. Insert the tube into the bottle. Using the tube like a drinking straw, draw up a 2-inch column of the solution. Put your finger over the open end of the tube to keep the solution in the tube.
  - ❑ Place the tube into the neck of the osmometer bulb, releasing your finger just as the tube contacts the bulb. An inch or more of the solution should remain in the tube.
  - ❑ Tap the bottom of the membrane to remove any air trapped in the bulb. There should be no air spaces in the solution in either the bulb or the tube. If there are gaps that cannot be removed by tapping, take the tube out and start again.

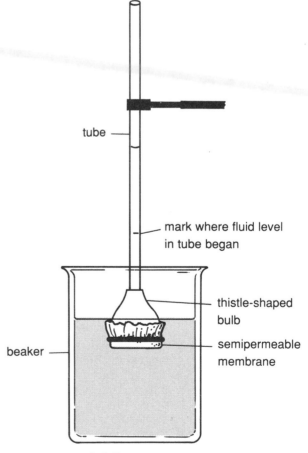

2-1 *Osmometer*

❑ Using a paper towel, dry the joint between the bulb and the tube. If the joint leaks, ask your instructor to help.

❑ Rinse the outside of the bulb with clean water.

❑ Mount the osmometer bulb in the solution.

❑ Fill the beaker of the osmometer with water to a depth of about 2 inches.

❑ Suspend the osmometer bulb in the water so that the membrane is covered but the water does not come near the joint of the bulb and tube. (Several methods of suspension can be used. Your instructor will demonstrate the method you should use.)

❑ Mark with a wax pencil the level of the solution in the tube.

II. Test for the presence of sugar.

- Some substances change color in the presence of certain chemicals. Often these substances are used to test for the presence of the chemicals.

- A *reagent test strip* is usually a piece of absorbent material containing a substance that changes color when a solution containing the proper chemical is placed on it.

- For this laboratory exercise, use the reagent test strip that tests for sugar in urine. The strip changes color in the presence of sugar.

- Each group must establish a set of controls for their reagent test strip.

  ❑ Using a clean dropping pipet, place a single drop of distilled water on a reagent test strip. Do not touch the pipet to the test strip. Note the color of the strip after ten seconds. This demonstrates a *negative reaction* (no change in color) since there is no sugar in the water.

  ❑ Using a clean dropping pipet, place a single drop of sugar solution (*Solution A*) on a reagent test strip. Be careful not to touch the pipet to the test strip. Note the color of the strip after ten seconds. Since there was sugar in the solution, you should see a *positive reaction* (change in color).

III. Set up the experiment.

- Solutions of **sucrose** (table sugar, a disaccharide) will be placed in the bulbs.

  ❑ There are two different concentrations of sucrose: *Solution A* contains twice as much sucrose per unit of volume as *Solution B*.

  ❑ **Invertase** (an enzyme also called *sucrase*) will be added to some of the sucrose solutions before they are placed in the bulbs. The sucrose solutions that contain invertase have the same concentration of this enzyme.

  ❑ Each group in the class will be given one of the following solutions to place in their osmometer bulb:

    1. Group 1–*Solution A*
    2. Group 2–*Solution A with invertase*
    3. Group 3–*Solution B*
    4. Group 4–*Solution B with invertase*

- The bottom container (beaker) will hold distilled water.

IV. Run the experiment.

- Set up the osmometers, mark the level of the fluid in the tubes, and test a drop of the fluid in the beakers of the osmometer to see if the fluid contains sugar.

- After ten minutes:

  ❑ Use a metric ruler to measure how far the fluid has risen in the tubes.

  ❑ Test a drop of fluid from the beakers for the presence of sugar.

  ❑ Record your results on the chart on page 15. Check *P* if the sugar test was positive, *N* if the sugar test was negative.

- Repeat the above procedure every ten minutes until the class hour ends.

- Toward the end of the class hour, the data from the groups will be exchanged. You will need all the data from all the groups in order to answer the following questions.

	Start	10 min.	20 min.	30 min.	40 min.	50 min.
Solution A	0 mm ☐ P ☐ N Sugar	____ mm ☐ P ☐ N Sugar	____ mm ☐ P ☐ N Sugar	____ mm ☐ P ☐ N Sugar	____ mm ☐ P ☐ N Sugar	____ mm ☐ P ☐ N Sugar
Solution A with Invertase	0 mm ☐ P ☐ N Sugar	____ mm ☐ P ☐ N Sugar	____ mm ☐ P ☐ N Sugar	____ mm ☐ P ☐ N Sugar	____ mm ☐ P ☐ N Sugar	____ mm ☐ P ☐ N Sugar
Solution B	0 mm ☐ P ☐ N Sugar	____ mm ☐ P ☐ N Sugar	____ mm ☐ P ☐ N Sugar	____ mm ☐ P ☐ N Sugar	____ mm ☐ P ☐ N Sugar	____ mm ☐ P ☐ N Sugar
Solution B with Invertase	0 mm ☐ P ☐ N Sugar	____ mm ☐ P ☐ N Sugar	____ mm ☐ P ☐ N Sugar	____ mm ☐ P ☐ N Sugar	____ mm ☐ P ☐ N Sugar	____ mm ☐ P ☐ N Sugar

*Questions to Answer After the Experiment

Carefully read the following discussions in your text: diffusion and osmosis, pages 51-53; catalysts and enzymes, pages 54, 57, 59-60; and sugars, pages 61-63.

I. From the results of the experiment, what can you conclude about the permeability of the membrane to sucrose? _____

_____

II. Was there a difference between the increase of *Solution A* and the increase of *Solution B* in the tubes?   ☐ yes   ☐ no   If so, what would account for the difference?

_____

_____

III. How does invertase (sucrase) affect sucrose? (Base your answer on the results of the experiment and on information in the laboratory exercise and text. You have enough information to figure out the answer.) _____

_____

Explain how you reached that conclusion. _____

_____

_____

IV. Was there a difference between the sugar contents in the beaker of *Solution A* and in the beaker of *Solution A with invertase*?   ☐ yes   ☐ no

If so, what would account for the difference? _____

_____

_____

_____

V. Was there a difference between the increase of *Solution A* and the increase of *Solution A with invertase* in the tubes?   □ yes   □ no   If so, what would account for the difference?

_____

_____

_____

_____

VI. What comparisons can you make between the results obtained from *Solution A with invertase* and those obtained from *Solution B with invertase*? _____

_____

_____

_____

Can you account for these differences? _____

_____

_____

_____

3A–Basic Cytology

Materials: cotton swabs, cork, coverslips, dissection kit, glass slides, methylene blue, microscope, nut, onion, single-edged razor

Goals:

To learn the basic technique of preparing a wet mount

To observe cell walls

To observe whole cells

To observe the effect of stains on specimens for the microscope

In your biological studies, you will need to know how to prepare a wet mount, a temporary microscope slide in which the specimen is mounted in water or some other fluid. After you have read about how to prepare a wet mount, we will practice the technique by doing what Hooke did to observe for the first time what he called cells.

Cells are the basic structural and functional units of all living organisms. Whether an organism is microscopic and single celled (like an ameba or a bacterium) or multicellular (like your body), a study of an organism's cells is important.

Cells from both plants and animals can be easily studied in the laboratory. The onion will represent plants for this laboratory exercise. Though it may appear dead, the onion is a living bulb that produces roots and leaves when planted. The cells in the lining of your own mouth will represent living "animal" cells.

How to Prepare a Wet Mount

Preparing the Slides and Coverslips

- Hold glass slides and coverslips *by their edges* so that you do not leave fingerprints on them.
- Thoroughly rinse a glass slide and a coverslip by following these instructions:
  - ❏ Be careful not to bend plastic coverslips. If you are using a glass coverslip, handle it gently; splinters from shattered glass coverslips easily enter the fingers and may require surgical removal.
  - ❏ Inspect plastic coverslips for excessive scratches. If too many scratches appear, discard the coverslip.
  - ❏ Use only water when washing the slides and coverslips. Soap film may kill or damage living specimens. If you cannot clean your slide completely by rinsing it in water, take it to your instructor and obtain another slide.
- Thoroughly dry the slide.
  - ❏ Shake excess water into the sink.
  - ❏ Blot the slide and coverslip with a paper towel.
  - ❏ Finish drying with a soft tissue.
- Set the glass slide and the coverslip on the edge of a book or table so that you can pick them up by the edges without getting fingerprints on them.

3A-1 *Method of handling glass slides*

Mounting the Specimen

- Place the specimen on the slide by following one of these techniques:
  - ❏ *If the specimen is small (unicellular or colonial) and already in a fluid medium,* use a dropping pipet to place a single drop of the specimen-containing medium on the center of the slide.

(continued on next page)

❏ *If the specimen is large (a tissue or a clump of organisms),* follow these steps:
1. Using a dropping pipet, place a small drop of water (or culture medium) on the slide.
2. Using forceps, place the specimen in the drop of water.
3. If necessary, prepare (smear or tease) the specimen.
4. If the specimen remains dry on top, place another drop of water (or culture medium) on top of the specimen.

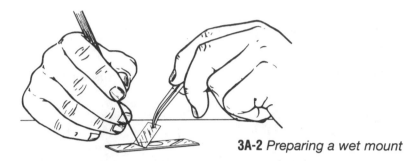

3A-2 *Preparing a wet mount*

- Place the coverslip on top of the specimen by following these instructions:
  ❏ Place the coverslip so that one edge is touching the slide and the coverslip is held at a 45° angle above the drop of water.
  ❏ Slowly lay the coverslip down on top of the water and specimen.
  ❏ If bubbles appear in the area you are going to view, tap the coverslip with the tip of a probe in order to remove the bubbles.
  ❏ If too many bubbles appear, take the wet mount apart and start again.
  ❏ If you have used too much water, you may need to blot dry the bottom of the slide before placing it on the microscope stage. You may also need to remove excess water from around the coverslip by lightly touching a paper towel to the water. Absorption will remove the water.

Cleaning Up and Putting Away the Wet Mount
- When you finish observing the slide, remove the coverslip and specimen. (If a stain was used, it is wise to use forceps.)
  ❏ If the specimen is microscopic in size, rinse it down the drain.
  ❏ If the specimen is large (a tissue or clump of organisms), wrap it in a paper towel and put the paper towel in the trash can.
- Rinse the slide and coverslip in running water.
- Shake the excess water into the sink.
- Place the slides and coverslips in the places provided.
  ❏ You do not need to dry the slide and coverslip completely.
  ❏ *Do not stack the slides or the coverslips.* When dry, they will be impossible to separate.

Observing Cork Cells

Over 300 years ago Robert Hooke discovered that certain plant tissues are made up of what he called "cells." To get a proper perspective of cytology, we will repeat his experiment. To see cork cells well, you must use a very thin slice of cork only one to two cells thick. If suitable slices of cork are provided for you, begin at Section II below. If you must cut your own, begin at Section I.

I. Cut a sliver of cork by following these instructions:
- Take the small cork stopper (piece of cork) and insert it into a hexagonal nut.
  ❏ Twist it carefully so that the flat surface of the cork does not become crooked inside the nut.
  ❏ As the cork reaches the other side, continue to turn it until it barely protrudes beyond the nut.

3A-3 *Slicing cork*

- Run a single-edged razor blade along the surface of the nut, carefully cutting into the cork. You do not need to get an entire cross section of the cork, but the section you use must be very thin.

II. Prepare a wet mount of cork by following these instructions:
- Pick up your cork slice carefully (it may crumble) and position it on top of the water of your wet mount.
- Add another drop of water on top of the cork slice before putting on the coverslip.
- If your coverslip "teeter-totters" on the cork, your slice of cork is too thick. Start again.

III. Observe the wet mount of cork on low power.
- When you observe wet mounts, remember that the microscope stage must remain parallel to the floor. Why is this necessary? _____

  _____

- Can you see any internal cellular structures in the cork cells?   ☐ yes   ☐ no

  Explain. _____

- You are, of course, observing dead cork. What cellular structure are you observing?

  _____

Onion Epidermal Cells

I. Observe onion epidermal cells.
- Obtain the scale of a small onion.
  - ❑ A *scale* is one of the layers of the onion.
  - ❑ The thin, transparent skin on the inside surface of the scale is the *epidermis* of the onion.
- Remove a layer of onion epidermis by following these instructions:

3A-4 *Removing the onion epidermis*

  - ❑ Take the scale and break it. At the edges of the broken scale, you should be able to see a portion of the epidermis.
  - ❑ Use your forceps to remove the thin sheet of cells.
  - ❑ Do not crush or wrinkle the epidermis. Otherwise, cells become damaged and air bubbles get trapped between the layers, making it hard to observe.
- Prepare a wet mount, using a small piece of onion epidermis no larger than the drop of water on your slide.
  - ❑ Place the onion epidermis so that it lies flat. If it begins to fold or curl, use probes to straighten it.
  - ❑ Put the second drop of water on it and then put the coverslip on. You may need your lab partner's help.
- Observe the onion epidermis cells under low power.
  - ❑ What is the general shape of one onion epidermal cell? _____

    _____

    Of a group? _____

    _____

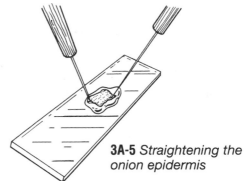

3A-5 *Straightening the onion epidermis*

  - ❑ What do the cork and onion cells have in common? _____

    _____

    _____

    _____

  *❑ Mark the terms that apply to onion epidermis:
  ☐ unicellular   ☐ multicellular   ☐ tissue   ☐ organ   ☐ system

R E O

II. Stain your onion epidermal cells and observe them again.

- Stain the cells by following these steps:
  - ❑ Carefully remove the slide from the stage and place it next to the microscope.
  - ❑ Place one drop of methylene blue on the slide at the very edge of the coverslip, in contact with the water under the coverslip.
  - ❑ At the opposite side, touch a paper towel to the water under the edge of the coverslip, allowing the paper to absorb the water. The stain will be drawn under the coverslip. (If the stain runs over the outside edges of the coverslip, you probably used too much water when you made your wet mount. Use paper towels to absorb the excess water and try again.

  - ❑ When the stain has contacted the onion epidermis, blot away any excess fluids on the slide or coverslip.

3A-6 *A method of staining cells in a wet mount*

  - ❑ Allow the stain to remain on the slide 3 to 5 minutes before observing the specimen. This permits the stain to enter the cells.

- Observe the stained onion epidermis on low and on high power.
  - ❑ What can you see that differs from your observation of an unstained onion epidermis? _____
  - ❑ Look among the cells until you find a dark, circular structure inside one of them. What is it? _____
  - ❑ Frequently, darker spots can be seen within this dark structure. What are they?

_____

_____

R E O

- In Area A, make a drawing of one onion cell with a few adjoining cells to show how the cells fit together. Follow these instructions:
  - ❑ Draw the internal structures for the main cell only.
  - ❑ Label only the structures you see in your specimen.
  - ❑ Use the power you feel is best, but be sure to indicate which power you used to prepare your drawing.

A

Human Cheek Epithelial Cells

I. Prepare a wet mount of your cheek cells (or those of your lab partner) by following these instructions:

- Collect some mucous epithelial cells by rubbing a cotton swab back and forth inside your cheek.
  - ❏ You should collect cells from only your own mouth.
  - ❏ To get the greatest concentration of cells, do not twirl the swab around, but use only one side.
- Remove the swab carefully, collecting as little saliva as possible.
- Smear the cells on the area of the clean slide that will be covered by the coverslip.
- Break off the used cotton head of the swab and discard it.
- Place one drop of diluted methylene blue stain on top of the smear. With the broken end of your swab (not the unused cotton head), spread the stain over all the cells without touching the slide with the stick.
- After this is done, carefully add the coverslip. Why do you need to be careful when you place the coverslip on top? _____

  _____

  _____

II. View the cheek cells under low power.

- Look for isolated cells, not clumps.
- How can you tell the epithelial cells from the other debris that appears on the slide?

  _____

*• These cells are called *mucous epithelial cells*. What does the word *mucous* tell us about the functions of these cells? (For help, use the index of your textbook.)

  _____

  _____

  _____

III. Draw a single cheek epithelial cell in Area B.

- After you have found the cell you wish to draw, center it and then adjust your microscope to high power.
- Draw one epithelial cell and label all the parts you see.

B

Comparing Onion Epidermal and Cheek Epithelial Cells

R
E
O

I. What are some of the similarities between the onion epidermal cells and the cheek epithelial cells? _____

_____

_____

_____

_____

II. What are some of their differences? _____

_____

_____

_____

_____

3B–Cellular Organelles and Processes

Materials: *Anacharis* (or *Elodea*) leaves, banana, methylene blue, dissection kit, (illuminator), cotton swabs, salt solution, microscope, glass slides, coverslips, concavity slides, iodine

Goals:
>   To study some specific cellular organelles
>   To observe cellular reaction to a salt solution

Anacharis is a common freshwater aquatic plant noted for its photosynthetic abilities. The edges of this plant's young leaves are thin enough to make possible microscopic viewing of living plant cells. You can see some colored organelles by observing these unstained, living plant cells. Also, some cellular processes and reactions can be demonstrated. Other plant organelles not visible in *Anacharis* can be seen in stained banana cells.

Observe *Anacharis (Elodea)* cells

I. Prepare a wet mount of an *Anacharis* leaf by following these instructions:
  - Use only young, light green leaves from the ends of the stem.
  - Use a concavity slide (a slide with a concave depression in it). This type of slide will permit the thick leaf to be mounted and will allow the coverslip to lie flat. Use enough water to fill the concave portion of the slide.
  - Be careful not to crush the leaf as you pick it up or mount it. (Often scissors and forceps help.)

II. Observe *Anacharis* cells, using both the high power and the low power of the microscope.
  - Be sure you are focused on cells on the margin (edge) of the leaf.
  - The green chloroplasts make the clear, unstained nucleus difficult to see.
  - By focusing at different depths in one cell, locate the large, clear area in the center of the cell (not the nucleus). What is this area called? _____
  - Observe the **cytoplasmic streaming** (carrying with it the chloroplasts) in the *Anacharis* cells.
  - If your specimen is not demonstrating any streaming, place the slide under an illuminator for 2 to 5 minutes. (Sometimes even this procedure does not help.)
  - If your specimen does exhibit cytoplasmic streaming, tell the instructor so that others can observe yours.
  *- Why would cytoplasmic streaming be valuable for cells that have many chloroplasts?

  _____

III. Make a drawing of two or three adjacent *Anacharis* cells in Area A. Use the power you think best for drawing them.

IV. Place the *Anacharis* leaf in a concentrated salt solution.
  - Because the cells may react quickly, do not remove the slide from the stage. One lab partner should observe the specimen while the other performs the following operations.
    - Using the same procedure used to stain onion epidermal cells in Lab 3A, draw a concentrated salt solution under the coverslip.
    - You may need to use 2 or 3 drops. The change may take up to 2 minutes.
  - Describe the change in the appearance of the cells. _____

  _____

  _____

• Describe the reasons for the change within the *Anacharis* cells. (You may need to do research in your text to explain the change.) ————————————————

——————————————————————————————————————

——————————————————————————————————————

Observe Leucoplasts in Banana Cells

R
E
O
I. Answer the following questions before beginning:

*• What are leucoplasts? ————————————————————————————

*• What is the major function of leucoplasts? ——————————————————

*• In what plant structures would you expect to find leucoplasts? ——————————

——————————————————————————————————————

R
E
O
II. Observe leucoplasts in banana cells.
• Using the broken end of a cotton swab (or a toothpick) make a smear wet mount of a small amount of mashed banana.
• Observe the slide on both the low power and the high power of your microscope.

What do you see? ———————————————————————————————
• Stain the slide with an iodine stain. (*NOTE:* Iodine turns starch dark.)
   ❏ Use the same procedure for staining as was used to stain the onion epidermis in Lab 3A.
   ❏ Observe the slide. What do you see now? ——————————————————

——————————————————————————————————————

R
E
O
III. Prepare a drawing of a stained banana cell in Area B and label as many parts as you can.

A

B

4–Photosynthesis

Materials: *Elodea,* glass funnels, glass beakers, test tubes, metal or plastic blocks (nonfloating material), metric ruler, thermometers, desk lamps, pH test papers, dilute acetic acid (vinegar), baking soda

Goals:

To observe the results of photosynthesis in an aquatic plant

To determine the conditions for photosynthesis in a plant

Elodea densa is a common freshwater plant that is known for its rapid growth and oxygen-producing ability. It produces stems that are 10-13 feet long and covered with short, flat leaves that grow in whorls of four. The most actively growing parts are the ends of the stems. The stem tips are composed of a rosette of immature leaves.

As photosynthesis takes place in many aquatic plants, the oxygen produced travels along tubes in the stem. The rate of photosynthesis can be measured by the amount of oxygen produced. If the stem of *Elodea* is cut, the oxygen produced during photosynthesis escapes and bubbles to the surface.

In this exercise you will measure the amount of photosynthesis happening in *Elodea* by measuring the oxygen given off. By setting up the same experiment under different conditions, you should be able to draw some conclusions regarding the ideal conditions for photosynthesis in *Elodea.*

An Apparatus to Measure Photosynthesis

I. The apparatus (Diagram 4-1)

- Prepare a large quantity of the proper medium in a container with a large opening.
- Fill the beaker with the proper medium.
- Place three or more blocks on the bottom of the beaker to support the funnel.
- Place the funnel in the beaker so that it rests on the blocks. (*NOTE:* The funnel's stem should be lower than the surface of the medium.)
- Fill the test tube with medium and place it above the funnel by following these instructions:
  - ❏ Place the test tube in the large container of the medium.
  - ❏ While the test tube is under the medium, cover the end of the test tube. (A glass plate can be used, but using your thumb to cover the end of the test tube works best.)
  - ❏ Remove the test tube from the medium, holding the cover in place so that no medium escapes.
  - ❏ Place the covered end of the test tube in the beaker under the level of the medium and remove the covering. If air gets into the top of the test tube, remove the test tube and repeat the process until your test tube contains no air.
- Move the test tube so that it covers the end of the funnel and can be suspended as shown in the diagram.

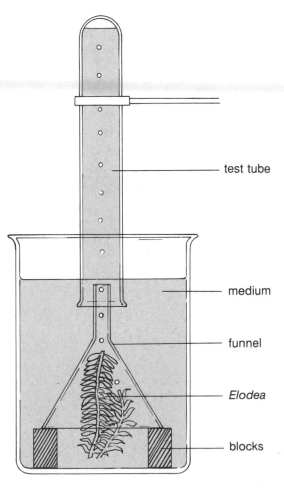

4-1 *Apparatus to measure photosynthesis*

II. The *Elodea*
- Cut a 5-8 cm section (or sections, if your glass funnels are large enough) of the growing end of an *Elodea* stem.
- Place the *Elodea* sections in the media of the beaker and gently shake them until all air bubbles are freed. (Gas introduced to the funnel with the *Elodea* will spoil the results of the experiment.)
- While holding the funnel in place, use forceps to place the *Elodea* section(s) in the funnel. The cut end should be pointing up the tube.
- When you set up experiments to compare the quantity of photosynthesis taking place, be sure you use *Elodea* pieces that are similar in length, quantity of leaves, and color.

Experiments to Determine Conditions for Photosynthesis

I. Devise a set of experiments to determine under which conditions *Elodea* carries on photosynthesis best.
- Choose from the following list a condition with which your class wishes to experiment.
  - ❏ *Light intensity* (Use different areas that naturally receive different light intensities such as a dim corner, a window ledge, a desk in the classroom, under a bright lamp, or you may use a light meter to set up areas with different light intensities.)
  - ❏ *pH* (Use vinegar and baking soda to arrive at media that have different pH values. Test papers will be needed to determine their pH.)
  - ❏ *Temperature* (Various temperatures can be established and maintained by using ice, hot water, or other methods.)
- Be sure you design an experiment that will involve only one experimental variable.
  - ❏ The light intensity can affect the temperature if steps are not taken to prevent it.
  - ❏ The experiment may need to be carried on for several hours, and constant temperatures are often difficult to maintain for that length of time without careful supervision.
- Plan to observe your experiments every 30-60 minutes for several hours.
II. Run the experiments and record your data on the chart on page 27.
III. Answer the following questions.
- What factor (experimental variable) did you test? _____
- Based on your data, is photosynthesis affected by the factor you were testing?
  ☐ yes   ☐ no
- At what range of the factor did photosynthesis happen at the fastest rate? _____
- At what range of the factor did photosynthesis happen at the slowest rate? _____
- What can you summarize regarding the rate of photosynthesis and the factor you were

  testing? _____

  _____

  _____

  _____

Conditions for Photosynthesis

Experimental Variable	Time	Oxygen in Test Tube	Temperature
Experiment 1: _____	_____ _____ _____ _____	_____ mm _____ mm _____ mm _____ mm	_____ _____ _____ _____
Experiment 2: _____	_____ _____ _____ _____	_____ mm _____ mm _____ mm _____ mm	_____ _____ _____ _____
Experiment 3: _____	_____ _____ _____ _____	_____ mm _____ mm _____ mm _____ mm	_____ _____ _____ _____
Experiment 4: _____	_____ _____ _____ _____	_____ mm _____ mm _____ mm _____ mm	_____ _____ _____ _____

- Were the other factors held constant?   ☐ yes   ☐ no
  - Were these factors held within acceptable limits to give reliable data?
    ☐ yes   ☐ no
    - If no, indicate which ones fluctuated too far. _____
      _____
    - If yes and the factor was not constant, indicate why you feel the fluctuation
      is acceptable. _____
      _____
      _____
  - What steps would you recommend to improve the experiment you performed?

    _____

    _____

5A–Mitosis and Meiosis

Materials: microscope, preserved slides of *Allium* root tips, l.s., and whitefish embryos prepared for viewing mitosis

Goals:

To clarify understanding of mitosis and learn its stages by drawing progressive diagrams

To observe cells in various stages of mitosis

To compare mitosis and meiosis

To clarify understanding of meiosis

> Cell division is one of the basic biological processes. To understand thoroughly what happens during mitosis, however, you must understand what happens to the chromosomes in each of the phases.
>
> After you master the process and significance of mitosis, you can understand meiosis (which forms gametes) and fertilization (which unites gametes). In order to grasp genetics and the concepts involved in the debate between biological evolution and creationism, you must understand the basic processes of mitosis and meiosis.

*A Description of Mitosis

To help your understanding of mitosis, use your text as a reference and fill in the following descriptions of the phases of **animal mitosis** before you begin your observations and drawings.

I. Prophase
- Outside the nucleus:
  - The centrioles _____ .
  - The aster _____ .
  - The nuclear membrane _____ .
- Inside the nucleus:
  - The chromosomes _____ .
  - The nucleolus _____ .
  - The centromere _____ .

II. Metaphase
- The centromeres of the chromosomes are located _____ .
- Metaphase ends as _____ .

III. Anaphase
- The sister chromatids _____ .
- The centromeres _____ .
- The daughter chromosomes _____ .

IV. Telophase
- Forming the nuclei:
  - The daughter chromosomes _____ .
  - At each centriole _____ .
  - The nuclear membrane _____ .
  - The nucleoli _____ .

- Outside the nucleus:
    - ❏ The spindle _____.
    - ❏ The centrioles _____.
    - ❏ The plasma membrane _____.
    - ❏ The cytoplasm _____.

Observing Mitosis in Plant Cells

[R] [E] [O] In certain plant parts, mitosis is carried on by almost all the cells. If these areas are properly stained, chromosomes in the various phases of mitosis are easy to see.

I. Observe mitosis in a prepared root tip of *Allium* (onion).
- Obtain a preserved slide of an *Allium* root tip.
    - ❏ Notice the way the root tip(s) has been sectioned (see p. ix). Name and describe this type of sectioning. _____
      _____
    - *❏ Mitosis is carried on in an area just above the root cap, a protective group of cells located at the very tip of the root. What is the name of this area? (Research in your text may be necessary.) _____
- Examine your slide under the microscope.
    - ❏ Using low power, locate the root cap and the area where mitosis is carried on.
    - ❏ Using high power, observe various stages of mitosis.
        - ○ Why do some of the root cells have no chromatin material? (Hint: how was the onion root cut to make this type of slide?) _____
          _____
        - ○ Find a cell in anaphase and as accurately as possible, tell how many chromosomes are found in an onion cell. _____
        - *○ You will probably not see all the chromosomes. How many chromosomes are in an onion cell? (Research in your text.) _____
        - *○ Account for the difference between the number you saw and the actual number.
          _____
          _____

[R] [E] [O] II. Draw a series of specimen drawings showing mitosis in *Allium* root tips.
- Make sure you draw typical specimens of the various stages of mitosis. If the first one you find is not good, look for another.
- Draw one cell in each of the following phases in the spaces provided on the next page.
    1. Interphase
    2. Prophase
    3. Metaphase
    4. Anaphase
    5. Telophase
    6. Daughter cells
- All the drawings must be individually labeled.
- A timesaving tip: It is not necessary for you to draw the interphase first. If you find a good metaphase, draw it in the metaphase space; then look for another phase. The drawings, however, must be in the proper boxes.

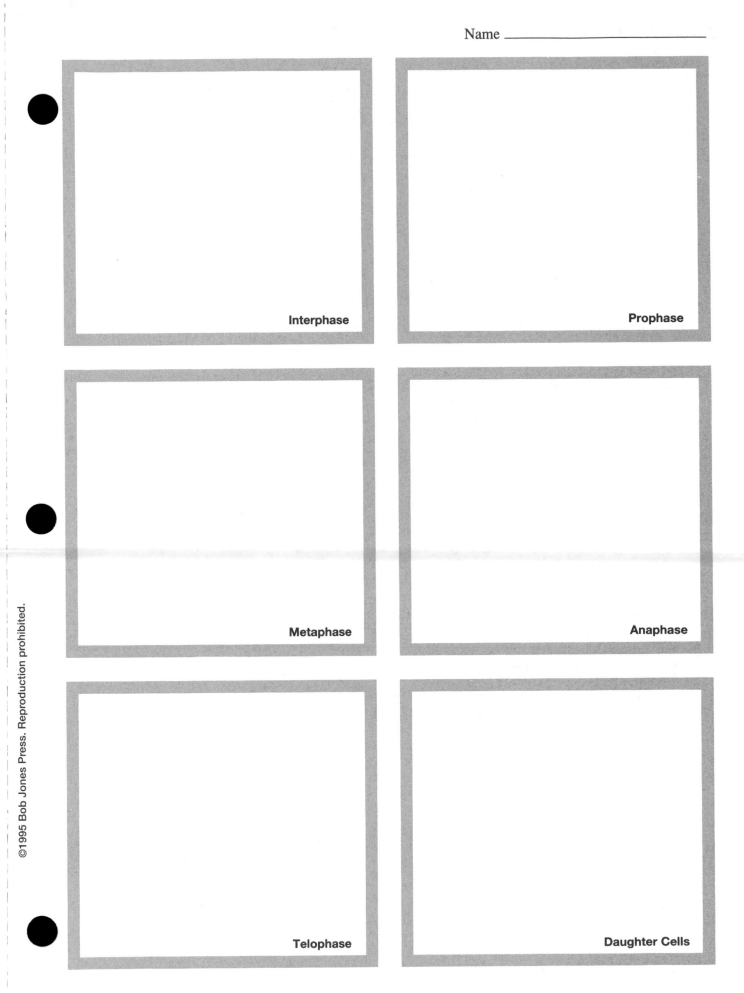

Name _____

Interphase

Prophase

Metaphase

Anaphase

Telophase

Daughter Cells

Observing Mitosis in Animal Cells

R
E
O

In embryos mitosis happens rapidly. Thus a slide of an embryo, if properly prepared, will reveal phases of mitosis.

I. Observe animal mitosis in a whitefish embryo.
- Obtain a preserved slide of a whitefish embryo.
- Observe the slide on high power, looking for the various stages of mitosis. You should find all the phases. In the proper spaces check the phases you find.
  - □ Interphase
  - □ Prophase
  - □ Metaphase
  - □ Anaphase
  - □ Telophase
  - □ Daughter cells
- How many chromosomes do you think a cell of a whitefish has? _____
  Based on your observations, can you be sure of this answer?　□ yes　□ no

  Explain why you can or cannot be sure. _____

  _____

  _____

R
E
O

II. Draw a series of specimen drawings showing mitosis in whitefish embryos.
- Make sure you draw typical specimens of the various stages of mitosis.
- Draw and label one cell in each of these points in the process:
  1. Interphase
  2. Prophase
  3. Metaphase
  4. Anaphase
  5. Telophase
  6. Daughter cells

R
E
O

*III. Compare mitosis in animals and plants. List several differences between mitosis in plants and animals by filling in the spaces below.

- In plants the _____

  _____

  while in animals the _____

  _____ .

- In plants the _____

  _____

  while in animals the _____

  _____ .

- In plants the _____

  _____

  while in animals the _____

  _____ .

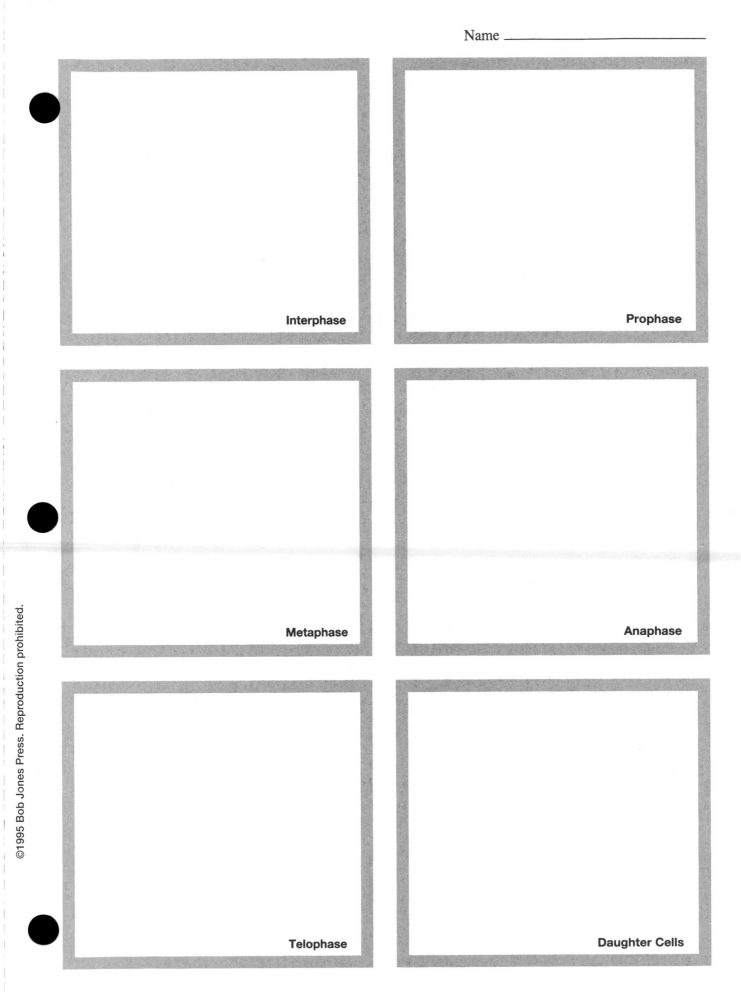

Interphase

Prophase

Metaphase

Anaphase

Telophase

Daughter Cells

*A Description of Meiosis

To help your understanding of meiosis, use your text as a reference and fill in the following descriptions of the phases of **meiosis in animals.**

I. First Division
- Prophase
  - ❑ Before going through meiosis, the mother cells must have the _____-ploid chromosome number.

  - ❑ The chromosomes _____ .
- Metaphase
  - ❑ The sister chromatids _____ .
- Anaphase
  - ❑ The sister chromatids _____ .

  - ❑ The homologous pairs of chromosomes _____

  _____ .

- Telophase
  - ❑ The homologous pairs of chromosomes _____ .

  - ❑ The cytoplasm _____ .

  - ❑ The result of the first division of meiosis is two _____-ploid cells, each con-

  taining _____ of each homologous pair of chromosomes found in the mother cell.

II. Second Division
- Prophase
  - ❑ Since the chromosomes do not uncoil after the first division of meiosis, the cells are ready to undergo the rest of the phases of meiosis almost immediately following the first division.
- Metaphase
  - ❑ The chromosomes in each cell (location) _____ .

  - ❑ The sister chromatids in each cell _____ .
- Anaphase
  - ❑ The sister chromatids in each cell _____ .
- Telophase
  - ❑ The sister chromatids in each cell _____ .

  - ❑ The cytoplasm in each cell _____ .

  - ❑ At the end of the second division of mitosis there are _____ cells, each of

  which contains the _____-ploid number of chromosomes. These cells are

  called the _____ .

Comparing Mitosis and Meiosis

Mitosis is the asexual reproduction of cells. Meiosis is the formation of gametes in preparation for sexual reproduction. The processes, while similar, have noticeable differences.

R
E
O

*I. Compare the phases.
- Compare mitosis and meiosis by filling in the chart below. All the information you need is in your text (see diagrams on pp. 115 and 121-22); however, some of the answers will require thought.

A Comparison of Mitosis and Meiosis			
Type and Phase	Stage has sister chromatids or daughter chromosomes	Chromosomes or chromatids moving toward, at, or away from the equatorial plane	Number of chromosomes or chromatids in each cell (2n=6)
Mitosis prophase	☐ Sister ☐ Daughter	☐ Moving toward ☐ At equator ☐ Moving away	☐ 3　☐ 9 ☐ 6　☐ 12
Meiosis prophase (1st division)	☐ Sister ☐ Daughter	☐ Moving toward ☐ At equator ☐ Moving away	☐ 3　☐ 9 ☐ 6　☐ 12
Mitosis metaphase	☐ Sister ☐ Daughter	☐ Moving toward ☐ At equator ☐ Moving away	☐ 3　☐ 9 ☐ 6　☐ 12
Meiosis metaphase (2nd division)	☐ Sister ☐ Daughter	☐ Moving toward ☐ At equator ☐ Moving away	☐ 3　☐ 9 ☐ 6　☐ 12
Mitosis anaphase	☐ Sister ☐ Daughter	☐ Moving toward ☐ At equator ☐ Moving away	☐ 3　☐ 9 ☐ 6　☐ 12
Meiosis anaphase (1st division)	☐ Sister ☐ Daughter	☐ Moving toward ☐ At equator ☐ Moving away	☐ 3　☐ 9 ☐ 6　☐ 12
Mitosis telophase	☐ Sister ☐ Daughter	No directional movement	☐ 3　☐ 9 ☐ 6　☐ 12
Meiosis telophase (2nd division)	☐ Sister ☐ Daughter	No directional movement	☐ 3　☐ 9 ☐ 6　☐ 12

R
E
O

*II. Answer the following questions comparing mitosis and meiosis.
- In metaphase, what is the name of the chromatin material that lines up on the equatorial plane for–
   - Mitosis? _____
   - Meiosis, first division? _____
   - Meiosis, second division? _____
- In anaphase, what is the name of the chromatin material that is moving toward opposite poles in–
   - Mitosis? _____
   - Meiosis, first division? _____
   - Meiosis, second division? _____

5B–Genetics
Part I–Monohybrid Problems with Simple Dominance

Materials: none

Goals:
To work problems to increase understanding of genetics
To measure knowledge and understanding of basic genetic principles

It is easy to watch someone else work a problem. Often, however, it is quite another thing to take a similar problem and work it out yourself. Only when you thoroughly understand the process can you work a problem "from scratch." If you can work the series of problems in this laboratory exercise outside of class, you probably understand the simple genetics presented in *BIOLOGY for Christian Schools*. If you cannot figure them out, you need more study and instruction.

If you have difficulty with these problems, seek help from your teacher. Many of the problems in this lab are "study problems" and will not be graded, but you are asked not to discuss your answers with anyone.

Determining Genotypes from Phenotypes

In humans, the ability to taste the chemical phenylthiocarbamide (PTC) is an inherited, dominant characteristic. For these exercises use the symbol T to represent the dominant allele and t to represent the recessive allele.

 I. The genotype for a person who cannot taste PTC would be written _____.

 II. The genotype for a person who can taste PTC would be written as either _____ or _____.

 III. Put a star in the answer above by the genotype for a person who is heterozygous.
  • Is there any difference between the phenotypes of these two people?   □ yes   □ no

  • Explain. _____

  _____

How to Fill in a Punnett Square

• Female genotypes are written on top of a Punnett square; male genotypes are written along the left side.
• The symbols used on the top and side of the Punnett square are **possible gametes,** not genotypes for individuals.
• The symbols you write inside the Punnett square are **possible gamete combinations** or the **possible genotypes** of the offspring.

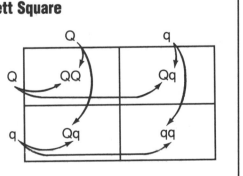

Using Punnett Squares

I. Using the Punnett square on the right, cross a homozygous male taster with a female nontaster.
   - In this Punnett square, is it possible to have the following offspring?
      - A. A heterozygous taster? □ yes □ no
      - B. A heterozygous nontaster? □ yes □ no
      - C. A homozygous taster? □ yes □ no
      - D. A homozygous nontaster? □ yes □ no

II. One of the offspring of the cross done above marries a person who is known to be heterozygous.
   - Is there any possibility of there being a nontaster in the next generation? □ yes □ no
   - To prove your answer, diagram the cross on the Punnett square to the right and circle the genotype of the nontaster (if there is one).
   - What is the phenotypic ratio of this cross? (Give the numbers and the description of what the numbers stand for.) _____

   _____

   _____

   - What is the genotypic ratio of this cross? (Give the numbers and the descriptions of what the numbers stand for.) _____

   _____

   _____

Suggestions for Solving Genetics Problems

1. Determine as many genotypes as you can.
   - Since a person who has the recessive phenotype must have the recessive genotype, you know the genotype of that person.
   - Since a person who has the dominant phenotype must have at least one dominant allele, note that as part of that person's genotype.
2. Determine if the person's parents or offspring tell you anything about the person's genotype.
   - If the parents are known to be purebred (homozygous) for a trait, that may give you some information regarding the individual's genotype.
   - If the offspring are known to be purebred (homozygous) for a trait, that may also give you information regarding the individual's genotype.
3. Put the information you have on a Punnett square.
4. Determine what you can based on the information you have.

III. Mr. Johnson cannot taste PTC, but his wife can. Mrs. Johnson's mother cannot taste PTC, but her father can.
   - Is it possible for the Johnsons to have a child that can taste PTC? □ yes □ no
   - Is it possible for the Johnsons to have a child that cannot taste PTC? □ yes □ no
   - Demonstrate your answers on a Punnett square.

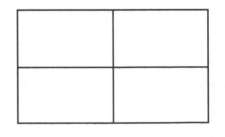

Name _____

Date _____ Hour _____

5B–Genetics
Part II–Problems with Pedigree Charts

Examine the Pedigree Chart below. It shows several generations of tasters and nontasters of PTC. Some of the genotypes are supplied. As you work out the problems below, you may need to fill in the genotypes of individuals *on the pedigree chart*.

Pedigree Chart

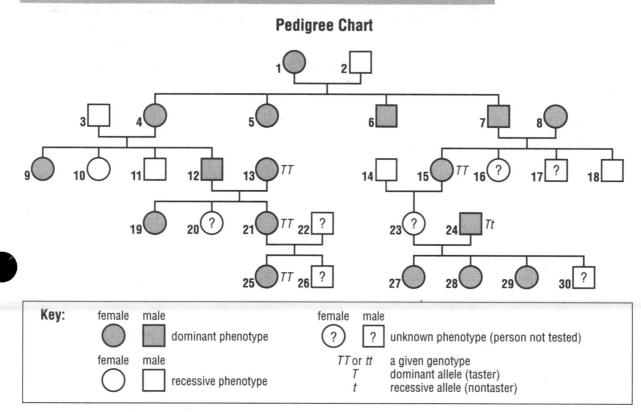

Key:

female	male	
⬤	⬛	dominant phenotype
○	☐	recessive phenotype

female	male	
(?)	[?]	unknown phenotype (person not tested)
TT or *tt*		a given genotype
T		dominant allele (taster)
t		recessive allele (nontaster)

Pedigrees and Pedigree Problems

[R] [E] [O] Be sure you have read the material about pedigrees in your text (pp. 136-37).

I. Answer the following questions regarding the pedigree of taster and nontaster.

- What is the phenotype of individual 1? _____

- What are the possible genotypes of individual 1? _____

- What is the phenotype of individual 2? _____

- What is the genotype of individual 2? _____

- Diagram the possible crosses for individuals 1 and 2 on the Punnett squares below.

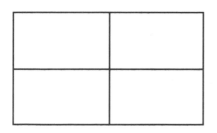

- Note carefully the phenotypes of the offspring of individuals 1 and 2 as given on the pedigree. Give the genotypes for the following individuals:

  4 _____   5 _____   6 _____   7 _____

- Would it be possible for any of their future brothers or sisters to exhibit the recessive

  trait?   □ yes   □ no   Explain your answer. _____

  _____

  _____

- Enter the genotypes for individuals 1, 2, 4, 5, 6, and 7 on the pedigree. Be sure to indicate those alleles you are not sure of by a dash (example: "T–" or "– –").

R E O II. What is the expected phenotype ratio for the crossing of individuals 3 and 4?

- Fill in the cross on the Punnett square to the right.
- Enter the phenotypic ratio from the Punnett square being sure to tell what the numbers

  stand for. _____

  _____

III. What is the genotype of individual 12? _____

IV. Individual 20 died in infancy.
- Is it possible to tell the child's phenotype?   □ yes   □ no

  If so, what is it? _____
- Is it possible to tell the child's genotype?   □ yes   □ no

  If so, what is it? _____

V. From the information given on the pedigree, is it possible to determine the phenotype of

  individual 22?   □ yes   □ no   If so, what is it? _____
- Is it possible to tell the genotype of his son (individual 26)?   □ yes   □ no

  If so, what is it? _____

VI. From information given on the pedigree, is it possible to tell the genotype of individual 8?

  □ yes   □ no   If so, what is it? _____
- Explain how you know or do not know. _____

  _____

VII. Is it possible to know the phenotype–
- of individual 16?   □ yes   □ no
- of individual 17?   □ yes   □ no

- If so, what are they?   16 _____   17 _____

- Explain how you know or do not know. _____

  _____

VIII. What must be the phenotype and genotype of individual 23? _____

IX. Is it possible that individual 30 expresses the recessive trait?   □ yes   □ no

  Is it possible that he expresses the dominant trait?   □ yes   □ no

- Which is more likely? _____

- Explain your choice. _____

  _____

5B–Genetics
Part III–Problems with Incomplete Dominance

> Read carefully the information about incomplete dominance in your text (pp. 132-33). Incomplete dominance problems can be worked easily on Punnett squares.

R
E
O
Simple Incomplete Dominance Problems

When a homozygous red radish plant is crossed with a homozygous white radish plant, purple radishes result.

I. Alleles in radishes
  - In incomplete dominance, both alleles are usually expressed with lowercase (small) letters.
    - Give the genotype of a white radish. _____
    - Give the genotype of a red radish. _____
  - Determine the possible gametes of–
    - A white radish _____
    - A red radish _____
II. Radish crosses
  - If the pollen from a red radish fertilizes the egg of a white radish, what will be the genotypes and the phenotypes of the offspring? Prove your answer on the Punnett square to the right. _____
    _____
  - If pollen from a red radish flower fertilizes the egg of another flower on the same plant, what will be the genotypes and phenotypes of the offspring? Why? _____
    _____
    _____
  - If two purple radishes are cross-pollinated, what are the genotypic and phenotypic ratios of the F_1 generation? Prove your answer by making the proper cross on the Punnett square to the right.
    Genotypic: _____
    Phenotypic: _____
  - If a red radish and a purple radish are cross-pollinated, what will be the phenotypic and genotypic ratios?
    Genotypic: _____
    Phenotypic: _____
  - Will the ratios given in the preceding question be the same if a white radish and a purple radish are crossed? Explain. _____
    _____

A Difficult Incomplete Dominance Problem

R
E
O

This problem is more complex, but if you understand the material already discussed, you can figure it out.

The litter resulting from the mating of two short-tailed cats contains three kittens without tails, two with long tails, and six with short tails.

I. Diagram a cross that will show the above results on the Punnett square to the right. First, however, you will need to give a key for the letters you choose to represent the alleles.

Key: _____

_____

_____

_____

II. What is the genotype of the parents? □ homozygous   □ heterozygous   □ one of each

III. Does the ratio of the kittens given in the statement agree with the ratio obtained from the Punnett square? Is it close enough for you to be sure you used the proper genotypes when

you diagrammed the cross? _____

_____

_____

5B–Genetics
Part IV–Problems with Multiple Alleles

Occasionally there will be more than one set (a pair) of alleles at a single locus. Three or more alleles, rather than just one set of contrasting traits, may be possible. Read carefully the material in your text regarding multiple alleles (p. 133).

Inheritance of the ABO Blood Types

The human blood types–A, B, AB, and O–are determined by multiple alleles, two dominant alleles and one recessive. They are often written–

Dominants: $I^A I^B$ **Recessive:** i

In this example the I represents the chromosome, and the A and B the gene. Of course, i represents the recessive gene on a chromosome.

I. Using the above symbols, indicate all the possible genotypes for the phenotypes given below. (*NOTE:* Two blood types have two possible genotypes; the others have only one.)

- Blood type A: _____
- Blood type AB: _____
- Blood type B: _____
- Blood type O: _____

II. A man who is heterozygous for blood type A marries a woman who is heterozygous for blood type B.
- Write their genotypes below.

  ❑ Man _____

  ❑ Woman _____

- Could a child with blood type O be born into this family?
  ☐ yes   ☐ no
  Prove your answer on the Punnett square to the right.
- Could a child with blood type A be born into this family?
  ☐ yes   ☐ no
- Could a child with blood type B be born into this family?
  ☐ yes   ☐ no
- Could a child with blood type AB be born into this family?
  ☐ yes   ☐ no

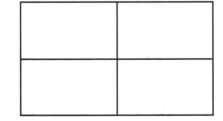

Additional Multiple Allele Problems

I. Is it possible for a woman with blood type O to have a child with blood type AB?
  ☐ yes   ☐ no   Explain your answer. (You may need to use a Punnett square to demon-

  strate the proper cross.) _____

  _____

  _____

  _____

  _____

  _____

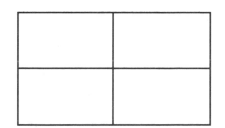

R
E
O

II. Is it possible for a man with blood type AB to have a child with type O blood?
☐ yes   ☐ no   Explain your answer. (You may need to use a Punnett square to demonstrate the proper cross.) _____

_____

_____

_____

_____

_____

_____

R
E
O

III. Is it possible for a woman with type A blood to have a child with type O blood?
☐ yes   ☐ no   Explain your answer. (You may need to use a Punnet square to demonstrate the proper cross.) _____

_____

_____

_____

_____

_____

5B–Genetics
Part V–Problems with Dihybrid Crosses

A dihybrid cross deals with two sets of characteristics at the same time. Read carefully the material on dihybrid crosses in your text (pp. 134-35).

The abilities of some people to taste PTC and roll their tongue into a U shape when it is extended from the mouth are dominant characteristics. We will call those who exhibit the dominant traits "tasters" and "rollers" and those who exhibit the recessive traits "nontasters" and "nonrollers." The capital letters R and T will be used for the dominant alleles, and the lowercase letters r and t for the recessive alleles in this exercise.

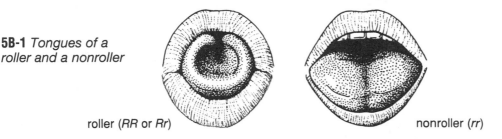

5B-1 *Tongues of a roller and a nonroller*

roller (*RR* or *Rr*)   nonroller (*rr*)

A Simple Dihybrid Cross

I. A man who is homozygous for tongue rolling and homozygous for the ability to taste PTC (genotype *RRTT*) marries a woman who is homozygous for both recessive traits.

- Write the genotype for his recessive wife. _____
- What possible gametes can the husband form? (Remember that a gamete will have **one of every homologous pair of chromosomes.** It is thus impossible to have an *RR* gamete or a *TT* gamete.) _____
- What possible gametes can the wife form? _____
- On the Punnett square on the right, cross these two people. What is the genotype of their offspring? *NOTE:* You should have only 1 genotype for the offspring, and that genotype *must have 4 letters*. If yours does not work this way, go back and check your work.

II. A man heterozygous for both rolling his tongue and tasting PTC marries a woman with the same genotype.

- Write the genotypes for them:

    man _____   woman _____

- What are the possible gametes they can form?

    man _____   woman _____

- Cross this couple on the Punnett square to the right.
- Give the resulting phenotypic ratio in the proper spaces.

    _____ Roller-taster(s)

    _____ Roller-nontaster(s)

    _____ Nonroller-taster(s)

    _____ Nonroller-nontaster(s)

Another Dihybrid Cross

In fruit flies, vestigial wings and hairy bodies are recessive traits that are caused by recessive genes located on different chromosomes. The normal alleles (long wings and hairless body) are dominant.

I. Using the above information, fill in the following chart with symbols for the alleles:

_____ is the allele for vestigial wings.

_____ is the allele for long wings.

_____ is the allele for hairless bodies.

_____ is the allele for hairy bodies.

II. Suppose a vestigial-winged, hairy-bodied male is crossed with a homozygous dominant female. (Work the Punnett squares for these questions on a separate sheet of paper. You will not turn it in.)

- What offspring would be expected? (Show genotypes and phenotypes as ratios.)

    ❑ Genotype: _____

    ❑ Phenotype: _____

    _____

- If these F_1 offspring are permitted to mate freely, what would you expect their offspring (the F_2) to be like? Show genotypes and phenotypes as ratios.

    ❑ Genotype: _____

    _____

    ❑ Phenotype: _____

    _____

5B–Genetics
Part VI–Problems with Sex-linked Traits

Carefully study the pedigree of Queen Victoria and Prince Albert on page 139 of your text and read the material regarding sex-linked traits on pages 136-40. Hemophilia, a recessive trait found on the X chromosome, is sometimes called "bleeder's disease." Traits on the X chromosome that are not found on the Y chromosome are usually written as superscripts (above and to the right) of the symbol for the chromosome–the X. The Y, which lacks the gene for this trait, is left without a superscript. Since hemophilia is recessive, we will use the letter h for the hemophilia gene and H for the normal, dominant gene.

I. Write the genotypes for the people described below. One phenotype given below is impossible and does not have a genotype. Put a star (*) in the blank for the impossible phenotype.
- A normal female who carries the gene for hemophilia: _____
- A normal male who carries the gene for hemophilia: _____
- A normal female without a gene for hemophilia: _____
- A normal male without a gene for hemophilia: _____
- A hemophiliac female: _____
- A hemophiliac male: _____

II. Answer the following:
- What is Queen Victoria's genotype? _____
- What is Prince Albert's genotype? _____
- Cross Queen Victoria and Prince Albert on Punnett Square A.
  - In the proper boxes of the Punnett square, write names of their offspring.
  - Is it possible to have a noncarrier female from Victoria and Albert? ☐ yes ☐ no
- On Punnett Square B, cross Beatrice of the first generation with Henry of Battenburg.
  - Show how they were able to have Alexander and Maurice, both males, but one with hemophilia and the other without the disease. (Write their names in the proper boxes.)
  - Is it possible to have a hemophiliac female from this cross? ☐ yes ☐ no

- On Punnett Square C, cross Alice of the first generation and Louis IV.
  - To show how they can have Elizabeth and Irene, both females, but one a carrier and the other a noncarrier, write their names in the proper spaces of the Punnett square.
  - Is it possible to have a hemophiliac female from this cross? ☐ yes ☐ no

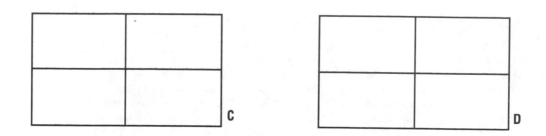

- If Frederick William married his cousin Alice (both of the second generation), could they produce a hemophiliac female? ☐ yes ☐ no
  Prove your answer on Punnett Square D. If there is a hemophiliac female, circle her genotype.
- Since there is no difference between the phenotype of a female carrier and the phenotype of a normal female, how have the people who compiled this chart been able to

  determine who were carriers and who were not? _____

  _____

  _____

- The current English ruling family (Queen Elizabeth II, fourth generation) has gone for five generations without a hemophiliac individual. This is because Edward VII, Victoria's son, did not have hemophilia. Explain how this fact eliminated the hemophilia

  gene from the current line of English rulers. _____

  _____

  _____

6–Genetic Research

Materials: library

Goals:

To learn about the current topics of genetic research

To make some decisions regarding genetic research

Genetic research makes headlines today more frequently than ever before. Scientists are not yet ready to announce a cure for all kinds of cancer or a way to replace a worn-out heart or liver with a cloned (genetically identical) replacement/transplant. Nor have they engineered a plant that will withstand heat, frost, drought, and flood and still produce abundant, edible, nutritious fruit. But many of the experiments being done today yield information that brings those and other genetic dreams closer to reality.

With all abilities come not only opportunities but also responsibilities. For example, when you begin to drive a car, you will have not only the opportunity to drive the car for good purposes (going to school or church, doing errands for the family) but also the opportunity to improperly use the car (going places you should not go, driving recklessly). It will be your responsibility to use the car as it should be used.

The same principle holds true for scientific information. Most people would rejoice at the announcement that scientists had learned to use a few blood cells to grow kidneys that can be implanted when needed and will not be rejected. Such information, however, could permit people to do things that may not meet with such universal approval and may even violate Scriptural or moral principles.

In this exercise you will be asked to read about a current area of genetic research or application of genetic knowledge and to speculate about the good and the bad that could result from the information being learned and used.

Your Research

I. In a periodical that has come out within the past two years, find an article that deals with current genetic research and/or application.
  - The article may deal with any of the following:
    - ❏ Genetic engineering
    - ❏ Recombinant DNA
    - ❏ Genetic screening
    - ❏ Cloning
    - ❏ Artificial reproduction (artificial insemination, test tube fertilization, surrogate motherhood)
  - The article may deal with humans, plants, animals, protists, bacteria, or the release of genetically altered organisms into the environment.

II. If possible, find other articles dealing with the same genetic research or application of knowledge.
  - This research can often be done by looking in other periodicals that came out about the same time.
  - Look for reactions of scientists, physicians, scientific groups, activist groups, political leaders, government agencies, and other groups regarding this or closely related research or applications.

Your Analysis

R E O In some of the following spaces you need to indicate "none." In those answers where you deal with Scriptural matters be sure to give references. Answer the questions in outline sections II-V on your own paper.

    I. Describe the genetic research or application.

* Who or what group did the research or experimentation? _____

_____

_____

* What organisms are currently involved in this genetic research or application?

_____

* What part of the organism(s) is currently involved? _____

_____

* What has been done? (Summarize the process of doing it, not the results.)

_____

_____

_____

_____

_____

_____

* What results have been achieved? _____

_____

_____

_____

_____

_____

_____

R E O   II. What are the projected outcomes of this genetic research or application?

* What is projected as the immediate outcome (benefits) of this genetic research or application? Mention any time frame that is given.
* What are the projected long-range benefits of this genetic research or application? Mention any time frame that is given.
* What drawbacks or potential problems connected with this genetic research or application are mentioned?

  III. What is your analysis of the present research and its present application?

* Were any Scriptural or moral principles violated in the discovery of the information (research)? If so, describe.
* Is the present application(s) of the information in violation of Scriptural or moral principles? If so, describe.
* What drawbacks not mentioned above do you see regarding the present use of the information?

  IV. What is your analysis of the future uses of this genetic research or application?

* What can you see this information contributing to in the future?
* What potential Scriptural or moral problems do you foresee from the use of this information?
* What drawbacks not mentioned above do you see regarding the future use of the information?

  V. What can you recommend to prevent present and/or future abuse of this knowledge and/or unacceptable applications of the knowledge?

7–Creationism: My Beliefs and Defense

Materials: a Bible

Goals:

    To think through information about creation and decide upon a Biblical position

    To defend a position on creationism Biblically and logically

> It is one thing to read and hear about creation and quite another to know what you believe. It is one thing to know what you believe and still another to defend your position. In this exercise you are asked to state your position on various creationist topics and to give your reasons for taking these positions. As you do this lab, think about how you would use this information to deal with someone who has not had the advantages of a Christian education that you have had.

*My Creationist Creed

A creed is a short statement of belief. It normally lists, without explanation, what a person (or group) believes. Of course, for a Christian, any creed must reflect Biblical positions. In the space below, write your personal creed regarding creationism. Using your own words, cover the main aspects of creationism. After each statement, list in parentheses the Scripture passages which support it.

I believe– _____

_____

_____

_____

_____

*My Answers to Some Evolutionist Statements

Below are several statements frequently used to defend evolutionary theory. Based on the information you find in Chapter 5 and other areas in the text (as well as outside references if necessary), answer the following arguments with logical, scientific, and if possible, Scriptural statements. Use additional paper if necessary.

    I. According to many evolutionists, reptiles are the evolutionary ancestors of birds. Microscopic examination shows that scales and feathers grow from the same types of tissues in the skin. Evolutionists use this fact to support their argument that scales evolved into feathers. Evolutionists disregard the fact that there is no fossil evidence of such evolution; they claim that fossils of feather evolution simply have not been located. What arguments would you use to support the creationist position that birds did not evolve from reptiles?

        _____

        _____

        _____

        _____

        _____

        _____

R
E
O

II. "Bigfoot" (sasquatch) has been sighted and even photographed repeatedly over the past several decades in the wilderness areas of the American Northwest. Some people claim that these creatures link apes and man. Assume that these organisms are real and that one is caught. There would be widespread publicity pointing out the organism's apelike and manlike characteristics and declaring that an evolutionary link had been found. If this information were presented by the press, what would be your position?

_____

_____

_____

_____

_____

_____

_____

R
E
O

III. Evolutionists often claim that *homology* indicates common ancestry. The fact that the "arms" of many vertebrates contain the same number of bones (illustration, top of p. 205 in the text) is often used as an example of homology. Fish, frogs, lizards, birds, rats, monkeys, and man all have digestive systems with a liver attached by a tube to the intestine just below the stomach. Evolutionists argue from this similarity that all these organisms can be traced to a common ancestor. How would you argue against this logic?

_____

_____

_____

_____

_____

_____

R
E
O

IV. Almost all the mammals of Australia belong to the order Marsupialia (pouched mammals, such as the kangaroo and koala–see pp. 444-45 in the text). Evolutionists generally believe that these are "lower mammals" because their reproduction does not involve a placenta, which is a "complex structure." Some evolutionists claim that there is no environmental pressure upon these marsupial mammals to develop into placental forms. Because of this, these pouched mammals contentedly continue to live in Australia. What arguments can you give against the evolutionary concept that marsupials are a "lower" form?

_____

_____

_____

_____

_____

_____

_____

_____

8–The Use of Biological Keys

Materials: animal specimens and photographs

Goal:

    To learn to use a biological key

> Included with this laboratory exercise is A Biological Key for Major Animal Classifications. You will use this general, artificial biological key to classify specimens (and some photographs of specimens) in the laboratory. You will have a limited amount of time to identify correctly the specimens and record properly all the information regarding your identifications. Before you come to class, carefully read the instructions, study the examples, and do the samples that are presented.

Preliminary Work

I. Read carefully the instructions on using a biological identification key in Facet 8A-1, pages 216-17 in your text. On page 56 is a glossary of terms used in the key. You may use this glossary while you identify organisms in the laboratory.

II. In order to receive credit for having correctly identified an organism, you will need to fill out all the information requested on the Specimen Identification Chart.

- The Sample Identification Chart (p. 54) is filled in for Specimen A, an American toad (illustrated on p. 406 of the text). Check carefully to see how all the information was obtained from the Biological Key.
- The chart has also been filled in for Specimen B, a grasshopper (illustrated in the top diagram on p. 375 of the text).
  - ❑ Note that no subphylum for this example appears in the Biological Key. Thus there is a line drawn in the space marked *SP* on the Sample Identification Chart.
  - ❑ Draw a line through any blank in the Classification of Specimen that does not apply.
- *● Try to identify the organisms listed below, and fill in the Sample Identification Chart for them.
  - ❑ Specimen C, the Gélapagos conch (snail) on page 360 of the text
  - ❑ Specimen D, the red-tail hawk on page 430 of the text
  - ❑ Specimen E, the caribou on page 473 of the text

III. On the lab day be prepared to identify as many of the specimens as you can.

- You may use only the key and the glossary given with this exercise.
- You will have a limited amount of time.
- You must fill in the Specimen Identification Chart accurately and completely to get credit for identifying the organism.
- After completing this exercise, you should know how to use a biological key, not simply be familiar with the divisions of the animal kingdom in the key. This key is highly artificial. The groupings will be discussed in more detail later.

Sample Specimen Identification Chart

Letter	Specimen Name	Numbers from Key Used to Identify Organism	Classification of Specimen*			
A	Grass frog	1, 2, 18, 19, 20, 24, 25	K: Animalia	C: Amphibia		
			P: Chordata	O: Anura		
			SP: Vertebrata			
B	Grasshopper	1, 2, 3, 5, 10, 12, 13, 15, 16	K: Animalia	C: Insecta		
			P: Arthropoda	O: Orthoptera		
			SP: ----------			
C			K:	C:		
			P:	O:		
			SP:			
D			K:	C:		
			P:	O:		
			SP:			
E			K:	C:		
			P:	O:		
			SP:			

*Key to symbols used: K: Kingdom   P: Phylum   SP: Subphylum   C: Class   O: Order

A Biological Key for Major Animal Classifications

This key deals with adult animals, not immature or larval forms. This simplified key should help you understand the use of biological keys. It is not a field guide but should be used to identify organisms in a laboratory exercise.

1. Autotrophic, perhaps producing flowers and seeds ....*Kingdom Plantae*
   Heterotrophic, not producing flowers and seeds ....*Kingdom Animalia* **2**

2. No backbone (an invertebrate) **3**
   Backbone (a vertebrate) or notochord ....*Phylum Chordata* **18**

3. Radial symmetry **4**
   Asymmetrical or with bilateral symmetry **5**

4. Soft body, usually transparent; thin tentacles; body with
      nematocysts ....*Phylum Cnidaria*
   Firm body with internal support; covered with epidermal
      plates which often have spines; tiny, hollow tube feet
      protrude from opening in the body covering and are
      used for movement ....*Phylum Echinodermata*

5. Exoskeleton ....*Phylum Arthropoda* **10**
   No exoskeleton; external shell or soft shell-less body **6**

6. External shell ....*Phylum Mollusca* **7**
   No external shell **8**

7. Coiled shell ....*Class Gastropoda*
   Shell of two similar parts ....*Class Pelecypoda*

8. Wormlike body without sensory tentacles on head ....*Phylum Annelida*
   Nonwormlike body, or sensory tentacles on head ....*Phylum Mollusca* **9**

9. Wormlike body with sensory tentacles on head ....*Class Gastropoda*
   Nonwormlike body, but eight or more tentacles used for
      grasping ....*Class Cephalopoda*

10. More than three pairs of legs **11**
    Three pairs of walking legs ....*Class Insecta* **12**

11. Four pairs of walking legs, body in two divisions ....*Class Arachnida*
    More than four pairs of walking legs; perhaps large pincers
      on some legs; often with large, segmented abdomen;
      usually aquatic ....*Class Malacostraca*

12. Wings **13**
    No wings **17**

13. Only transparent wings **14**
    Nontransparent wings **15**

14. Capable of inflicting sting with last abdominal segment ....*Order Hymenoptera*
    Not capable of inflicting sting (may be able to bite) ....*Order Diptera*

15. Large, often colorful wings covered with scales
      which easily rub off ....*Order Lepidoptera*
    Thick, hard, or leathery wings **16**

16. Pair of hard wings covering a folded pair of thin,
      transparent wings ....*Order Coleoptera*
    Pair of leathery wings covering a pair of straight, thin,
      transparent wings ....*Order Orthoptera*

17. Piercing, sucking mouthparts for obtaining blood ....*Order Siphonaptera*
    Chewing mouthparts ....*Order Hymenoptera*

18. No vertebrae (backbone) ....*Subphylum Cephalochordata*
    Vertebrae (backbone) ....*Subphylum Vertebrata* **19**

19. Jaws or beak **20**
    No jaw or beak ....*Class Agnatha*

20. Skin is covered with scales **21**
Skin lacks scales **24**

21. Fins; breathing by means of gills **22**
No fins; breathing by means of lungs ....*Class Reptilia*

22. Mouth on ventral (lower) side of body ....*Class Chondrichthyes*
Mouth at terminal (front) end of body ....*Class Osteichthyes*

23. Legs or legless, no dorsal (top) and ventral
(bottom) shell ....*Order Squamata*
Legs, and dorsal (top) and ventral (bottom) shell ....*Order Testudinata*

24. Skin is naked (no hair, scales, or feathers)
and slimy ....*Class Amphibia* **25**
Skin with feathers or hair **26**

25. Tail ....*Order Caudata*
No tail .... *Order Anura*

26. Body covered with feathers .... *Class Aves*
Body covered with hair ....*Class Mammalia* **27**

27. Hooves **28**
No hooves **29**

28. Odd number of toes, each with a hoof ....*Order Perissodactyla*
Even number of toes, each with a hoof .... *Order Artiodactyla*

29. Eats other animals **30**
Eats vegetable matter **31**

30. Teeth for eating meat .... *Order Carnivora*
No teeth; usually eats insects ....*Order Insectivora*

31. Enlarged front teeth for gnawing **32**
No enlarged front teeth for gnawing **33**

32. Legs suitable for crawling .... *Order Rodentia*
Hind legs suitable for jumping ....*Order Lagomorpha*

33. Enlarged trunk, used for breathing and for grasping ....*Order Proboscidea*
Tendency to stand erect on two hind limbs .... *Order Primates*

Glossary for Key to Major Animal Classifications

abdomen The body region posterior to (below or behind) the thorax

asymmetry Different shapes, sizes, and structures of body parts; therefore, the animal cannot be divided into like external halves

bilateral symmetry Animal can be divided into matching external right and left sides

dorsal Toward the back or upper side of an animal

epidermal plates Small, hard plates joined beneath the epidermis to give shape and support

exoskeleton A system of external plates that protect and support the animal

gill A respiratory structure in aquatic organisms through which oxygen and carbon dioxide are exchanged

nematocyst A stinging cell, characteristic of coelenterates, that contains poisonous barbs, coiled threads, or a sticky substance

notochord A tough, flexible rod, located along the dorsal side of an animal; provides support for the animal's body

radial symmetry Animal can be externally divided in half like a pie; has no right or left side

tentacle A long, slender, movable extension of an animal's body

terminal end The extreme end of an animal's body

trunk A flexible extension of an animal's head used for grasping, feeding, and breathing

ventral Toward the underside, or "stomach side," of an animal

Specimen Identification Chart

#	Specimen Name	Numbers from Key Used to Identify Organism	Classification of Specimen*
			K: C: P: O: SP:
			K: C: P: O: SP:
			K: C: P: O: SP:
			K: C: P: O: SP:
			K: C: P: O: SP:
			K: C: P: O: SP:
			K: C: P: O: SP:
			K: C: P: O: SP:
			K: C: P: O: SP:
			K: C: P: O: SP:

*Key to symbols used: K: Kingdom   P: Phylum   SP: Subphylum   C: Class   O: Order

#	Specimen Name	Numbers from Key Used to Identify Organism	Classification of Specimen*	
			K:	C:
			P:	O:
			SP:	
			K:	C:
			P:	O:
			SP:	
			K:	C:
			P:	O:
			SP:	
			K:	C:
			P:	O:
			SP:	
			K:	C:
			P:	O:
			SP:	
			K:	C:
			P:	O:
			SP:	
			K:	C:
			P:	O:
			SP:	
			K:	C:
			P:	O:
			SP:	
			K:	C:
			P:	O:
			SP:	
			K:	C:
			P:	O:
			SP:	

*Key to symbols used: K: Kingdom   P: Phylum   SP: Subphylum   C: Class   O: Order

9A–Bacterial Basics

Materials: Petri dishes; divided Petri dishes; agar; nutrient agar (beef extract, peptone); test tubes; transfer loop; Bunsen burner; laboratory cultures of *Bacillus cereus, B. subtilis, Rhodospirillum rubrum, Sarcina lutea,* and *S. subflava;* incubator; preserved slide of bacteria types; dropping pipets; distilled water; cotton; gauze

Goals:
> To observe the laboratory techniques for handling and culturing bacteria in an experiment
> To observe bacterial growth rates under different conditions
> To observe different types of bacteria

In this laboratory exercise several types of living bacteria will be cultured under laboratory conditions. These cultures will be prepared one day, and then they will be observed 24, 48, and 72 hours later. The instructor will set up the laboratory cultures as a demonstration. You will observe these cultures and record the observations during the first few minutes of class for the next several days.

The species of bacteria used in this lab are nonpathogenic; however, if a culture becomes contaminated with bacteria from the air, pathogenic bacteria could be cultured. Therefore, you must handle live bacteria only under the instructor's supervision. **Under no circumstances should any student open any bacterial culture in the laboratory without the presence and supervision of the instructor.** You can easily make your observations for this laboratory exercise through the glass of the culture container.

Materials Used in Culturing Bacteria

Carefully observe the following pieces of equipment in the laboratory. You should be able to recognize them and know what they are used for.

Equipment
- The **Petri dish**, a flat dish with a flat lid, is used for culturing bacteria, molds, and similar organisms on solid culture media.
- The **autoclave**, a piece of equipment used to sterilize materials for culturing bacteria, normally contains a closed chamber which can be heated and will keep its contents under pressure. Adequate heat and pressure will kill even spores.
- The **incubator**, a piece of equipment containing a chamber which can be kept at a specific temperature, is used to culture organisms like bacteria.
- A **culture slant** is a test tube of solid culture medium which has been cooled at an angle, forming a large surface area of the culture medium on which to grow bacteria.
- A **transfer loop** is a piece of wire with a small loop at one end and a handle on the other. The wire can be heated to destroy bacteria on it and can then be used to transfer bacteria from one culture to another.

Culture Media
- **Beef extract** is a paste made of beef. It serves as a nutrient source in culturing many bacteria.
- **Peptone** is an enzyme which digests protein. It is added to many bacterial culture media since many bacteria are not able to digest some proteins.

(Continued on next page)

- **Agar** is a solidifying agent obtained from certain algae; it is used to solidify the culture media on which bacteria grow.
- **Nutrient broth** is a mixture of beef extract, peptone, and water and is used for growing certain species of bacteria.
- **Broth culture** is a culture of bacteria in a fluid medium (like nutrient broth).
- **Nutrient agar** is a mixture of beef extract, peptone, water, and agar and is used for growing bacteria on a solid medium.

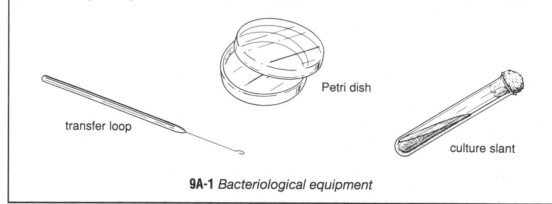

Petri dish

transfer loop

culture slant

9A-1 *Bacteriological equipment*

Techniques Used in Culturing Bacteria

The techniques described will be demonstrated while your instructor sets up bacterial cultures for your observation.

I. Preparing the apparatus and the media
- After the proper media are set up in the proper containers, they must be sterilized in an autoclave to destroy all living materials in them.
- After the containers are removed from the autoclave, they should not be opened until time to transfer the culture material into them.

II. Preparing the environment–close windows and turn off fans and other blowers. The fewer air currents there are, the less chance there is of contamination.

III. Opening different containers of bacterial cultures
- Open a culture slant.
  - ❏ After opening a culture slant, pass the lip of the test tube through a flame to destroy stray bacteria.
  - ❏ Keep the open culture slant at an angle or even parallel to the floor to avoid as much as possible having airborne bacteria settle on the agar.
  - ❏ Never set the cotton stopper down on a table while working with bacteria, but replace it as soon as possible.
  - ❏ Just before replacing the stopper, pass the lip of the test tube through a flame to destroy contaminating bacteria.

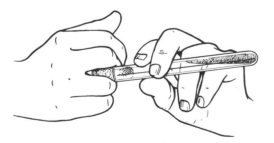

The proper way to hold a culture slant

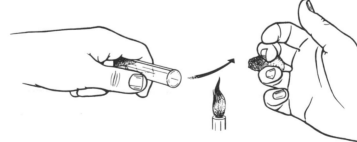

After opening a culture slant, pass the lip of the test tube through a flame.

9A-2 *Opening a culture slant*

- Open a Petri dish.
  - ❑ When opening a Petri dish, turn the dish upside down so the agar is in the upper section of the dish.
  - ❑ Open the dish only partway to avoid as much as possible having airborne bacteria settle on the agar.
  - ❑ When finished with the bacteria, close the Petri dish as soon as possible.
- Use a broth culture.
  - ❑ Broth cultures pose special problems because they cannot be held at an angle and frequently must be poured.
  - ❑ Take special care to leave broth cultures open as little as possible.
  - ❑ Pour any excess broth into a strong, bacteria-killing solvent.

IV. Transferring bacteria from one culture to another by using a transfer loop
- Burn the transfer loop in a flame until it is red-hot. This destroys any living material which may be on it. Allow the loop to cool for a few seconds.
- Touch the loop of wire at the end of the transfer loop to the bacteria being transferred.

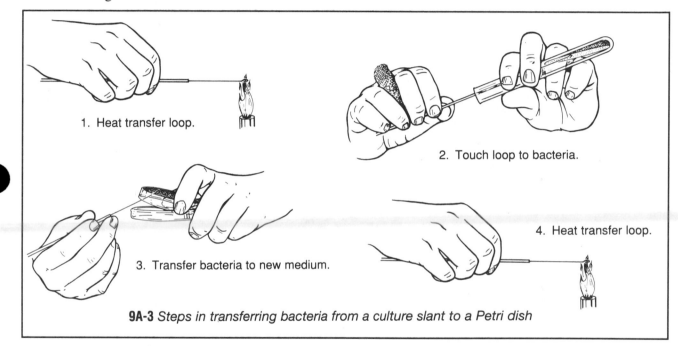

1. Heat transfer loop.

2. Touch loop to bacteria.

3. Transfer bacteria to new medium.

4. Heat transfer loop.

9A-3 *Steps in transferring bacteria from a culture slant to a Petri dish*

- Quickly take the transfer loop to the sterile culture medium prepared to receive the bacteria. Take care not to touch the transfer loop to the dish containing the culture medium.
- The transfer loop should be immediately burned in a flame until it is red-hot to destroy any bacteria which may be left on the loop.

R E O Observing Bacteria

In this segment you will observe various bacterial cells and colonies through a microscope and then observe living cultures of bacteria.

I. Observe bacteria with the microscope.
- In the lab will be three microscopes on oil-immersion power (940×-1,000×), each focused on a different preserved and stained bacterium.
- From your observation, decide on the type of bacterial shape and type of colony in each of the microscopes and record your answers below.

Microscope	Name and Description of Shape	Type of Colony (if any)
A		
B		
C		

R E O II. Observe bacterial cultures.
- Observe living cultures of the following bacteria on nutrient agar. Write a detailed description of each bacterial growth, including color, size of growth, texture, shape of growth, and any other visible factors.

  ❑ *Bacillus subtilis:* _____

  _____

  ❑ *Rhodospirillum rubrum:* _____

  _____

  ❑ *Sarcina lutea:* _____

  _____

  ❑ *Sarcina subflava:* _____

  _____

*• From your knowledge of etymologies and bacterial colonies and shapes, determine the shape, the type of colony, and any other characteristics each of the bacteria above has. Record your answers below.

  ❑ *Bacillus subtilis:* _____

  ❑ *Rhodospirillum rubrum:* _____

  ❑ *Sarcina lutea:* _____

  ❑ *Sarcina subflava:* _____

Bacterial Growth Rates

Two identical culture dishes, each with the same four bacteria *(Bacillus subtilis, Rhodospirillum rubrum, Sarcina lutea,* and *Sarcina subflava),* will be prepared by your instructor. They will be placed in streaks on nutrient agar in a divided Petri dish. The direction of the streaks tells which bacteria is which (see Diagram 9A-4). One Petri dish will be kept in a dark incubator at a constant temperature of about 39° C. The other will be kept in the classroom near a window so that there will be a change in temperature and amount of light.

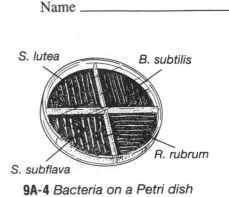

9A-4 *Bacteria on a Petri dish*

*I. Read the questions in Part III below. These are the questions you will be expected to answer after three days of observing these bacteria.

II. Record your observations in the proper spaces below. (Be sure you observe thoroughly enough to answer questions later.)

In Incubator

	24 hours	48 hours	72 hours
B. subtilis:			
R. rubrum:			
S. lutea:			
S. subflava:			

In Classroom

	24 hours	48 hours	72 hours
B. subtilis:			
R. rubrum:			
S. lutea:			
S. subflava:			

If you miss an observation, obtain data from someone else in your class. You must put the person's name with the data you obtain from him, or using the information will be considered plagiarism. Because observations and methods of recording differ, data you obtain from someone else will be different in answering the questions.

III. Answer the following questions.

- Which bacterium grows the fastest in the incubator? _____

  In the classroom? _____

  If different bacteria grow best in each of these circumstances, account for this difference. _____

  _____

  _____

- Were there any noticeable differences in other species of bacteria grown under the different sets of conditions?   ☐ yes   ☐ no   What were they? _____

  _____

  Why would you expect differences? _____

  _____

- Were there any noticeable similarities in growth rates in the various species of bacteria?   ☐ yes   ☐ no   What were they? _____

  _____

  Why would you expect some species of bacteria to grow at the same rate as others?

  _____

  _____

- All these bacteria were grown on nutrient agar. Could the difference in growth rates have anything to do with the medium?   ☐ yes   ☐ no
  Would it be possible for the slowest-growing bacteria in this experiment to grow faster on some other medium?   ☐ yes   ☐ no   Explain your answer. _____

  _____

  _____

- In our growth rates experiment, there are too many variables to make any definite conclusions about why there was a difference in the bacterial growth rates. What could be done to correct this problem? _____

  _____

- We have considered temperature, food, and light as possible reasons that some bacteria grow faster than others. Name two other conditions which could affect the growth rate of bacteria.

  1. _____

  2. _____

- Is it possible that even if each bacterium were given optimum conditions for growth, the growth rates would still differ?   ☐ yes   ☐ no   Explain. _____

  _____

  _____

9B–Bacteria and Antibiotics

Materials: Petri dish, nutrient agar, a nutrient broth culture of *Bacillus cereus,* antibiotic disks, forceps, a strong acid

Goal:

To observe the effects of various antibiotics on bacteria

In this laboratory exercise a nonpathogenic species of bacteria will be exposed to several different antibiotics. All antibiotics are not equally effective against all bacteria. Tests using antibiotic sensitivity disks are sometimes performed to reveal which antibiotic to use in fighting a particular species of bacteria. You will be able to judge the effectiveness of the different antibiotics by observing the growth of the bacteria around the antibiotic.

The species of bacteria used in this lab is nonpathogenic. The teacher will set up the culture as a demonstration. **Under no circumstance should any student open any bacterial culture in the laboratory without the presence and supervision of the instructor.** You can easily make your observations for this laboratory exercise through the clear lid of the culture container.

I. Your instructor will prepare a *sensitivity test plate.*
   - A few drops of a well-mixed broth culture of *Bacillus cereus* will be poured into a sterile Petri dish containing nutrient agar.
   - The dish will be tilted back and forth until the entire agar surface has come in contact with the broth. This will make an even culture of *B. cereus.*
   - Place four different-colored paper disks, each containing a different antibiotic, on the moist surface of the nutrient agar and tap them lightly.

*II. Read the questions in Part III that you will be asked to answer. Then record your observations in such a way that you will be able to answer the questions from them.

Antibiotic Effectiveness Chart			
Antibiotic	Color	24 Hours	48 Hours

*III. Answer the following questions:
- Which antibiotic most effectively prevents growth of *B. cereus*? _____

  Least effective? _____
- Do your experimental results indicate how effective these antibiotics would be against

  other bacteria? □ yes □ no Explain. _____

  _____

  _____

  _____

- What clinical advantage might be gained by preparing an antibiotic sensitivity test plate of an unknown throat bacterium suspected of causing sore throats?

  _____

  _____

  _____

10A–Protozoans

Materials: microscope; glass slides; coverslips; living cultures of amebas, paramecia, and euglenas; preserved slides of amebas, paramecia, euglenas, *Plasmodium,* and as many other different protozoans as possible; dropping pipets; hand lens; glycerine or methyl cellulose; carmine powder; cotton fibers; toothpicks

Goals:

To observe living protozoans

To note the differences among various protozoans and the various protozoan phyla

To note the similarities among the protozoans within each phylum and characteristics common to all protozoans

Protozoans were at one time classified in the kingdom Animalia (and thus are often discussed in zoology books) in a separate phylum called "Protozoa." In the modern 5-kingdom system, these tiny organisms are placed in the kingdom Protista, and several of the designations that were once classes in the phylum "Protozoa" became phyla in the kingdom Protista. In the 5-kingdom system, Protozoa is a subkingdom containing 4 phyla that are motile and are (or may be) heterotrophic.

This laboratory exercise is designed to aquaint you with the major protozoan phyla. When possible, living specimens have been chosen to demonstrate the major characteristics of the phyla. Searching for, chasing, observing, drawing, and labeling living protozoans is interesting, fun, and profitable.

*Preliminary Work

Use information from your text to fill in these comparison charts of the protozoan phyla, using the ameba, paramecium, and euglena as representative members. After each phylum, place an X in the boxes that are under column headings that describe that phylum.

Comparison of Basic Characteristics / Comparison of Reproductive Processes

	Heterotrophic	Autotrophic	Unicellular	Colonial	Freshwater	Salt Water	Binary Fission or Mitosis	Cyst Formation	Conjugation
Phylum Sarcodina (Ameba)									
Phylum Ciliophora (Paramecium)									
Phylum Mastigophora (Euglena)									

Comparison of Body Structures

	Flagella	Cilia	Pseudopodia	Contractile Vacuole	Food Vacuole	Single Nucleus	Micro- and Macronuclei	Ectoplasm and Endoplasm	Pellicle	Gullet	Eyespot
Phylum Sarcodina (Ameba)											
Phylum Ciliophora (Paramecium)							X				
Phylum Mastigophora (Euglena)							X				

How to Handle Live Protozoan Cultures Properly

- Live cultures of the various protozoans are not "pure"; that is, there are other organisms in the culture. Do not be surprised if you see some unidentifiable organisms on your slide. Do not spend much time with these "odd" organisms.
- Cultures sometimes turn "sour"; that is, the cultured organisms die.
  - ❏ If this happens, or if for some reason living cultures are not available to you, examine a preserved slide of the organism.
  - ❏ If you use a preserved slide, answer questions dealing with live observation according to your research in the text.
- Care for the cultures properly.
  - ❏ Keep the lids on the culture dishes. (Lids, however, should not be screwed on tightly.)
  - ❏ Use each pipet for only one culture dish. Do not mix the pipets. Contaminating one culture with another often leads to souring.
  - ❏ Do not take the cultures to your desk.
  - ❏ Keep slides and coverslips clean and free of soap film.

Phylum Sarcodina

The phylum Sarcodina contains those unicellular organisms that move using pseudopods. We will examine the ameba (*Amoeba proteus* or a similar species) as an example. Actually, there is considerable diversity among members of this phylum, but the typical ameba clearly shows the major phylum characteristics.

The Ameba

R E O

I. Prepare and observe a wet mount of living amebas by following these instructions:
- Obtain an ameba and prepare a wet mount from its culture.
  - ❏ Amebas usually stay close to the bottom of the culture or crawl on some object.
  - ❏ Amebas can be drawn into a dropping pipet.
    - ○ Squeeze the bulb of a dropping pipet in the air.
    - ○ Place the pipet directly above the place where the ameba should be.
    - ○ Release the bulb to suck up *one drop*.
    - ○ Put the entire drop on the slide.
  - ❏ Wait a minute before placing the coverslip on top of the ameba culture on your slide. This allows the ameba to attach to the slide and begin to move.
- Scan the entire slide on low power.
  - ❏ Scan from right to left; then move the slide a little lower and scan left to right. Repeat until you have scanned the entire slide.

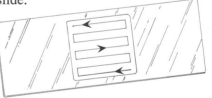

10-1 *How to scan a microscope slide*

  - ❏ Everything that moves is not an ameba.
- Be sure the culture medium does not evaporate. Using the pipets from the ameba culture, add more medium to the edge of the coverslip as necessary.
- Observe the movements of the ameba for a while on both high and low power.
- Observe the amebas that other students have found and let them observe yours.
- Carefully observe the cellular structures of the ameba. Try to locate all the structures listed in the Comparison of Body Structures chart on page 67.
- You may see an ameba engulfing food or dividing. If your ameba appears to be doing either, inform your instructor so that you can share it with the class.

R E O

II. Answer the following questions about amebas.
- Whether or not your ameba engulfed any food particles while you observed it, describe the process of obtaining food and describe how the food is digested.

_____

_____

- As you observed the ameba on your slide, what type of locomotion (movement) did

  the ameba use? _____

  Describe the locomotion. _____

  _____

  _____

- What type of cytoplasm fills the pseudopods? _____

  _____

- Is more than one pseudopod present at one time? ☐ yes   ☐ no
  If so, does more than one grow at a time?   ☐ yes   ☐ no
- Amebas can respond to several types of stimuli. Describe the taxes of the ameba. You

  may need to research in your text for a complete answer. _____

  _____

  _____

R E O

III. Draw an ameba in Area A.
- Draw one of the live amebas you observed under the microscope.
- Label the drawing as completely as you can.

R E O

Other Sarcodines

*I. Choose one of the following sarcodines, research it, and prepare a brief report about it (at least a half page, no more than a full page). Tell how it is similar to the ameba and how it differs from it. (You will need to use reference books other than the text.)
- *Arcella*
- *Difflugia*
- *Actinosphaerium*
- *Actinophrys*
- *Globigerina*
- *Entamoeba coli*

II. If preserved slides are available, make a specimen drawing to illustrate your report.

*III. Prepare a schematic diagram to illustrate your report.

A

Phylum Ciliophora

The phylum Ciliophora contains many diverse organisms unified by the fact that they all possess cilia. Some have cilia covering their entire body, like the paramecium, which will serve as our typical organism for the phylum. Others, like the *Vorticella,* have only a band of cilia. Some ciliates are found in sewage, some in only acidic water, some in clean ponds, and others in our bodies.

The Paramecium

R E O

I. Study a wet mount of living paramecia.
- Prepare a wet mount from the paramecium culture. Paramecia may be found throughout the culture.
- Scan the entire slide.
  - ❏ Paramecia move rapidly and will need to be chased across the slide.
  - ❏ The box below contains three methods you can use to slow down or stop your paramecium. Use the method your instructor designates.

Methods of Slowing Protozoan Movement

Coverslip Pressure

1. As the culture medium evaporates, the coverslip will press on the organism and slow its movement.
2. A paper towel on the edge of the coverslip can be used to speed the process. Your lab partner can draw off small portions of water while you chase the organism.
3. Do not permit the medium to evaporate completely. Replenish it by placing a drop of medium beside the coverslip and letting some of it seep under the coverslip.

Cotton Fibers

1. Before you place the coverslip on the medium, you can place a small quantity of cotton fibers on the medium.
2. These serve as obstacles, blocking the path of protozoans and thus localizing their activities.

Thicker Medium

1. Special media (glycerine, methyl cellulose, or commercially prepared products) can be used to slow protozoans.
2. Because these media are thicker than water, the protozoans must move more slowly through them.

- Be careful not to confuse other protozoans in the culture with paramecia. A paramecium looks like the slipper-shaped illustration in your text and is easy to recognize.
- Observe the paramecia on both high and low powers. Observe the paramecia that other students have found and let them observe yours.
- Carefully observe the cellular structures of the paramecium. Try to locate all the structures belonging to the paramecium discussed in the Comparison of Body Structures chart on page 67.
- Sometimes paramecia can be seen during fission or conjugation. If a paramecium appears to be doing either function, inform your instructor so that you can share the observation with the class.

II. Observe various functions of the paramecium.

R E O

- Observe the reaction of paramecia to obstacles.
    - ❑ If you do not have cotton fibers in your wet mount, remove the coverslip carefully and place a few cotton fibers under the coverslip. (This observation can be done only if the paramecium is not in a thickened medium.)
    - ❑ Carefully observe the movement of the paramecium in response to the cotton fibers.
        - ○ Describe the movement of the paramecium. (Be sure to include the names of the cellular structures involved in its movement.) _____
        _____
        _____
        - ○ By its response to the cotton, would you say the paramecium has taxes?
        ❑ yes ❑ no   Explain. _____
        _____

R E O

- Observe the operation of the contractile vacuole.
    - ❑ Look carefully at a resting or confined paramecium and observe the contractile vacuole in operation. Describe what this looks like. _____
    _____
    _____
    - ❑ Why is the operation of the contractile vacuole essential to the paramecium?
    _____
    _____

R E O

- With a toothpick, place a few grains of carmine powder onto your slide.
  - ❑ When the paramecium takes in food, it takes in the carmine powder also.
  - ❑ Trace the path of the powder as it enters the paramecium and moves within it.
    - ○ How do paramecia obtain their food? _____

      _____

    - ○ After they have obtained food, what process of digestion do paramecia use?

      Explain. _____

      _____

R E O

III. Describe reproduction in paramecia.
- Describe the process of conjugation (sexual reproduction) in paramecia.

  _____

  _____

- Describe asexual reproduction (binary fission) in paramecia. _____

  _____

  _____

R E O

IV. Draw a paramecium in Area B.
- Draw one of the live paramecia you observed with the microscope.
- Label the drawing as completely as you can.

R E O

Other Ciliates

*I. Choose one of the following ciliates, research it, and prepare a brief report about it (at least a half page, no more than a full page). Tell how it is similar to the paramecium and how it differs from it. (You will need to use reference books other than your text.)
  - *Prorodon*
  - *Stentor*
  - *Colpoda*
  - *Halteria*
  - *Tetrahymena*
  - *Vorticella*

II. If preserved slides are available, make a specimen drawing to illustrate your report.

*III. Prepare a schematic diagram to illustrate your report.

B

Phylum Mastigophora

The flagellates are unusual because many of them are both heterotrophic and photosynthetic, as is our typical organism, the euglena. Not all flagellates possess chlorophyll; some are heterotrophic, and a few are parasitic. The euglena is a small protozoan compared to the ameba and the paramecium we have previously studied, but it is easier to find on a slide because most laboratory cultures of euglena are more densely populated.

R E O

The Euglena

I. Observe wet mounts of living euglenas.
- Prepare a wet mount from a euglena culture. Euglenas will be found throughout the entire culture.
- Scan the slide. Euglenas can move rapidly but usually will not leave the microscope field very rapidly. Occasionally it will be necessary to use coverslip pressure or a thicker medium to slow their movement.

- Observe the euglenas on both high and low powers. Observe the euglenas that other students have found, and let them observe yours.
- Carefully observe the cellular structures of the euglena. Try to locate the structures belonging to the euglena discussed in the Comparison of Body Structures chart on page 67.

R E O
II. Answer the following questions concerning euglenas.
*• Describe the two types of movement euglenas can have.

1. _____

2. _____

- Were you able to observe these two types of movement?   ☐ yes   ☐ no

What did you note about the way your euglena moved? _____

_____

_____

*• Explain how euglenas can make their own food. _____

_____

*• Explain how euglenas obtain food (other than by manufacturing it). _____

_____

*• What type of asexual reproduction do euglenas have? _____

What type of sexual reproduction? _____

R E O
III. Draw a euglena in Area C.
- Draw one of the live euglenas you observed under the microscope.
- Label the drawing as completely as you can.

R E O
Other Flagellates
*I. Choose one of the following flagellates and prepare a brief report about it (at least a half page, no more than a full page). Tell how it is similar to the euglena and how it differs from it. (You will need to use reference books other than your text.)
- *Phacus*
- *Bodo*
- *Trypanosoma*
- *Giardia*
- *Peranema*
- *Trichomonas*

II. If preserved slides are available, make a specimen drawing to illustrate your report.
*III. Prepare a schematic diagram to illustrate your report.

C

Phylum Sporozoa

The phylum Sporozoa contains organisms which, as adults, lack methods of movement. (Frequently, stages in their cycle may have pseudopods or other forms of movement.) They also form spores at some stage in their life cycles. They are all parasitic and often have complex life cycles. The *Plasmodium,* which is responsible for malaria, will be the organism we study as an example of this phylum.

R E O
*I. Study carefully the life cycle of the *Plasmodium* on page 267 of your text.
II. Observe a preserved slide of the various stages of the *Plasmodium* life cycle.

10B–Algae

Materials: microscope; glass slides; coverslips; preserved specimens of Proto-coccus, Chondrus, Fucus, Corallina, and kelp; preserved slides of desmids, diatoms, *Protococcus, Spirogyra, Spirogyra* in conjugation, *Ulothrix, Vaucheria,* and dinoflagellates; living cultures of *Spirogyra, Protococcus,* and *Vaucheria;* forceps; scissors; dropping pipets; colored pencils; pond water; reference books for algae and protozoans

Goals:

To observe algae specimens and note the differences among them

To understand the classification of algae

To understand the importance of the algae as a group

To identify examples of the kingdom Protista

The term *algae* refers to five phyla in the kingdom Protista (pp. 268-76) and one group of organisms in the kingdom Monera (p. 233). This lab deals with the algae of the kingdom Protista. To complete parts of this laboratory exercise, you may need to consult additional references such as a dictionary, an encyclopedia, or perhaps a botany or microbiology text.

When working on this lab, keep in mind that you are responsible for each example you observe. You should know its common name (often a part of its scientific name and thus italicized) and to what phylum it belongs, and you should be able to recognize it. When you are asked to observe a specimen but not required to draw it, make mental notes at least. In order to avoid confusion regarding the phylum to which an organism belongs, it is wise to complete all the exercises for one phylum before doing another. You do not need to do the phyla in sequence.

Remember when working with this lab a *preserved slide* is a microscope slide which has a specimen mounted on it, and a *preserved specimen,* or *mounted specimen*, is a specimen in a jar or in plastic, not designed to be used on the microscope.

*Preliminary Work

Algae Classification

- One of the major differences among the algal phyla is the color pigments found with the chlorophyll, which often give the algae found in nature slightly different colors.
- At one time algae were classified in the kingdom Plantae. Give two reasons that this would have been the logical classification for most algae.

    1. _____

    2. _____

- Under the present system of classification, one group of algae is placed in the kingdom

    Monera. What characteristics place blue-green algae in this kingdom? _____

    _____

    _____

- All of the algal phyla other than the blue-green algae are classified in the kingdom Protista. Give at least one reason that the algae in the kingdom Protista should not be classified as

    plants. _____

    _____

R
E
O
Vocabulary Study

- What are phytoplankton? _____
  _____

- The body of an alga that is not differentiated into leaves, roots, and stems (the vegetative body of an alga) is called the _____.

- What is a holdfast? _____

- What are sessile algae? _____

- Long, chainlike colonies of algae are called _____.

- What is a pyrenoid, and what does it do? _____
  _____

- The splitting of an algal colony to form two colonies is called _____.

- Identical gametes that unite to form a zygote are called _____.

- What are heterogametes? _____

- What is conjugation? _____

- A spore formed by the union of gametes is called a(n) _____.

- What is a zoospore? _____

Phylum Chlorophyta–The Green Algae

Chlorophyta, the green algae, is a large phylum. It contains many varied species. Some are tiny, microscopic spheres; others have unusual geometric shapes. Some of these unicellular algae float; others have flagella and swim toward the light. The larger, filament-forming varieties are the usual components of "pond scum," the mat of green, slimy threads that forms on the top of many nutrient-rich water supplies. Microscopic observations of these organisms reveal fascinating structures.

R
E
O
I. Example: **Protococcus** *(Pleurococcus)*
- *Protococcus* is unusual because it frequently lives on tree bark or on the surface of moist soil. Observe a mounted specimen of *Protococcus*.
- Observe *Protococcus* through a microscope.
  - If a living culture is available, prepare a wet mount of the culture and observe it on high and low powers.
  - If a living culture is not available, observe a preserved slide of the organism.
- In Area A draw 3 or 4 cells of this alga, labeling cell walls, chloroplasts, and any other cellular structures you find.

R
E
O
II. Example: **Desmid**
- Observe a preserved slide of desmids.
- Draw in Area B the outlines of 5 different shapes of desmids found on the slide.

  *• Give one structural difference between desmids and diatoms. _____
  _____

R
E
O
III. Example: **Spirogyra**
- Observe *Spirogyra* through a microscope.
  - If a living culture is available, prepare a wet mount.
    - Place a drop of culture medium on a slide.
    - Using forceps and scissors, cut a few short strands of *Spirogyra* and place them on the slide.
    - Be careful to observe cells that are not crushed or broken.
  - If a living culture is not available, use a preserved slide.

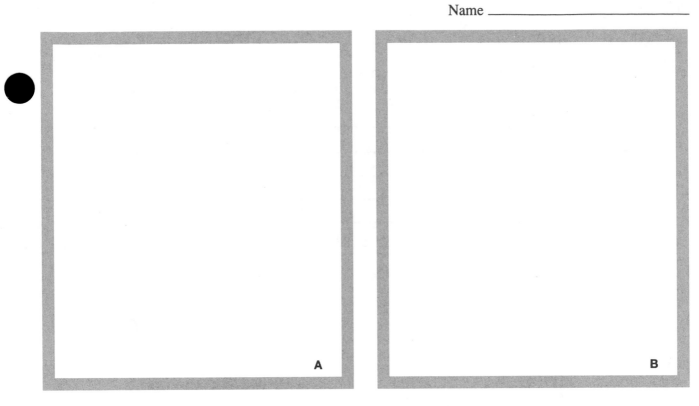

A

B

- Make a specimen drawing in Area C of a normal filament of *Spirogyra*.
  - ❑ The filament should be 3 to 5 cells long.
  - ❑ Draw the filament, showing how the cells are joined.
  - ❑ Label the following if possible: sheath, cytoplasm, chloroplast, pyrenoid, and nucleus.

- Observe a preserved slide of *Spirogyra* in conjugation.
  - ❑ Make a specimen drawing in Area D of *Spirogyra* in conjugation.
  - ❑ Label all the following parts and stages: conjugation tube, zygote, zygospore, empty cell, filament, and normal cell.

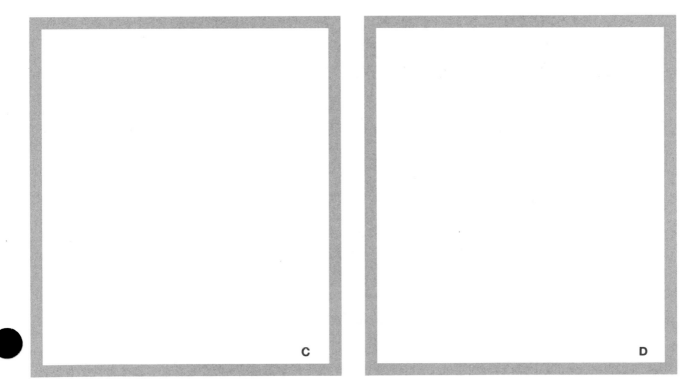

C

D

R
E
O

IV. Example: ***Ulothrix***
- Observe a preserved slide of *Ulothrix*. Check the structures you observed on the slide.
  □ filament □ nucleus □ chloroplast □ holdfast □ gametes
- In the chart below, compare the structures of *Ulothrix* and *Spirogyra*. Describe how they are different or how they are alike.

Ulothrix	*Spirogyra*

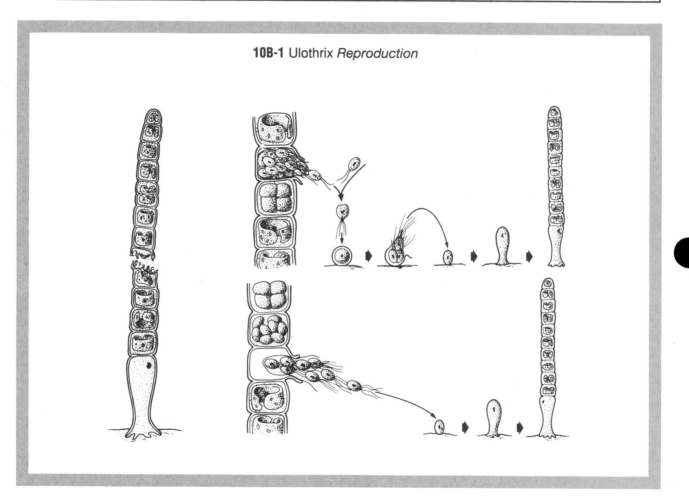

10B-1 Ulothrix *Reproduction*

R
E
O

*- Label the diagram of *Ulothrix* (Diagram 10B-1)
  ❏ Label all of the following structures: filament, isogametes, zoospores, zygote, zygospore, chloroplast, and holdfast.
  ❏ Draw different-colored circles around examples of each of the following types of reproduction. Indicate in the spaces below which color represents each type of reproduction.
    ○ Asexual by fragmentation, forming a new filament _____
    ○ Asexual by cell division (forms new cells within filament) _____
    ○ Sexual by isogametes (forms zygote, which forms filament) _____
    ○ Asexual by zoospores' forming a new filament _____

Phylum Chrysophyta

The phylum Chrysophyta contains three different groups of algae: the yellow-green algae, the golden brown algae, and the diatoms. These three groups are placed in a single phylum because they contain similar pigments, because they store their food as oils, and because they have silica in their cell walls.

I. Example: **Diatoms**
- Scan the preserved slides of diatoms and observe the various shapes.
- Draw in Area E the outlines of five differing diatoms.
- Diatoms have been used for many different purposes because of their hard, silica-containing cell walls. List four uses of diatom cell walls.

1. _____

2. _____

3. _____

4. _____

E

II. Example: *Vaucheria*
- Observe *Vaucheria* through a microscope.
  - ❏ If a living culture is available, prepare a wet mount.
    - ○ Place a drop of the culture medium on a slide.
    - ○ Using forceps and scissors, cut a few short strands of *Vaucheria* and place them on the slide.
    - ○ Be careful to observe cells that are not crushed or broken.
  - ❏ If a living culture is not available, use a preserved slide.
  - ❏ While observing *Vaucheria,* look for reproductive structures, chloroplasts, and nuclei. Which of these did you find? (Tell the type of reproductive structures.)

  _____

  _____

  _____

*• Label the diagram of *Vaucheria* (Diagram 10B-2).
  - ❏ Label the following structures: zoospore, moving zoospore, zoospore forming new filament, sperm, antheridium releasing sperm, archegonium containing egg, and zygote.
  - ❏ Draw different-colored circles around examples of each type of reproduction. Indicate in the spaces below which color represents each type of reproduction.

    - ○ Asexual by fragmentation, forming a new filament _____

    - ○ Asexual by zoospore _____

    - ○ Sexual by heterogametes (forms zygote, which forms filament) _____

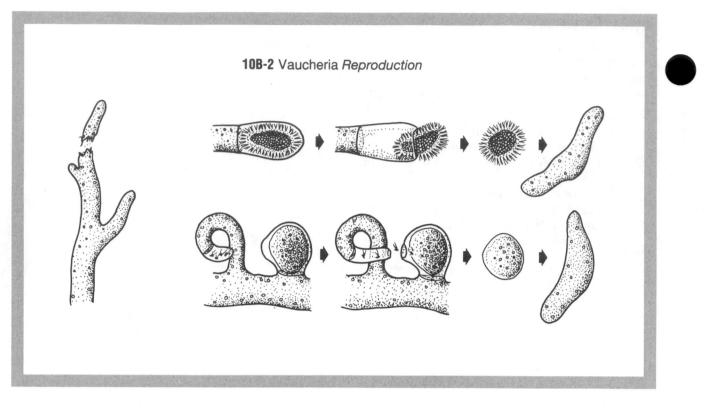

10B-2 Vaucheria *Reproduction*

Phylum Phaeophyta

Although the phylum Phaeophyta is one of the smallest phyla in number of species, the sizes of its individual organisms more than make up for their small number. Some of the larger brown algae may have colonies over 100 feet long. Some areas of the ocean are almost overrun with "algae forests" made up of members of this phylum. Although these appear to be plants with large leaves and stems, they actually lack true tissues and are colonies.

R
E
O

I. Example: *Fucus*
- Observe the mounted specimen of *Fucus*.
- Identify the receptacle and the air bladder, describing the differences between them.

	Receptacle	Air Bladder
Size		
Shape		
Location on thallus		
Function		

R
E
O

II. Example: **Kelp**
- Observe the mounted specimen of kelp.
- Research kelp in other sources and write on your own paper a brief statement describing its appearance, use, and importance to man. Identify your sources.

Phylum Pyrrophyta

The dinoflagellates of the phylum Pyrrophyta are often called the "fire algae" because of the reddish to yellowish color these organisms can give to water. Although many of these are harmless, some cause extensive damage.

*I. Some members of this phylum have bioluminescent properties. This explains a common phenomenon that bothers many when they first see it. What is this phenomenon?

_____

What are bioluminescent properties? _____

II. Example: **Dinoflagellates**

*• *Gymnodinium* is a marine genus, some species of which cause the red tides of Florida. Research red tides and tell how an alga that is usually considered food can kill large

quantities of fish. _____

_____

_____

• *Peridinium,* a common freshwater genus, is illustrated in Diagram 10B-3.

*□ Using the information in your textbook, label the following structures on the diagram: flagella, grooves, and cellulose plates.

□ Observe a preserved slide of freshwater dinoflagellates.

○ Were you able to find *Peridinium?* □ yes □ no

○ Describe two other dinoflagellates you may have seen.

1. _____

_____

_____

2. _____

_____

_____

10B-3 Peridinium

Phylum Rhodophyta

Members of phylum Rhodophyta, the red algae, are multicellular and red. Most members of the phylum are marine organisms. The red algae are similar to the brown algae except for the foods they store and the pigments they contain.

I. Example: **Chondrus,** Irish moss

• Observe the preserved specimen of this marine alga in the laboratory.

*• This alga is economically important. Research to find out what substance is derived

from this alga and how it is used. _____

_____

_____

II. Example: **Corallina**

• This marine alga is important in reef formation. It extracts calcium-containing substances from seawater and deposits them in its cell walls.

• Observe the preserved specimen of this marine alga in the laboratory.

Observing Pond Water

Although many other organisms are found as plankton, most easily recognizable plankton belong to the kingdom Protista. Observing pond water can be interesting and profitable. You can often see organisms that you have studied as well as unfamiliar examples of phyla that you have studied.

R
E
O

  I. Observe pond water from the laboratory culture through a microscope.
- Make a wet mount of the material at the bottom of the culture.
- Make another wet mount of the material near the surface of the culture.

- Why is it advisable to take samples from both areas? _____

  _____

- Various keys and other reference books are available in the classroom for you to use in identification of the organisms you find.

II. List each organism that you observe under the appropriate heading below.

- Organisms studied–give name and phylum. _____

  _____

- Organisms not studied but recognized–describe and, if possible, give the names and phyla of the organisms. _____

  _____

  _____

- Organisms not recognized–describe and name if possible. _____

  _____

  _____

R
E
O

III. Draw in Area F several of the organisms that you found in pond water but had not studied.
- Try to find out the names of what you have and the groups to which they belong.
- Label each of your drawings as completely as possible.

F

11–Fungi and Lichens

Materials: microscope; hand lens; living cultures of *Rhizopus nigricans, Penicillium notatum,* and yeast; preserved slides of *Rhizopus nigricans, R. nigricans* forming zygotes; *Penicillium, Aspergillus, Coprinus,* c.s. and l.s., and lichen c.s.; preserved specimens of puffballs, mushrooms, bracket fungi, and lichens; methylene blue; glass slides; coverslips; dropping pipets; immersion oil

Goals:

> To observe fungi specimens
> To note the difference between types of fungi
> To note the difference between fungi and other organisms
> To understand how the fungi are classified
> To observe and classify lichen specimens

> The smallest kingdom, kingdom Fungi, contains a group of organisms that we frequently consider disgusting. Although their existence may be reserved to dark, musty corners, the fungi are still important organisms. Occasionally you will have to research in other books for answers as you are working on this exercise. The fungi were once considered plants; therefore most general botany texts have chapters covering the fungi.
>
> Technically lichens are not placed in a phylum or any classification in the biological taxonomic system. Lichens are duo-organisms–consisting of an alga and a fungus living together.

*Preliminary Work

I. Fungi Classification and Characteristics

- What is the primary reason fungi are not classified as algae? _____

_____

- What is the primary reason fungi are not classified as plants? _____

_____

_____

- Give two examples demonstrating how fungi are destructive.

    1. _____

    2. _____

- Give two functions of fungi that benefit man.

    1. _____

    2. _____

II. Fungal Vocabulary

- What is mycology? _____

- What are hyphae? _____

- What are aerial hyphae that produce new filaments called? _____

- What are mycelia? _____

- What are rhizoids? _____

- What part of the fungus both produces and disperses spores? _____

- What are haustoria? _____

- What is a sporangiophore? _____
- When spores are not in an enclosure and are formed by repeated divisions, what is the spore-producing structure called? _____
- What is an ascus? _____
- What is a basidium? _____
- What are basidiospores? _____

Phylum Zygomycota

The phylum Zygomycota contains the organisms we normally think of as fungi. These organisms are usually sessile, produce spores, and resemble algae in structure. These fungi bear asexually produced spores in the sporangia. Sexual reproduction takes place when specialized hyphae unite. Examples of this phylum are common and abundant; they are often found literally under every step you take.

R E O **Example: *Rhizopus nigricans***
  I. *Rhizopus nigricans* is a black-colored mold that often grows on bread.
  II. Using the stereomicroscope or a hand lens, observe cultures of *R. nigricans*.
  - Describe what you see, including any fungal structures you can identify.

_____
_____
_____

  - *R. nigricans* produces hyphae that are clear or white. What causes its dark appearance? _____

R E O III. Observe a preserved slide of *R. nigricans,* w.m., on high power.
  - Make a drawing in Area A that will include sporangiophores, sporangia, hyphae, mycelia, stolons, and rhizoids.
  - Label these structures on your drawing.

A   B

R E IV. *R. nigricans* reproduces sexually by forming zygotes by conjugation.
- Observe a preserved slide of *R. nigricans* with zygotes.
- Draw in Area B a zygote with two parent hyphae.
- What is the difference between a zygote and a zygospore? _____

_____

R E O *Other Examples of Phylum Zygomycota
Choose any example of class Phycomycetes not previously used in this exercise. Some examples you might like to choose from are *Pilobolus* (cap-thrower fungi) and *Glomus*.
- Observe laboratory specimens or preserved slides of your example, if possible.
- Consult at least one other text for information about your specimen.
- Make a drawing of your example (specimen drawing if possible, schematic drawing if necessary) and label it completely.
- Write a description of the structure, habitat, and economic significance of your specimen.

Phylum Ascomycota

The second phylum we will study is Ascomycota. Often these organisms appear very similar to the zygomycotes, but differ in their spore-forming structures. Some of the ascomycotes, however, have varied and unusual structures.

R E O **Example: *Penicillium***
I. *Penicillium* is a common mold of fruits and is the original source of the antibiotic penicillin.
II. Using the stereomicroscope or a hand lens, observe the laboratory culture of *Penicillium notatum*. Describe what you see, including any fungal structures you can identify.

_____

_____

III. Observe a preserved slide of *Penicillium*
- Look for conidia and conidiophores.
- Below are diagrams of conidia and conidiophores. Which one exhibits the structures found in *Penicillium*? ☐ Diagram 11-1 ☐ Diagram 11-2
- Label the diagram appropriately.

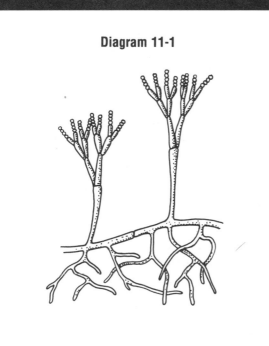

Diagram 11-1

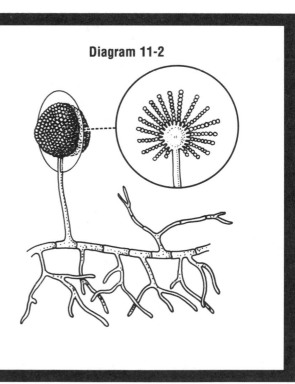

Diagram 11-2

*IV. Does *Penicillium* have a use besides being a source of antibiotics? □ yes □ no

If so, what is it? _____

Example: *Aspergillus* ("powdery mildews")
Observe a preserved specimen of the genus *Aspergillus*.
- Based on your observation and reading, why is the name "powdery mildews" appropriate? _____

*• What effect do powdery mildews have on plants? _____

_____

Example: Yeasts
I. A drop of yeast culture will be mixed with a stain (methylene blue) and placed on a slide for you to observe. The slide will be set up for oil-immersion viewing (1,000×).
- Draw a few yeast cells in Area C. If possible, include some that are budding. Label your drawing as completely as you can.
- Smell the yeast culture and see if you detect an alcohol odor. What chemical process does this odor indicate? _____

_____

_____

_____

*II. What are some ways yeasts profit man? _____

_____

_____

The Imperfect Fungi
One group in the phylum Ascomycota are not known to reproduce sexually. They are few in number, and, except those that are parasitic to man, they have only minor importance.

*I. Example: **Athlete's foot**
Find information about the athlete's foot fungus. Describe the fungus itself. Then describe the common disease it causes, how the disease is spread, how it can be prevented, and how

it can be cured. _____

_____

_____

*II. Example: **Ringworm**
Find information about the ringworm fungus. Describe the fungus itself. Then describe the common disease it causes, how the disease is spread, how it can be prevented, and how it

can be cured. _____

_____

_____

R E O

*Other Examples of Phylum Ascomycota

Choose any example of class Ascomycetes not previously covered in this exercise. Some examples you might like to choose from are *Neurospora, Taphrina, Morchella* (morel), cup fungi, and *Peziza*.

- Observe laboratory specimens of your examples, if possible.
- Consult at least one other text for information about your specimen.
- Draw your example (specimen drawing if possible, schematic drawing if necessary) and label the drawing completely.
- Write a brief description of the structure, habitat, and economic significance of your specimen.

Phylum Basidiomycota

The basidiomycotes are a widely varied group of fungi. They range from those having extremely large vegetative and fruiting bodies to others that have very small ones. Some are harmful parasites; others are saprophytes. Some contain deadly poisons; others are prized as food. A number have several hosts during their intricate life cycles.

R E O

Example: Rusts and Smuts

I. The rusts and smuts are usually parasitic fungi with many hosts. Many of them are parasites on food crops and can be extremely harmful.

*II. *Puccinia* is the genus that contains many rusts, including the common wheat rust. Compare the life cycle given in other books with the life cycle in Diagram 11-3. Fill in as many labels on the diagram as you can.

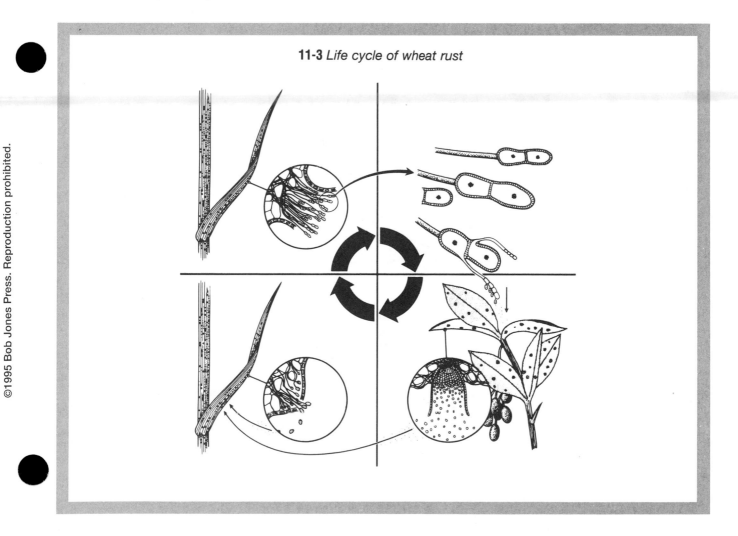

11-3 *Life cycle of wheat rust*

Example: Puffballs

Observe preserved and dried specimens of puffballs.

*• Where are the basidia and basidiospores (''spores'') located on the puffballs?

_____

*• How are the spores released? _____

_____

R
E
O

Examples: Bracket (shelf) Fungi

Observe preserved specimens of bracket, or shelf, fungi and note differences and similarities among the various species.

*• Where are the basidia and basidiospores located on the shelf fungi?

_____

*• How are spores released from these fungi? _____

R
E
O

Example: Mushrooms

I. Observe preserved specimens of mushrooms.
  • Note the cap, gills, stipe, and hyphae of the various species.
  • Note the different colors, sizes, and textures of the various species.

*II. Label as many structures as you can in Diagram 11-4.

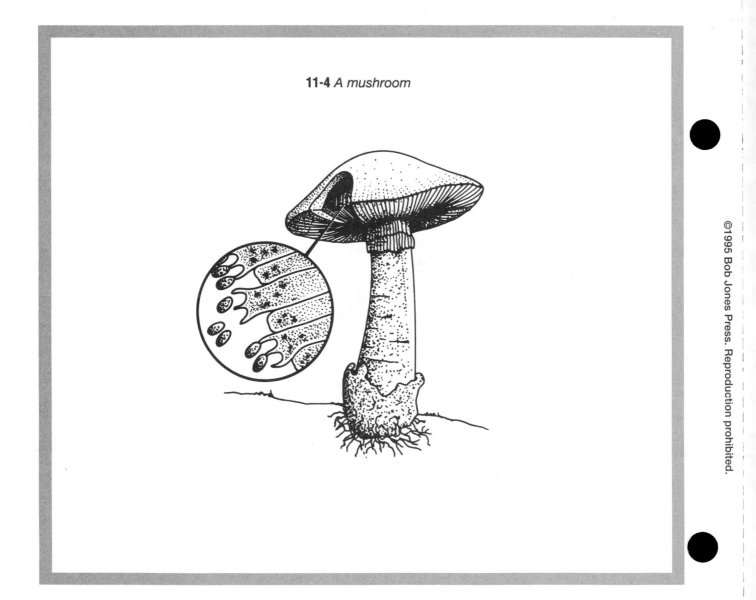

11-4 *A mushroom*

R E
● III. Observe the preserved slide of *Coprinus*, c.s.
(Be sure to use the cross section of the cap.)
- Find the gills and locate the basidia and basidiospores.
- In Area D, make a drawing that includes a section of a gill with basidia and basidiospores.
- Label the drawing as completely as possible.

R E O
IV. Choose any two specific mushrooms and research them in other texts. Briefly describe them, telling their habitat, importance, and a couple of unusual facts.

- Name of mushroom: _____

_____

Description: _____

_____

_____

_____

_____

_____

_____

_____

_____

_____

D

- Name of mushroom: _____

Description: _____

_____

_____

_____

_____

R E O
*Other Examples of Phylum Basidiomycota

Choose any example of class Basidiomycetes not previously covered in this exercise. Some examples you might like to choose from are earthstars, stinkhorns, apple cedar rust, and corn smut.
- Observe laboratory specimens of your examples, if possible.
- Consult at least one other text for information about your specimen.
- Draw your example (specimen drawing if possible, schematic drawing if necessary) and label it completely.
- Write a brief description of the structures, habitat, and economic significance of your specimen.

The Lichens

Lichens are not fungi, but they do contain fungi. Actually they are a symbiotic set of organisms, living together as one for the benefit of both.

R
E
O

*I. What two organisms are always found in a lichen? Trace the organisms to phylum and class if possible.

1. _____

2. _____

II. Your instructor will supply you with several different lichen specimens labeled by letters. There will be at least one of each of the three types of lichens. Identify the type of each specimen and describe it in the chart below.

Example	Type of Lichen	Description of This Specimen
A		
B		
C		

R
E
O

III. Observe slide of a lichen, c.s., stained to show the alga in one color and the fungus in another.
- Draw in Area E a section showing the alga and fungus.
- Label the structures you are able to identify.

E

12A–Plant Identification

Materials: live and preserved plant specimens

Goals:
> To learn major classifications in the plant kingdom
> To recognize various plant characteristics in specimens

> It is one thing to see plant characteristics in photographs or drawings, but it is quite another to recognize those characteristics in actual specimens. In this laboratory exercise you will list characteristics you would look for when identifying the major plant groups and then use your list to identify specimens. The more specimens you correctly identify, the better your grade.

*Before Class

I. Fill in the Plant Classifications Chart on pages 91-92.
- List characteristics for each classification, using characteristics that you can distinguish by sight. (For example, ''Has cell walls made of cellulose'' would be a poor characteristic to list since you cannot tell this by looking at a specimen.)
- Try to list characteristics that apply only to a particular taxonomic group. (''Has chlorophyll'' would be a poor characteristic to list since nearly all plants have chlorophyll.)
- As you identify the specimens in class, you will be permitted to refer to the Plant Classifications Chart only. Put on it all the information you will need.
- You may not list names of plants on your Plant Classifications Chart.

II. Make sketches of the types of leaf venations on the back of the Plant Classifications Chart. You may draw variations of the venation to help you as you fill in the Specimen Chart. (Remember, you can put no names of plants on your Plant Classifications Chart.)

In Class

I. Various specimens will be present in the lab. Some will be fresh; others preserved. Some will be entire plants, while others will be pieces of a plant.
- Each specimen will be numbered, and you will be asked to identify it accordingly on the Specimen Chart.
- You must list your reasons for each identification by listing the letters for the appropriate characteristics from your Plant Classifications Chart. (See Sample Specimen Chart.)
- If the specimen has leaves, you must list the type of leaf venation it has in order to get credit for that specimen.
- If the specimen has needles or scales, you must write ''needles'' or ''scales'' in the venation section of the Specimen Chart to get credit for that specimen.
- Some of the specimens will have their common and/or scientific names on them. If they are not labeled, you do not need to list their names on the Specimen Chart.

II. This exercise is limited to the 45 minutes available in class. There will be no lab time after school.

Sample Specimen Chart

	Name	Classification	Reasons for Identification	Venation
1	Sugar Maple	Dicot	A, C, D	S. Pal.
2	Iris	Monocot	A, E	Parl.
3	White Pine	Conif	E	Needles
4				
5				
6				
7				
8				
9				
10				
11				

Note: These letters are for example only and are not intended as accurate answers.

Plant Classifications Chart

I. Phylum Bryophyta† *(Bryo)*‡

   A. Lacks vascular tissue; most living specimens about one inch high _____

   B. _____

   C. _____

   D. _____

   E. _____

II. Phylum Lycophyta† *(Lyc)*‡

   A. _____

   B. _____

   C. _____

   D. _____

   E. _____

III. Phylum Pterophyta† *(Pter)*‡

   A. _____

   B. _____

   C. _____

   D. _____

   E. _____

IV. Phylum Coniferophyta† *(Conif)*‡

   A. _____

   B. _____

   C. _____

   D. _____

   E. _____

V. Phylum Anthophyta

   • Class Monocotyledoneae† *(Monocot)*‡

     A. Leaf venation: parallel _____

     B. _____

     C. _____

     D. _____

     E. _____

   • Class Dicotyledoneae† *(Dicot)*‡

     A. Leaf venation: pinnate or palmate _____

     B. _____

     C. _____

     D. _____

     E. _____

† Use only these levels of classification when identifying the specimens.

‡ The abbreviations in parentheses may be used when filling in the Specimen Chart.

Leaf Venations§

Parallel (Parl.)‖

Simple Palmate (S. Pal.)‖	Palmately Compound (Pal. C.)‖

Simple Pinnate (S. Pin.)‖	Pinnately Compound (Pin. C.)‖	Bipinnately Compound (Bipin.)‖

§ It is suggested that you draw a couple of modifications of the leaves (heavily lobed, etc.) above so that you can more easily recognize them. When identifying succulent leaves, you will have to make an educated guess. Succulent leaves are often very thick, and the venation does not show.

‖ Use the abbreviations in parentheses as you fill in the Specimen Chart.

Name _____

Specimen Chart

	Name	Classification	Reasons for Identification	Venation
1				
2				
3				
4				
5				
6				
7				
8				
9				
10				
11				
12				
13				
14				
15				
16				
17				
18				
19				
20				
21				
22				
23				
24				
25				
26				
27				
28				
29				
30				
31				
32				
33				
34				
35				

	Name	Classification	Reasons for Identification	Venation
36				
37				
38				
39				
40				
41				
42				
43				
44				
45				
46				
47				
48				
49				
50				
51				
52				
53				
54				
55				
56				
57				
58				
59				
60				
61				
62				
63				
64				
65				
66				
67				
68				
69				
70				
71				
72				

12B–Plant Organs

Materials: microscope; stereomicroscope or hand lens; preserved slides of leaf, c.s.; *Ranunculus* young root, c.s.; *Ranunculus* stem, c.s.; *Zea* stem, c.s.; fresh lettuce, spinach, or geranium leaves; glass slides; coverslips; dormant twigs; plants rooting in water; leaf with epidermal hairs; scalpel; collection of leaves; forceps

Goals:

To observe some of the plant organs and tissues

To understand better the anatomy and physiology of plant leaves and stems

Plants have their own ways of handling the basic functions necessary for survival. Observing some of their special structures will help you better understand the functions of leaves, roots, and stems.

Leaves

Plant leaves are usually the major photosynthetic organs of the plant. Foliage leaves, which are the type you will work with in this exercise, display the typical characteristics of leaves. We will note some of the varieties of foliage leaves and then observe their specialized design for carrying on photosynthesis.

Gross Structure

R E O

I. Leaf venations
- Make a collection of leaves typical of the various types of leaf venations.
- Press and mount your leaves on paper, one type per page. You may have several specimens with the same type of leaf venation on the same page.
- On each page write the common names of the specimens you have collected and the names of several other plants with the same type of leaf venation.
- You should have examples of the following types if possible:
  - ❏ parallel
  - ❏ simple pinnate, pinnately compound, bipinnately compound
  - ❏ simple palmate, palmately compound
  - ❏ scales
  - ❏ needles
  - ❏ modified leaves such as bracts and thorns

R E O

II. Leaf margins
- Make a collection of leaves with different margins and shapes.
- Press and mount your leaves on paper, one type of leaf margin or leaf shape per page. You may have several specimens with the same type of margin or shape on the same page.
- On each page write the common names of the specimens you have collected and list the names of several other plants with the same type of leaf margin or leaf shape.
- You should have examples of at least the following margins:
  - ❏ entire
  - ❏ undulate serrate
  - ❏ dentate
  - ❏ any two others
- You should include at least the following shapes:
  - ❏ linear
  - ❏ cordate
  - ❏ deltoid
  - ❏ lobed
  - ❏ circular
  - ❏ at least one other

Microstructures

R E O

I. Draw a cross section of a leaf from a preserved slide.
- Draw five to fifteen cells of each type of tissue (for example, five to fifteen upper epidermal cells, five to fifteen palisade mesophyll cells adjacent to the epidermal cells). Continue until you have a section of the leaf from top to bottom, including the vein. Include guard cells and stomata if possible.
- Draw in Area A.
- Include a vein (not the large vein in the middle of the leaf). Try to find a vein cut in cross section, not one that has been cut longitudinally.
- Be careful not to draw a torn segment of leaf.
- Label all parts.

A

R E O

II. Study and draw a wet mount of a leaf epidermis.
- Using your forceps or your fingers, carefully peel a piece of epidermis from a geranium, spinach, or lettuce leaf.
- Make a wet mount of this tissue and observe the epidermis by using a microscope.
- What is the position of the guard cells?   □ open   □ closed
  What does this tell you about the photosynthetic activity of the leaf at the time you took off the epidermis? _____
  _____
- What is the approximate ratio of guard cells to epidermal cells in this epidermis specimen? _____
  - Would you expect this ratio to be different in other plants?   □ yes   □ no
  - Why or why not? _____
  _____
- Draw in Area B a section of epidermal tissue, including two stomata with guard cells and several epidermal cells. Label your drawing completely.

R E O

III. Observe a leaf with epidermal hairs under a stereomicroscope or a hand lens. Observe the area near the margin of the leaf. Describe what you see. _____
_____
_____

B

Roots

Roots anchor plants, help them absorb water and dissolved substances, and provide storage. In this section you will observe the structures of roots that do all these functions. Carefully note which structure of the root accomplishes each function.

Gross Structure

Draw schematic diagrams of a taproot system and a fibrous root system. On both root system drawings, label primary and secondary roots.

Microstructure

I. Observe the preserved slide of a young *Ranunculus* root, c.s. Follow these instructions:
- Scan the entire slide.
- Draw in Area C a pie-shaped section of the root (triangular, touching both the center of the root and the outside–see Diagram 12B-1 on the next page).
- You may need to move the slide while you make this drawing because what you are drawing is probably larger than the field of view of the microscope.
- Include all the tissues found in the root. Label all the parts.

C

R E O

R E O

12B-1 *Drawing a pie-shaped section*

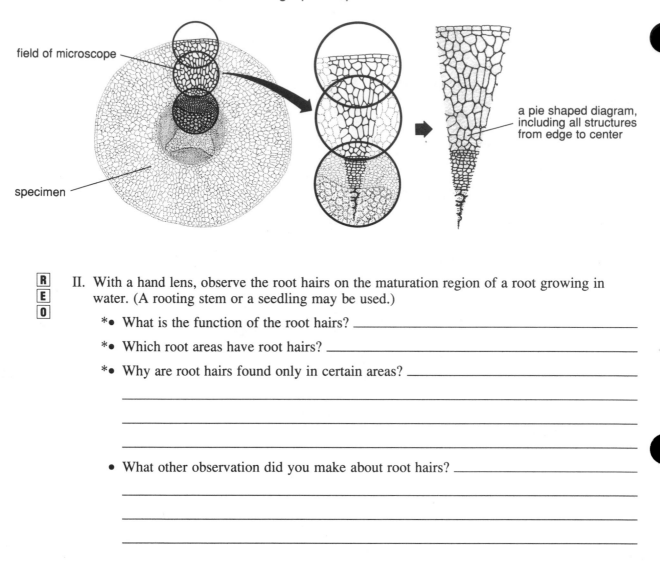

field of microscope

specimen

a pie shaped diagram, including all structures from edge to center

R
E
O

II. With a hand lens, observe the root hairs on the maturation region of a root growing in water. (A rooting stem or a seedling may be used.)

*• What is the function of the root hairs? _____

*• Which root areas have root hairs? _____

*• Why are root hairs found only in certain areas? _____

_____

_____

_____

• What other observation did you make about root hairs? _____

_____

_____

_____

Stems

Although some plants (such as cactus) have stems that are the primary photosynthetic structures and even the storage organs of the plant, in this section we will observe stems that use typical structures to accomplish the usual function of manufacturing and displaying leaves.

Gross Structure

R
E
O

I. Observe a dormant twig section. Answer the following:
   - My twig number is _____.
   - How many years old is the twig? _____

     How do you know? _____

     _____

     _____

   - Was the rate of growth the same each year?
     ☐ yes   ☐ no   How do you know?

     _____

     _____

     _____

     _____

   - What is the leaf arrangement of this plant?
     ☐ opposite   ☐ alternate   ☐ whorled
   - How many nodes were produced during the most recent growing season (last summer)? _____

II. Using a scalpel, make a longitudinal section of an apical (terminal) bud.
   - Do not use the apical bud of any of the twigs used earlier.
   - Draw the dissected apical bud and label all the parts you observed in Area D.

D

Microstructure

R
E
O

I. Observe a preserved slide of a *Ranunculus* stem, c.s.
   - Scan the entire slide.
   - Make a drawing of a pie-shaped section of the stem in Area E (triangular, touching both the center of the stem and the outside; see Diagram 12B-1). You may need to move the slide while you make the drawing because what you are drawing is probably larger than the field of view of the microscope.
   - Label all the parts.
   - *Ranunculus* is a dicot. Is the *Ranunculus* stem typical of this class?   ☐ yes   ☐ no

R
E
O

II. Observe the preserved slide of a cross section of *Zea* (corn) stem.
   - Follow the directions given above to make a drawing of the stem in Area F.
   - *Zea* is a monocot. Is the *Zea* stem typical of this class?   ☐ yes   ☐ no

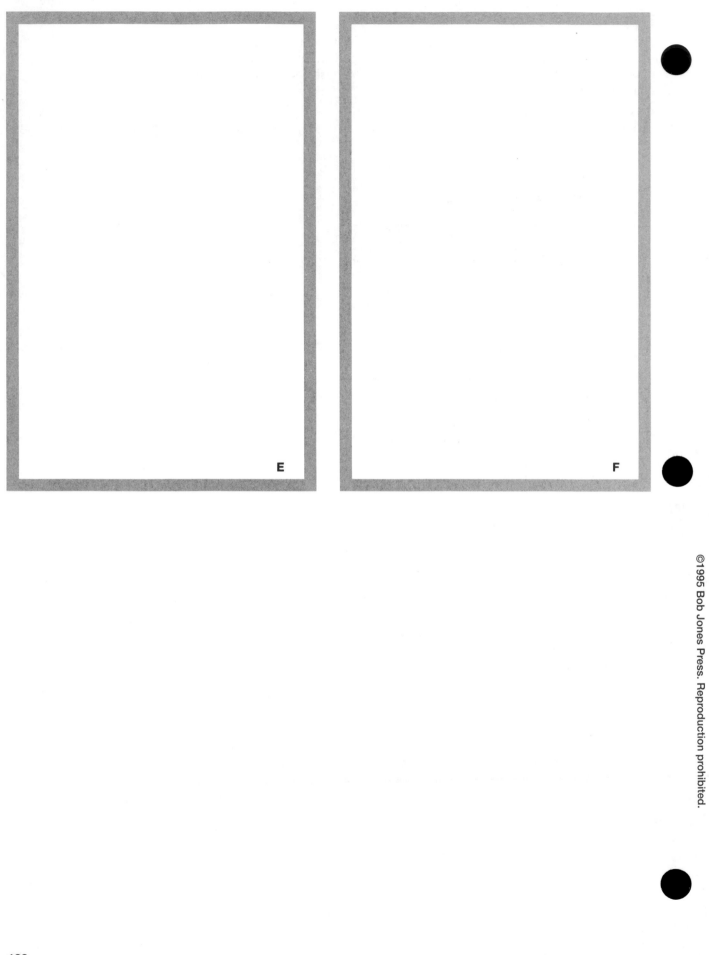

E

F

Name _____

Date _____ Hour _____

13–Flowers, Fruits, and Seeds

Materials: fresh flower specimens (gladioli); fresh fruit specimens (including at least a pome, drupe, berry, modified berry and a pod); scalpel; large kitchen knife; single-edged razor blade; seeds

Goals:

To observe the structures of a typical flower and to learn the structures of various flowers

To observe various kinds of fruits and learn their parts

To observe and learn the structures of a typical seed

> The sexual reproductive parts of angiosperms are found in structures called flowers. There are many types of flowers, but they all have certain characteristics in common. Note these characteristics as you study the flowers and their products, the fruits and the seeds.

Flowers

Not all flowers are variations of the rose, lily or daisy. Many flowers lack showy petals, many have very unusual structures, but most of them share the same basic floral parts.

*I. Observe and label the diagrams of various flowers in Diagram 13-1 on pages 102-3.

   • On each diagrammed flower, label as many of the following structures as you can: pistil, stigma, style, ovary, ovule, stamen, anther, filament, pollen, petals, sepals, and receptacle. (*NOTE:* Not all these are visible in all the flowers illustrated. Use your knowledge of these structures to assign the labels.)

   • By the names of the various flowers in Diagram 13-1, indicate whether the flower
      ❑ is complete or incomplete.
      ❑ is male, female, or both.
      ❑ has a superior ovary or an inferior ovary.
      ❑ contains a single ovule or multiple ovules.
      ❑ is from a monocot or a dicot.

II. Dissect a flower.

   • Using your scalpel, carefully dissect a live flower to see the various internal structures. Examine with a hand lens if necessary.

   • Draw in Area A a longitudinal section of your flower. Label all parts.

   • Indicate whether your flower is complete or incomplete; is male, female, or both; has a superior or inferior ovary; contains a single ovule or multiple ovules; is a composite flower or not a composite flower; comes from a monocot or dicot plant.

   _____

   _____

   _____

   _____

   _____

A

13-1 *Flowers*

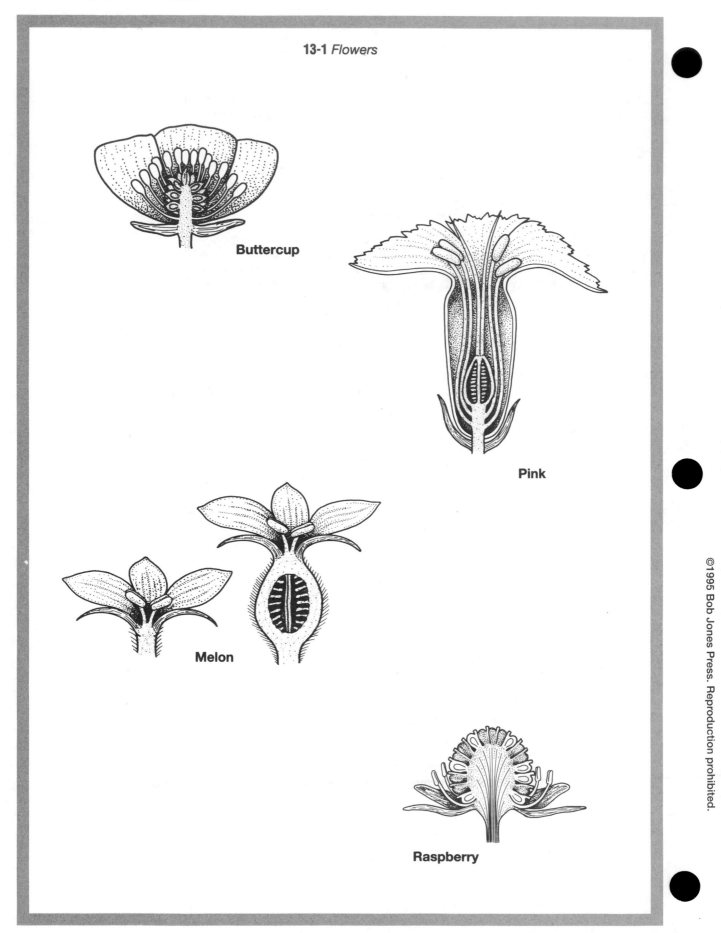

Buttercup

Pink

Melon

Raspberry

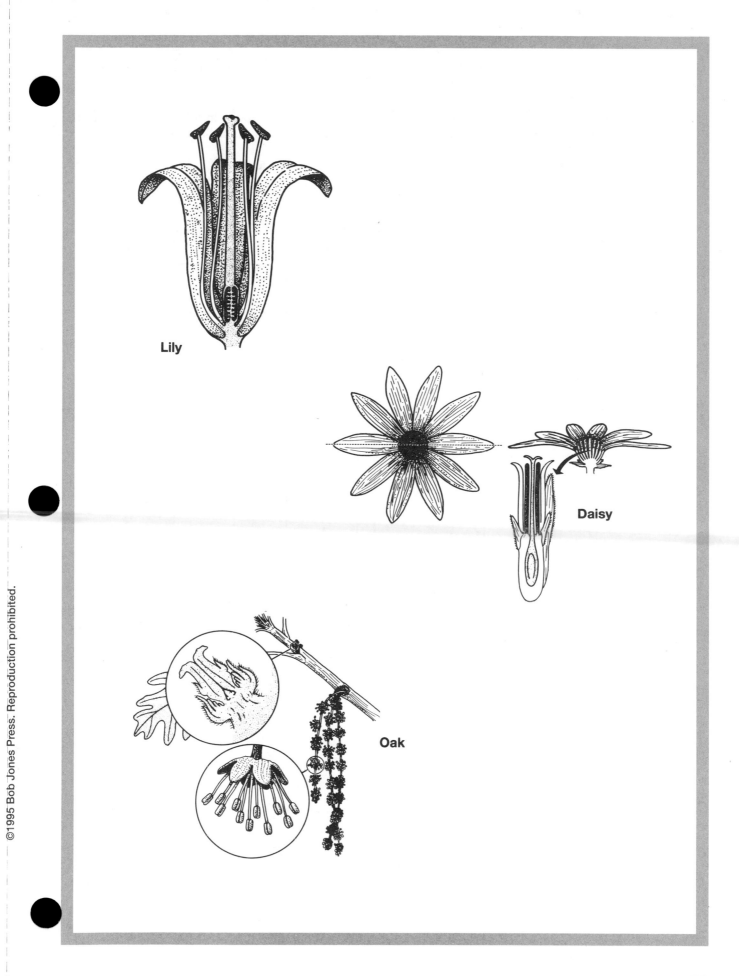

Lily

Daisy

Oak

Fruits

A fruit is a ripened ovary. Although many fruits are like the familiar apple and orange, many are quite different. Fruits have been classified into groups based on the different ways their structures develop.

R E O   I. Using a scalpel and/or knife, dissect the examples of fruits found in the lab. (Your teacher may assign a different fruit to each laboratory group to dissect, or the fruits may already be dissected for you.)

R E O   II. Use A Key to Common Fruit Types (p. 105) to identify the type of each of the fruit specimens.

Fruit Types

Specimen	Name of Fruit	Fruit Type
A		
B		
C		
D		
E		
F		

Specimen	Name of Fruit	Fruit Type
G		
H		
I		
J		
K		
L		

B

III. Draw in Area B a longitudinal section of the fruits your teacher selects and label the parts indicated by the fruit type. Research may be necessary.

- *Pome:* Label receptacle, ovary, remains of flower parts, pedicel, ovary wall, and seeds.
- *Drupe:* Label pedicel, remains of flower parts, ovary (outer layer and inner layer), and seed.
- *Berry:* Label pedicel, remains of flower parts, skin, ovary, section of fruit, and seeds.
- *Pod:* Label pedicel, remains of flower parts, ovary, and seeds.
- *Modified Berry:* Label pedicel, remains of flower parts, skin, ovary, section of fruit, and seeds.

A Key to Common Fruit Types

1. Single ovary which may have one or more chambers for ovules, usually without other floral parts . . . . (Simple Fruit) 3

   Collection of ovaries, usually with other floral parts . . . . (Compound Fruit) 2

Compound Fruits

2. Several separate ovaries of a single flower which ripen individually, usually on an enlarged receptacle . . . . **Aggregate fruit**

   Several ovaries from separate flowers which ripen fused together, usually on an enlarged receptacle . . . . **Multiple fruit**

Simple Fruits

3. Fruit dry at maturity . . . . (Dry Fruit) 4

   Fruit fleshy at maturity . . . . (Fleshy Fruit) 9

Dry Simple Fruits

4. Fruit open when ripe 5

   Fruit closed when ripe 6

5. Ovary wall thin. Single-chambered ovary with many seeds. Opens along one or two sides when ripe . . . . **Pod**

   Ovary wall thin. Multiple-chambered ovary, each chamber with many seeds. Opens when ripe . . . . **Capsule**

6. Fruit with thin wing formed by ovary wall . . . . **Samara**

   Fruit without wing 7

7. Thick, hard, woody ovary wall enclosing a single seed . . . . **Nut**

   Thin ovary wall 8

8. Ovary wall fastened to a single seed . . . . **Grain**

   Ovary wall separated from a single seed . . . . **Achene**

Fleshy Simple Fruits

9. Fleshy portion develops from receptacle enlargement. Ovary forms leathery core with seeds inside . . . . **Pome**

   Ovary fleshy 10

10. Ovary two-layered; outer layer fleshy, inner layer forming hard, woody stone or pit, usually enclosing one seed . . . . **Drupe**

    Entire ovary fleshy 11

11. Thin-skinned fruit, with divided ovary, usually with each section containing seeds . . . . **Berry**

    Thick, tough skinned, with divided ovary, usually with each section containing seeds . . . . **Modified Berry**

Seeds

The three basic parts of a seed are the embryo plant, stored food, and a seed coat.
The diversity of these structures found in different plants, however, is almost as
wide as the diversity found in the floral parts and fruit types.

R E O
I. Observe the seed(s) found in the lab. (Your teacher may assign a different seed to each
laboratory group, or may give each group a few seeds to observe and dissect.)
   - Use a hand lens to observe the exterior structures of the seed(s).
   - Seek to identify the following structures:
     - ❏ The *hilum* (point where the seed was attached to the ovary).
     - ❏ The *micropyle* (point where the pollen tube entered the ovule).
   - Draw the seed you observed in area C, labeling as many parts as you can.

R E O
II. Dissect the seed(s) supplied by your instructor.
   - You will need to use a sharp scalpel or a single-edged razor blade to dissect most
seeds.
     - ❏ If your dissection instrument is dull, you will damage the structures.
     - ❏ The size or hardness of some seeds makes using a sharp instrument dangerous.
       - ○ If possible, hold the seed with forceps or other instruments when you are
attempting to cut it open.
       - ○ If your seed is very hard (a nut or a pit) you may need to use special instru-
ments to open it. Your teacher will give you special instructions.
   - Often a single, well-placed cut will reveal all of the structures listed below. Some
seeds, however, will require additional cuts. Some seeds (like nuts) must be taken
apart in pieces to reveal all of the structures.
   - Once you have dissected the seed, seek to find the following parts:
     - ❏ The *embryo plant,* composed of the *epicotyl, hypocotyl,* and *radicle*
     - ❏ The cotyledon(s)
     - ❏ The endosperm
   - Is the seed you dissected a monocot or a dicot?   ☐ monocot   ☐ dicot

R E O
   - Draw the seed you dissected in Area D, labeling as many parts as you can.
     - ❏ You may need to draw both halves of your dissected seed in order to get all of
the parts in your drawing.
     - ❏ You may need to "reconstruct" some of your dissected seed in order to draw it.
III. After everyone is finished, observe their dissected seeds and their drawings.

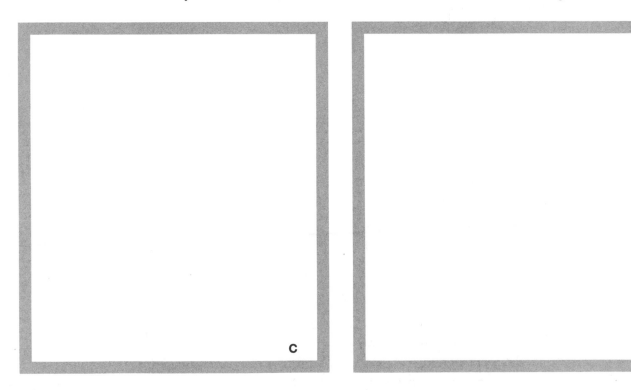

C

D

14A–**Porifera**

Materials: preserved slides of *Grantia,* c.s. and l.s., and *Grantia* spicules; preserved specimens of various sponges; dissection kit; hand lens; microscope; glass slides; coverslips

Goals:

    To observe typical sponges

    To draw some conclusions regarding the structure and unique specializations of sponges

> You will study these unusual animals in phylum Porifera by observing preserved specimens. Before you begin, read carefully the Life Process Chart for *Grantia.* You are responsible for knowing the structures and functions of each organism covered in the laboratory exercises as an example of the particular phylum you are studying.

R **E** **O** **Example: *Grantia***

    I. Study the picture of *Grantia* in your text on page 342.

   II. Without using the microscope, observe a cross section and a longitudinal section of *Grantia* found on a preserved slide. Measure the height and width of these sections of *Grantia*–

    _____ mm high by _____ mm wide.

  III. Scan both the c.s. and the l.s. of a *Grantia* preserved slide under a microscope.

    • How is the sponge structure of *Grantia* classified?   ☐ simple   ☐ complex

    Why? _____

    _____

    • After studying your text and a preserved slide prepared for observing spicules, describe the spicules of a *Grantia.* _____

    _____

    _____

    _____

    _____

    _____

    _____

    _____

    _____

    _____

    _____

R **E** **O** IV. Draw a portion of a *Grantia* cross section in Area A by following these directions:

    • Include sections of both cell layers and the mesenchyme.

    • Label as many different structures as you can see.

A

Example: Bath Sponge

R E O

I. Observe a preserved specimen of a bath sponge.

- What structures are you able to see? _____
- Classify the structure of a bath sponge: ☐ simple   ☐ complex

Why? _____

R E O

II. Observe the spongin network of a bath sponge.
- Use a hand lens to observe the spongin fiber network of a bath sponge.
  ❏ Observe sections of a dry bath sponge and of a wet bath sponge.

  ❏ What differences are you able to observe? _____

  _____

  _____

R E O

- Make a wet mount of the spongin fibers of a bath sponge.
  ❏ Use a very small piece of sponge.

  ❏ Describe what you see. _____

  _____

  _____

  ❏ Draw in Area B several of the spongin fibers as seen on low power of your microscope.

B

Life Process Charts

The 9 basic life processes that all animals accomplish are described on page 338 of your text. As you read about and study the various animal phyla, you will learn about the methods and structures they use to accomplish these life functions. To help you associate the different organisms with their structures and methods and to make sure that you have grasped all the information you need to know, you will fill in Life Process Charts for the representative animals of several phyla.

Unless you are told otherwise, you will find in your text most of the information you need to fill in these charts. When you finish them, they will serve as excellent study guides as well as reveal how carefully you have read.

On pages 109-10 a Life Process Chart has been completed for the sponge *Grantia*. Because *Grantia* is a simple organism, not all the spaces on the chart have been used. The entry in the column labeled Notes describes, defines, or explains the entry in the Structure column. The lack of special structures for a particular function *does not* indicate that an organism does not accomplish that function. You should explain in the Notes column the way it accomplishes that function. Normally, the first time you use a term in a Life Process Chart, you should define it in the Notes column.

Life Process Chart

Organism _____ Sponge *(Grantia)* _____

Phylum _____ Porifera _____ **Class** _____ **Genus** _____ *Grantia* _____

Structure	Notes

Movement *(structures responsible for movement, types of movement)*

	Sessile; it does move its environment (water) into incurrent pores and out the excurrent pore (osculum). (See *Collar cells* under Nutrition below.)

Body Covering *(what covers the body, how it protects the animal)*

Epidermis	One cell layer thick. (Some sponges, like *Grantia,* have spicules that stick through the epidermis for protection.)

Support *(structures responsible for support, what they are made of)*

Spicules	Made of lime; help to support. (*NOTE:* spicules of other sponges are made of silica and spongin.)
	Much support comes from "fullness" caused by mesenchyme filling between cell layers.

Nutrition *(structures of digestion, methods of ingestion, types of food, assimilation)*

Collar cells	Food is carried in by currents made by collar cells, engulfed by collar cells, and digested in vacuoles of the collar cells.
	Nondigestible material is egested.
	Food: algae, protozoans, bacteria, etc.

Respiration *(structures used in gas exchange for respiration)*

No structures	Gases are exchanged between cells and water environment.

Structure	Notes

Circulation *(structures responsible for internal movement of substances)*

Amebocytes	Cells in the mesenchyme; in larger sponges these cells transport substances.
	Most circulation takes place by diffusion.

Excretion *(structures for the collection and elimination of soluble wastes)*

No structures	Wastes are released by diffusion.

Responses *(structures for receiving stimuli and for responses, level of responses)*

No structures	Osculum sometimes can be closed in response to substances in water.
	Collar cells can change their rate of flagellar movement.

Reproduction–Asexual *(structures for and types of asexual reproduction)*

Gemmules	Some freshwater sponges produce gemmules to survive unfavorable conditions.
Budding	Most sponges reproduce by buds and regenerate by fragmentation.

Reproduction–Sexual *(structures for sexual reproduction)*

Testes	Eggs and sperm are produced by one sponge or by separate sponges.
Ovaries	

Other Notes *(habitat, size range, unusual examples, etc.)*

Most are marine; some, freshwater.
Many are small; a few, large.
Simple sponges usually have only one cavity; complex sponges may have thick walls and many cavities.
Bath sponges have a spongin network of fibers.
They are asymmetrical or radially symmetrical.

14B–Cnidaria

Materials: preserved slides of plain and budding hydra, a cross section of a hydra, hydra with ovaries, and hydra with testes; preserved specimens of coral; living cultures of hydra and brine shrimp or *Daphnia;* spring water; dissection kit; hand lens; microscope; dilute acetic acid; culture dishes; pipet; glass slides; concavity slides; coverslips

Goals:

To observe typical cnidarians

To draw some conclusions regarding the structure and unique specializations of cnidarians

To compare sponges and cnidarians

Although many widely varying animals belong in the phylum Cnidaria (Coelenterata), they all have body forms and responses similar to the hydra. Therefore, you will study the hydra in detail as a representative cnidarian, and then observe other examples.

Example: Hydra

I. Study the life processes of the hydra and prepare a Life Process Chart for the hydra.

II. Draw the hydra.

- In Area A, make an *outline drawing* of an entire hydra *with bud* from a preserved slide. Use only low power.
  - ❑ The entire hydra will not fit into the microscope field. You will need to move the slide several times as you draw.
  - ❑ Label as many structures as you can find. (Carefully look for sexual reproductive structures.)
- Using high power, draw a portion of hydra wall, c.s., in Area B.
  - ❑ This drawing should *include internal structures,* not just be an outline.
  - ❑ Label as many of the cellular structures of hydra as you can.
- In Area C, using *low power,* prepare an outline drawing of an entire hydra with ovaries and testes. Label the ovaries and testes.

A

III. Observe a living hydra.
- To obtain a living hydra for observation:
  - ❑ Fill a clean culture dish with spring water (or treated, "aged," or pond water).
  - ❑ Using a dropping pipet, follow these instructions to obtain a specimen from the culture:
    - ○ Flush a stream of water from the pipet onto the hydra you have selected in order to dislodge the specimen.
    - ○ Draw the dislodged hydra into your pipet and flush it onto the culture dish.
- Observe your living hydra and the hydras of other students in your class during the hour. Identify as many different forms of locomotion or movement as you can. Describe as many forms as you observe. _____

_____

_____

_____

R
E
O

- Study the nerves and the responses of the hydra.
  - ❑ The hydra's nervous system consists of a *nerve net*. From the information in your text (and possibly other research), describe a nerve net.

_____

_____

B

C

❑ Observe the responses of the hydra.
  ○ Very gently swirl the water around the hydra. What is its reaction?

  _____

  _____

  ○ After the hydra has recovered from the above experiment (which may take several minutes), touch your probe as gently as possible to its base. What is

  its reaction? _____

  _____

  ○ After the hydra has recovered from the above experiment, touch your probe as gently as possible to one of its tentacles. What is its reaction?

  _____

  _____

  ○ After the hydra has recovered from the above experiment, arrange your probe so that the hydra will "touch" the probe of its own power. What is its

  reaction? _____

  _____

  _____

[R] [E] [O] • Observe the feeding process of the hydra.
  ❑ Using a dropping pipet, place a few living *Daphnia* or brine shrimp in your culture dish near the hydra. Be careful not to add the food so rapidly that you disturb the hydra.
  ❑ Using a hand lens, watch carefully the actions of your hydra. Note especially any activity in the mouth region.
  ❑ From your observations, describe the feeding process of the hydra.

  _____

  _____

  _____

  *❑ Describe digestion in a hydra by answering the following questions.
  ○ In what structure of the hydra does extracellular digestion take place?

  _____

  ○ What cells provide the necessary enzymes for this digestion?

  _____

  ○ What happens to the partially digested food? _____

  _____

  ○ What happens to the substances that cannot be digested?

  _____

  *• Typical food for a hydra includes _____ .
  • Observe the reaction of the hydra to acid.
  ❑ Carefully remove your hydra and set it in a large drop of spring water placed on a concavity slide.
  ❑ Place a coverslip over the slide and observe the hydra (or sections of it) with a microscope.
  ❑ After it has recovered from the transfer and you have been able to focus on cells of its tentacles, place a small drop of the dilute acetic acid on the edge of the coverslip.
  ❑ Watch the hydra carefully. For the best results, one partner should put the acetic acid on the slide while the other partner observes the reaction through the microscope.

[R] [E] [O]

❑ What did you observe as the acid reached the hydra? _____
_____
_____

R
E
O

• Draw conclusions from your observations of the movement, feeding, and reactions of the hydra.
   ❑ How specialized to different stimuli are the responses of the hydra? In other words, is the hydra able to respond differently to various kinds of stimuli?
   ☐ yes   ☐ no
   ❑ To what degree? _____
   _____
   _____

• To remove your hydra, flush the slide with spring water while holding it over a separate culture container for "used" hydra. **Do not** return the hydra to its original culture.

R
E
O

Example: Coral

I. Observe the preserved coral specimens in the classroom. What structure are you actually

observing? _____

*II. Compare a living coral organism and a hydra. _____
_____
_____
_____

R
E
O

Example: Jellyfish

I. Observe and describe the preserved jellyfish in the classroom. _____
_____
_____
_____

II. Compare a jellyfish and a hydra (diagrams may be helpful). _____
_____
_____
_____
_____
_____

14C–Worms 1
Platyhelminthes and Nematoda

Materials: culture of living planarians; spring water; culture dish; dissection kit; hand lens; Epsom salts; glass slides; preserved slides of beef tapeworm *(Taenia saginata)* scolex, proglottid, and bladders in meat; preserved specimens or preserved slides of *Ascaris lumbricoides, Necator americanus,* and *Trichinella spiralis;* illuminator

Goals:

To observe planarians and other flatworms

To draw conclusions about the structure and special characteristics of flatworms

To compare planarians and various flatworms to previously studied organisms

> In this laboratory exercise you will observe free-living and parasitic flatworms (phylum Platyhelminthes) and some significant roundworms (phylum Nematoda). Although Annelida may be the most familiar of the worm phyla, these two phyla contain organisms which are far more significant to humans because of the diseases they cause.

Platyhelminthes

Phylum Platyhelminthes contains simple organisms with only three basic cell layers: an ectoderm, a gastroderm, and a mesoderm. Various structures develop from these cell layers. Some of these structures correspond to many of the organs and systems in more complex animals. The flatworms exhibit two "ways of life": free-living and parasitic. We shall examine the planarian as an example of the free-living variety.

Free-Living Flatworms–The Planarian

R
E
O

*I. Fill out the Life Process Chart for the planarian.
   • Read the sections in your text that deal with phylum Platyhelminthes (pp. 347-49, 352-53).
   • Prepare a Life Process Chart for the planarian.

Laboratory Techniques for Handling Planarians

• Fill a clean culture dish with fresh spring water.
• Move the planarian by following these instructions:
   □ Agitate the water around the planarian (make small currents with a dropping pipet) until it floats about in the water.
   □ Quickly draw it into a dropping pipet.
   □ Quickly put it into the container you have ready. Speed is important, for if the planarian "uncoils" and attaches itself to the side of the pipet, it is often difficult to move.
• On occasion it will be best to put your planarian on a glass slide in order to restrain it and to view its ventral surface easily. If you use a concavity slide, a coverslip can be placed on it. However, if you use a flat slide, the coverslip will squash the planarian.

II. Observe the movement of planarians.
- Obtain a planarian by following the instructions in the box.
- Study the two different means by which the planarians move.

R E O

   ❑ Ciliary movement
   - Where are the cilia located on the planarian? _____
   - After observing the planarian moving by using its cilia, describe this type of

      movement. _____
   ❑ Muscular movement
   - Place a few grains of Epsom salts into the water right next to the planarian. Watch carefully as the Epsom salts dissolve near it.
   - After you have observed the movement that results, remove and discard the grains of salt and add some fresh spring water to dilute the salt.
   - Describe muscular movement in comparison to the ciliary movement you

      have described above. _____

      _____

      _____

   *○ Where are the structures for muscular movement located?

      _____

- Briefly compare the structures for movement in the planarian to structures for move-

   ment in the hydra. _____

   _____

   _____

III. Observe the responses of planarians.

R E O

- Observe the responses to touch.
   ❑ With a clean probe, touch very lightly the lateral surface of the planarian. What

      is the response? _____
   ❑ Touch lightly an auricle (side point of the head). What is the response?

      _____

   ❑ Touch lightly the posterior end. What is the response? _____

      _____

R E O

- Observe the responses to current.
   ❑ Fill a clean pipet with water and slowly force the water out to produce a current.
   ❑ Direct the current to one side of the planarian in the culture dish. (Take about 30 seconds to empty one pipet of water. Have several pipets ready.) What is its

      response? _____
   ❑ Direct a current toward the side of the planarian's head. What is its response?

      _____

   ❑ Direct a current toward the posterior end, directly behind the planarian. What is

      its response? _____

      _____

R E O

- Compare the degree of specialization (how specific the organism's responses are) in

   the planarian and in the hydra. _____

   _____

   _____

IV. Investigate the ingestion and digestion of planarians.
- Place your planarian on a glass slide, using the techniques described in the box (p. 115).
- Look for the planarian's food-getting structures.
  - ❏ Holding the slide above your head, look for the mouth and pharynx of your planarian.
  - ❏ Describe the mouth's location on the body. _____

  _____

  - ❏ Describe the appearance and the function of the pharynx. _____

  _____

*• Describe the digestion of planarians.
  - ❏ Describe the area within the planarian where digestion begins. Be sure to use the proper name for this structure. _____

  _____

  _____

  - ❏ After the structure described above completes preliminary digestion, what happens to the small particles of food to complete digestion? _____

  _____

  _____

Parasitic Flatworms

There are many different types of parasitic Platyhelminthes. You will study two of the most common human parasites: the beef tapeworm *(Taenia saginata)* and the human liver fluke *(Clonorchis sinensis)*. These two pathogenic organisms are examples of different classes in the phylum Platyhelminthes.

I. Study the beef tapeworm.
- Using low power, observe preserved slides of the following stages (structures) in the life cycle of the beef tapeworm: scolex, mature proglottid, and bladders in meat.
- Study the life cycle of the beef tapeworm.
  - ❏ Carefully study the outline of the beef tapeworm's life cycle given below.
  - ❏ From your observations, complete Diagram 14C-1 of the stages of the beef tapeworm's life cycle.
  - ❏ Add labeled drawings in the three circles of the diagram.
  - ❏ Add the following labels in the places they belong: *intestine of man, intestine of cow, blood vessel of cow, contaminated meat, adult tapeworm, egg containing six-hooked larva.*

Life Cycle of a Beef Tapeworm

- Eggs of the tapeworm are eaten by the cow.
  - ❏ Eggs hatch in the intestine as a six-hooked larva.
  - ❏ The larva bores through the intestinal wall, enters the blood stream, and is carried to a muscle.
- The larva burrows into the muscle.
  - ❏ In the muscle, the larva becomes a bladderworm (cyst).
  - ❏ Inside the "bladder" is an immature scolex.
- The muscle infected with the bladderworm is eaten by man.
  - ❏ If the meat is not cooked enough or treated to kill the bladderworm, the bladderworm hatches in the human's intestine.
  - ❏ The scolex (head) of the tapeworm embeds itself in the lining of the intestine.
- The adult tapeworm lives in the intestine of man.
  - ❏ The scolex produces proglottids (the chain of which may be over ten feet in length), which contain hundreds of eggs.
  - ❏ The ripe proglottids are passed in the feces.
  - ❏ Cows graze on grass fertilized with infected feces.

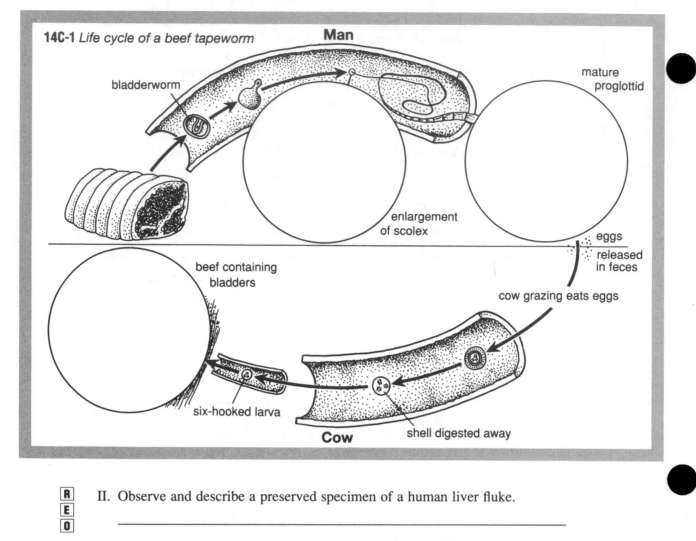

14C-1 *Life cycle of a beef tapeworm*

Man

bladderworm

mature
proglottid

enlargement
of scolex

eggs
released
in feces

beef containing
bladders

cow grazing eats eggs

six-hooked larva

shell digested away

Cow

R
E
O

II. Observe and describe a preserved specimen of a human liver fluke.

_____

_____

_____

Nematoda: Roundworms

The roundworms (phylum Nematoda) are surprisingly alike in their body structure but are extremely diverse in their habitats and life cycles. In this laboratory section we will observe some of the organisms that are pathogenic to humans.

R
E
O

*I. Prepare a Life Process Chart for the *Ascaris*.

II. Observe preserved specimens or slides of various roundworms and describe them (color, length, shape, etc.).

R
E
O

• Human *Ascaris (Ascaris lumbricoides)* _____

_____

• Hookworms *(Necator americanus)* _____

_____

• Trichina worms *(Trichinella spiralis)* _____

_____

14D–Worms 2
Annelida

Materials: dissection kit, hand lens, living earthworms, preserved earthworm, dissection pan, plastic bag, ether, alcohol

Goals:

To introduce dissection techniques

To observe the structures of an earthworm

To compare the earthworm to other organisms

The organisms in phylum Annelida are very diverse. For classroom observation the most common of the annelids is an excellent choice, even though it may not be considered typical of all of the organisms in this phylum.

In this laboratory exercise you will be asked to dissect an earthworm. This is the first laboratory dissection you are asked to do for this course. To prepare for it, be sure you read the information in the Dissection Techniques box and define the terms indicated in the box. These terms will be commonly used in describing dissection procedures.

Dissection Techniques

General Instructions

These instructions apply to all dissections in this laboratory manual.

- Read carefully the entire exercise before you begin. This reading can prevent many wrong cuts.
- Reread the directions before you begin to cut.
- Make sure you have identified the correct structures by comparing them to drawings before you cut.
- Handle the specimens delicately. Preserved structures often tear and break easily.

Temporarily Storing a Dissection Animal

- Put your name and lab hour on a plastic bag with a permanent marker.
- Wrap the organism in a very wet paper towel.
- Place the organism and the wet paper towel in the plastic bag. Gently squeeze out most of the air, and tie the bag closed.
- Organisms wrapped in this manner may be kept for a few days without great deterioration.

Dissection Vocabulary

Define the following terms. Be sure you know how they apply to each animal before you begin a dissection. **The terms *right* and *left* in the instructions refer to the organism's right and left, not yours.**

- Anterior: _____
- Posterior: _____
- Dorsal: _____
- Ventral: _____
- Median: _____
- Longitudinal: _____
- Transverse: _____

continued on next page

- Lateral: _____

- Cephalic: _____

- Caudal: _____

Earthworm Dissection

R
E
O

External Structures

I. Examine your specimen carefully.
- Rub your fingers lightly across its surface.
- As you touch the skin of the earthworm, you should feel tiny bristles.

  ❑ What are these bristles called? _____

  ❑ How many are there on each segment? _____

  ❑ On what area of the body do these bristles appear? _____
  _____

  ❑ How do they help in locomotion? _____
  _____

II. Does the earthworm have definite anterior and posterior ends that can be determined by sight? ☐ yes ☐ no

Explain your answer. _____
_____

- Locate the prostomium. What is its function? _____
_____

- Locate the anus. What is its function? _____
_____

III. Examine the clitellum.
- How many segments are there in the clitellum? _____
*• What is the function of the clitellum? _____
_____

IV. Examine other body openings.
- Using a hand lens, try to locate the nephridiopores. How many are there on each segment? _____

- Examine segment 14 and locate the female pore through which eggs leave the body. (*NOTE:* Segments are numbered beginning at the mouth and continuing toward the anus.)
- Locate the male pore in segment 15. Sperm leave the body through this opening.
- Try to locate the openings in the furrows between segments 9 and 10 and segments 10 and 11 through which sperm enter the body. (These are sometimes impossible to locate.)

Opening the Body Cavity

I. Place your specimen in a dissection pan with the dorsal side up.
II. Pin the anterior and posterior ends to the pan, using care not to put the pins through any internal organs.
III. Place your scissors slightly to the left of the mid dorsal line about an inch posterior to the clitellum. Carefully cut through the body wall. Then extend the cut anteriorly to the prostomium. *Be careful not to cut anything but the body wall.*

IV. Separate the edges of the cut and look into the body cavity.
- Observe that the wall is separated from the intestine by a space. What is this space

  called? _____
- Notice that the space is divided by partitions extending from the body wall to the

  intestine. What are these partitions called? _____

- Using forceps and probes, carefully break these partitions segment by segment until the internal structures found in the anterior end of the worm are entirely exposed for study.
- To hold the body wall open, pin it to the wax in the dissection pan.

R E O **Locating the Earthworm's Muscular Structures**

I. Locate the circular and longitudinal muscles in one or two of the segments of your worm. (This is sometimes difficult with small preserved worms.)

*II. Suppose that the worm's circular muscles have already contracted and its setae have anchored its anterior end to the soil. In the earthworm's movements, what structures will

function next and what movement will result? _____

_____

R E O **Locating the Earthworm's Interior Digestive Structures**

I. Locate the *pharynx,* a thick-walled area posterior to the buccal cavity. What is the purpose

of the thick walls? _____

II. Locate the *esophagus,* which extends from the pharynx to segment 14. What is the function

of the esophagus? _____

III. Locate the *crop,* a large, thin-walled area posterior to the esophagus. What is the function

of this structure? _____

IV. Locate the *gizzard,* a thick-walled area posterior to the crop. What is the function of the

gizzard? _____

V. Locate the *intestine,* which extends from the gizzard to the anus. What is the function of

the intestine? _____

VI. Make an outline drawing of the digestive system in the earthworm outline provided in Diagram 14D-1. Be sure to include all the structures italicized in the digestive section (above), and be sure they are in the correct body segments.

14D-1 *Earthworm digestive structures*

R
E
O

Locating the Earthworm's Circulatory Structures

I. Find the dorsal blood vessel on your specimen. It appears as a dark, brownish-colored vessel running along the medial surface of the intestine. In many specimens you can see this structure lying on the intestine.

II. Remove the seminal vesicles by lifting them out from the left side of the body.

III. Look in segment 11 for a pair of stout tubes coming from the dorsal blood vessel and extending ventrally. These ''hearts,'' or aortic arches, are often discolored because they contain blood. What is the function of these structures? _____

_____

IV. Look at each segment from 7 to 11 for the rest of the aortic arches. You will have to remove the septa to see these clearly.

V. Near the posterior section of your cut, use probes to move the intestine to the right and try to find the ventral blood vessel. (This structure is often difficult to locate.) Does it look any different from the dorsal blood vessel?   □ yes   □ no

R
E
O

VI. Make an outline drawing of the circulatory system in the earthworm outline provided in Diagram 14D-2.
- Include and label the dorsal blood vessels, the ventral blood vessels, the aortic arches. Be sure they are in the correct segment.
- Make the drawing as though it were being viewed laterally.

14D-2 *Earthworm circulatory structures*

R
E
O

Locating the Earthworm's Excretory Structures

I. Nephridia are located in every segment except for the first three and the last one.
- Extend the body wall incision posteriorly about two inches.
- Carefully open the body wall in this area, trying not to tear the septa.
- Carefully remove the intestine from the area.
- Use a hand lens or stereomicroscope to find the nephridia. (In some specimens the nephridia are difficult to find.)

*II. To what human organ do the nephridia of the earthworm correspond? _____

Locating the Earthworm's Nervous System

Locating these structures may be difficult, and if you have not been careful in your dissecting, you may have destroyed them.

I. In the area of segments 2 and 3, dorsal to the buccal cavity, the "brain," or suprapharyngeal (*supra* "above," and *pharyngeal* "pharynx") ganglia, is located. Try to find them.

II. Two nerve fibers extend from the suprapharyngeal ganglia, pass around the pharynx, and join below the pharynx at the subpharyngeal (*sub* "below," and *pharyngeal* "pharynx") ganglion. Try to locate the subpharyngeal ganglia.

III. The ventral nerve cord extends from the subpharyngeal ganglia. Remove a part of the intestine from the posterior part of the body and try to locate the nerve cord.

IV. Note the small ganglion present in each segment. Also note the small nerves going from each of these ganglia into the body wall.

V. In Diagram 14D-3, label the suprapharyngeal ganglia, subpharyngeal ganglion, ventral nerve cord, nerve cord ganglia, and nerves to body segments.

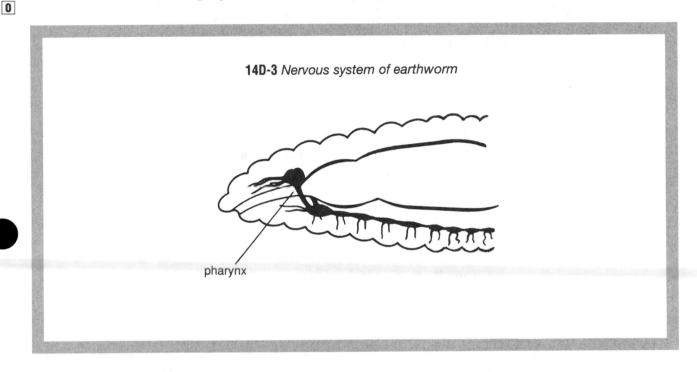

14D-3 *Nervous system of earthworm*

pharynx

Locating Earthworm's Reproductive Structures

I. The parts of the reproductive system are found in the first fifteen segments.

II. Segments 9 to 13 contain pairs of white structures called *seminal vesicles*. Sperm are stored in these organs.

III. Segments 9 and 10 contain pairs of small, white, spherical structures called *seminal receptacles*. These organs receive sperm from other earthworms.

IV. Locate the small ovaries, in which the eggs develop. They are under the seminal vesicles.

Testing Reactions of a Live Earthworm

To see how an earthworm responds to various stimuli, you will need to test a living earthworm. Place a living specimen in a clean dissection pan that has a number of crumpled, wet paper towels in it. Keep the earthworm wet. After you have finished the experiments, return the worm to the laboratory culture.

R
E
O
Testing the Earthworm's Response to Touch
I. Touch the posterior end lightly with a probe. (**Do not stab it.**)
- Pause until the earthworm is moving slowly.
- Repeat several times.
- What is the worm's reaction? _____

_____

II. Do the same to the anterior end. What is its reaction? _____

_____

III. As the worm lies on the paper towels, touch its body near the middle as low on its side as

you can. What is the reaction? _____

_____

R
E
O
Testing the Earthworm's Response to Light
I. Remove the towels from the dissection pan, cover the pan, and keep the worm in the dark for several minutes.
II. Peek inside (keeping it as dark as possible) to find the worm's anterior end.
III. Still keeping conditions as dark as possible, shine the flashlight or illuminator on the

worm's anterior end. What is its reaction? _____

R
E
O
Dissection of a Live Earthworm

Under supervision, two students will anesthetize a live earthworm with ether and follow the directions given earlier for opening the body cavity. All students will observe the specimen and then answer the following questions. After the class's observation, the worm will be put to death with alcohol.

I. What moving structures indicate that the earthworm is alive? _____

_____

II. How do the aortic arches beat? □ in unison □ in a rhythm □ without coordination

III. Other than movement, what are the major differences between the preserved specimen and

the live specimen? Can you explain these differences? _____

_____

15A–**Malacostracans**

Materials: preserved crayfish, dissection kit, dissection pan, culture dish, preserved slides of malacostracans, preserved specimens showing crayfish life cycle, preserved specimens of other malacostracans, plastic bag

Goals:

To observe arthropod characteristics in the crayfish

To note the variety of appendages and the specialization of internal parts of a crayfish

To observe other malacostracans and compare them to the crayfish

> You will begin this laboratory exercise by studying crayfish appendages, noting their varied shapes and functions, and then studying the life processes of a crayfish. As you observe other malacostracans or other arthropods, you will find that although their structures vary greatly, the basic body plan is the same in all of them.

External Anatomy of the Crayfish

R
E
O
The Segments of the Exoskeleton

I. Place your crayfish in a dissection pan and carefully observe the dorsal side of your specimen.

- As you find each of the structures italicized below, label them on Diagram 15A-1. *NOTE:* You will need to draw in details in order to label all the structures.
- Examine the hard, chitinous *exoskeleton* covering the crayfish and note that the body is divided into two main regions, the *cephalothorax* and the *abdomen.*

II. Examine the cephalothorax, the anterior region of the crayfish.

- Note that the cephalothorax is covered by a single piece of exoskeleton called the *carapace.*
  - ❑ The anterior extension of the carapace, which forms a horny beak between the eyes of the crayfish is called the *rostrum.*
  - ❑ Locate the *cervical groove* on the carapace, which marks the division between the *head* and the *thorax.*
- Note the segments of the cephalothorax.
  - ❑ There are either 13 or 14 segments in the cephalothorax, depending on whether the segment preceding the one bearing the antennules is considered a true segment.
  - ❑ On the ventral side these segments are easy to locate if you remember that there is one set of appendages per segment.

III. Examine the abdomen of the crayfish

- How many segments (not appendages) are there in the abdomen? _____ The last segment is called the *telson.* Label it on Diagram 15A-1.
- Although it is not a segment, locate the anal opening on the ventral side of the abdomen.

The Appendages of the Head

If possible, continue to label Diagram 15A-1 with the italicized structures discussed in this section.

R
E
O
I. Appendages of sensation

*• What is an appendage? _____

_____

- Although they do not fit the definition of a true appendage, locate the stalked *compound eyes.*

15A-1 *External structures of the crayfish*

- Locate the most anterior appendages, the *antennules*.

  - How many antennules are there? _____
  - They are used for balance, taste, and touch.
- *● Other appendages near the antennules are the long *antennas*.

  - How many of these are there? _____
  - They are used for taste and touch.

II. Appendages of the mouth
- Turn your crayfish ventral side up in the dissection pan and locate all the mouthparts.
- Compare what you find with those drawn in Diagram 15A-2.
- Do not remove them.
  - The 1 pair of *mandibles* (or true jaws) are just posterior to the antennas. They are small hard coverings of the mouth that pulverize food.
  - The 2 pairs of *maxillae* are just posterior to the mandibles and assist in chewing.
  - The 3 pairs of *maxillipeds* (or jaw feet) are posterior to the maxillae. (When counting these appendages, do not be fooled by their branched appearance.) Maxillipeds are used to hold food in place.
- Mouthpart movement
  - Human mouthparts move vertically (up and down). In what direction do the

    mouthparts of a crayfish move? (Note especially the mandibles.) _____
  - Does this characteristic reinforce the idea that the mouthparts are appendages?
    ☐ yes   ☐ no

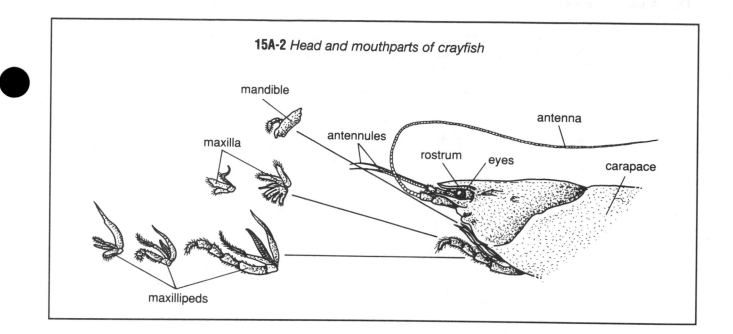

15A-2 *Head and mouthparts of crayfish*

- Remove the mouthparts, including the maxillipeds, from *one* side of your crayfish. (You still have the other side of the organism to work with if you are unsuccessful the first time.)
  - ❑ Remove the maxillipeds; then locate and remove the other mouthparts.
  - ❑ To remove the appendage, grip the base with forceps and pull the entire append-age out.
- Draw in Area A all the mouth appendages you have removed from the crayfish.
  - ❑ Label the drawing completely.
  - ❑ Draw the appendages in the order they were in the crayfish, the most anterior at the left of the drawing and the most posterior at the right.

The Appendages of the Thorax

As you locate each of the appendages discussed below, label them on Diagram 15A-1.

   I. The *thoracic appendages* move either the organism or the materials around the organism.

     How many pairs of appendages does the thorax have? _____

A

   II. The most obvious appendages of the thorax are the *chelipeds*. Note the large *pincers* (the claws), which are used for protection and capturing food.

  III. The next 4 pairs of appendages are *walking legs*. Carefully examine these thoracic append-ages. How do these legs differ from one another? _____

_____

      Do all the walking legs have pincers? Which do? _____

_____

The Appendages of the Abdomen

    I. The abdomen has 5 pairs of appendages called *swimmerets*. Label these on Diagram 15A-1.

   II. Carefully examine preserved male and female crayfish.
- In the male, the most anterior swimmerets are modified. In the female, the anterior swimmerets are greatly reduced in size.
- What sex is your crayfish? ☐ male ☐ female

*III. The sixth abdominal appendages are called the uropods. They grow from the *telson*. Together these structures form a powerful tail fin. How would the crayfish use these?

_____

_____

[R] [E] [O] Internal Anatomy of the Crayfish

Read all the following directions carefully before starting your dissection. The following procedures must be done *in order*. You will be expected to know the functions and locations of the organs that have been italicized.

Opening the Body Cavity

    I. Place your animal in the dissection pan with its dorsal side up.

   II. Carefully insert the point of the scissors under the dorsal surface of the carapace at the posterior edge of the cephalothorax. Cut anteriorly along the midline of the body to the rostrum.

  III. Reposition the scissors just behind the eyes and make a transverse cut.

  IV. Carefully remove the two pieces of the carapace without disturbing the structures underneath.

The Respiratory Structures

    I. Note carefully the exposed *gills* and study their structure.
- Remove a few gills and place them in a culture dish of water. Observe and describe their structure. _____
- Carefully remove the rest of the gills.

*II. Gills are able to exchange gases only when they are wet. Explain how the crayfish can spend many hours at a time on land. _____

_____

The Circulatory Structures

    I. For easier handling of the animal, remove the legs attached to the thorax.

   II. Carefully separate the dorsal tissues in the thorax and locate the mid dorsal *heart*.
- Locate the main *blood vessels* attached to the heart.
- * The crayfish, as well as most other arthropods, has an open circulatory system.

     ❏ How does an open circulatory system work? _____

_____

     ❏ Does an open circulatory system circulate materials as efficiently as a closed circulatory system? ☐ yes ☐ no Why or why not? _____

_____

❑ Explain why being forced to lie on its back would cause death for a crayfish.

_____

*● Do crayfish have red blood? ☐ yes ☐ no
If not, what color is their blood? (You will need to do research to find the answer.

Observing a preserved specimen is not sufficient.) _____

The Reproductive Structures
I. Look between the digestive glands (described in the next section) to find the reproductive structures.
- If your crayfish is a male, look for a small pair of white gonads *(testes)* and coiled ducts.
- If your crayfish is a female, look for a large mass of dark-colored *eggs* (inside the ovaries). (Diagram 15A-5 on p. 367 of your text is of a female.)
II. Remove these reproductive structures so that you can see the digestive structures.

The Digestive Structures
I. The two light-colored masses extending along each side of the body cavity beyond the

cervical groove are the *digestive glands*. What is their function? _____

_____

II. To expose the *intestine,* insert the point of the scissors underneath the dorsal side of the exoskeleton covering the abdomen. Cut posteriorly to the telson.
- Open the abdominal exoskeleton along the cut. The intestine appears as a tube on the dorsal side of the abdominal muscles.
- Do not confuse the intestine with the dark-colored dorsal blood vessel.
III. Trace the intestine anteriorly to the portion of the cephalothorax where the intestine joins the large, thin-walled *stomach.*

Removing the Viscera
I. Remove most of the internal organs (viscera) of the crayfish by following these instructions.
- Just behind the eyes, cut the bands of muscles leading to the stomach. These muscles hold the stomach in place.
- Pull the stomach posteriorly and cut the short esophagus located just below the stomach.
II. Carefully lift out the organs all in one piece. What is attached to the organs that keeps

them all together? _____

The Excretory Structures
I. Clean out the remaining tissue in the head to expose the *green glands* (kidneys) just posterior to and below the antennules. They are soft, small, and only slightly green.
II. The careful student may also be able to find the small, saclike bladder, which is connected to the green glands.

The Nervous System
I. At the front of the head cavity, between the eyes, note the "brain," a tiny mass of white tissue.
II. Trace the nerves that go from the brain to the antennas and the eyes.
III. Trace the *nerve cord* back from the brain to the abdomen by cutting the hard tissue on the floor of the thorax with the scalpel.
- Spread the abdomen apart and pull out the large muscles. (This is the portion of the shrimp and the lobster, and occasionally the *fresh* crayfish, that we eat.)
- The nerve cord should now be exposed on the ventral side of the abdomen.

  *● The swellinglike portions of the nerve cord are called the _____ .
IV. Why is it an advantage for the crayfish to have its nerve cord on the ventral side rather

than on the dorsal side, as it is in humans? _____

_____

R
E
O

Drawing the Dissected Crayfish

I. Do not begin these drawings until *after* you have completed your dissection.

II. In the crayfish outlines in Area B, draw a *dorsal view* of the viscera of your specimen. Let different outlines include different body segments so that the organs will not overlap in your drawings (suggested combinations: digestive/excretory, reproductive/circulatory, nervous/respiratory).

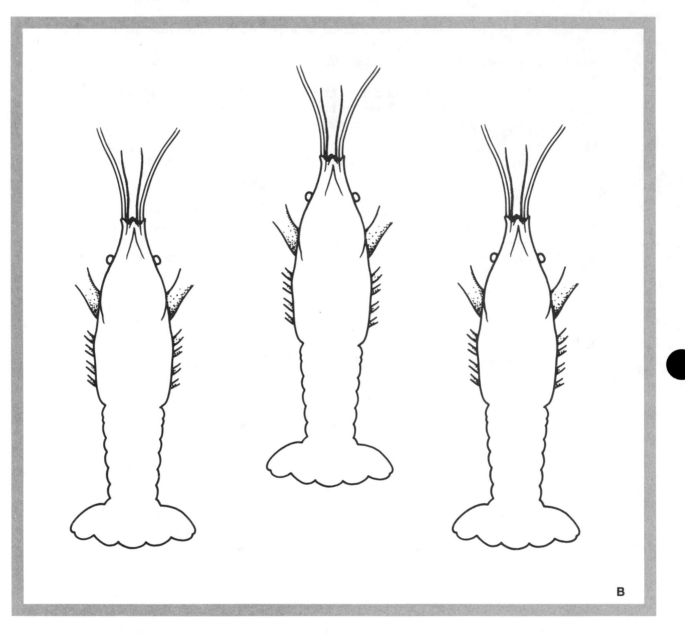

B

*Life Process Chart: Crayfish

R
E
O

I. Fill out a Life Process Chart for the crayfish.
- Be careful *not* to repeat material covered in the Anatomy section of this laboratory exercise.
- Include an extensive Other Notes section in your Life Process Chart.

R
E
O

II. Add to your Life Process Chart a final section called Other Malacostracans.
- Choose two of the following: *Cyclops,* ostracod (seed shrimp), *Daphnia,* barnacle, fiddler crab, brine shrimp *(Artemia),* blue crab, edible shrimp, lobster.
- Do research in another source about the two malacostracans you choose. Then write one or two paragraphs covering their unusual features, their habitats, and their economical and environmental importance.

15B–The Grasshopper

Materials: preserved specimen of "Lubber" grasshopper *(Romalea microptera)*, dissection kit, dissection pan

Goal:

To observe the major insect characteristics as seen in the grasshopper

> The order Orthoptera, the straight-winged insects, includes the grasshopper, cockroach, cricket, and praying mantis. Because of its large size, the "Lubber" grasshopper is often used in the science laboratory. It is native to the states on the Gulf Coast. Its wings are small compared to its body, making the "Lubber" a poor flier.

R E O External Anatomy of the Grasshopper

I. Examine the preserved specimen, taking care not to dissect or damage the specimen in any way. Locate all the following structures. Use a hand lens if necessary.

- Antennas (Note the segments of the antennas and compare the length of the antennas to the grasshopper's body length.)
- Compound eyes
- Simple eyes
  - ❏ The simple eyes are located between the compound eyes.
  - ❏ How many simple eyes are there? (Research may be necessary.) _____
- Thorax
- Head
- Tympanum–What is the purpose of the tympanum? _____
- Jumping leg–Identify these parts of the leg, beginning at the base (the part closest to the body) and progressing toward the tip.
  - ❏ Trochanter
  - ❏ Femur
  - ❏ Tibia
  - ❏ Tarsus (the foot)–Which section of the leg is the largest? _____
- Forelegs–How do the forelegs and the jumping legs differ?
  - ❏ In appearance: _____
  - ❏ In function: _____
- Forewings–The forewings are thick, heavy wings that are not used in flight. What is their purpose? _____
- Hind wings–You may need to lift the forewings in order to see these structures. Look for the fine veins in the hind wings.
- Abdomen
- Spiracles–Where are the spiracles located? _____
- Ovipositor–Does your organism have an ovipositor? ☐ yes ☐ no

  What does the answer to this question indicate? _____

II. On Diagram 15B-1, label all the external structures listed above. (*NOTE:* You will need to draw in details in order to label all the structures.)

15B-1 *Grasshopper*

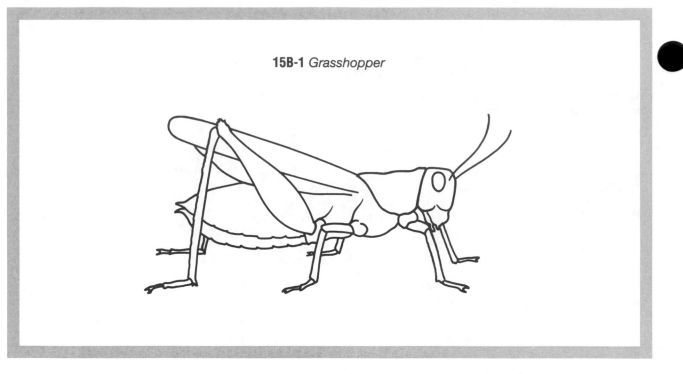

III. On your specimen, locate all the mouthparts listed below.
- Label the mouthparts on Diagram 15B-2.
- In the spaces below, tell how many of each mouthpart the grasshopper has.

    ❑ Labrum: _____

    ❑ Mandible (jaws): _____

    ❑ Labium: _____

    ❑ Labial palp: _____

    ❑ Maxilla: _____

    ❑ Maxillary palp: _____

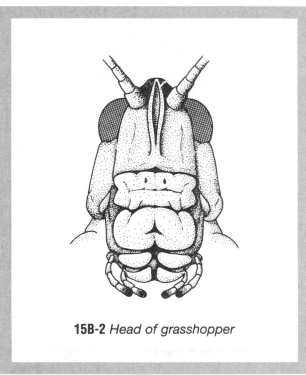

15B-2 *Head of grasshopper*

R E O   Preparing a Life Process Chart for the Grasshopper

I. Read Chapter 15B and take notes on the grasshopper and other members of the Class Orthoptera. Do additional research in another text.

II. Fill out a Life Process Chart and include all the information you learned in this laboratory exercise. Do not copy from the exercise.

15c–Insect Orders

Materials: visuals of insects, live cultures of fruit flies *(Drosophila melanogaster)* and flour beetles *(Tribolium sp.)*

Goals:

To learn about some of the diversity among insects

To use and enhance research, writing, and oral skills

To learn how insects affect man

To learn about some of the techniques man uses to control insects

To learn about insect metamorphosis

> The majority of organisms in the animal kingdom are insects. In class Insecta, there are over 20 orders, representing thousands of different species. The population of each species is thousands to billions. In this exercise, we will study the major orders of insects (based on number of species) to survey the "insect kingdom."
>
> Insects are one of the most successful animal forms; in many respects they compete with man for dominance on the land's surface. In the second part of this exercise, you will observe living insect cultures. Following these observations, you will be given information about the role of insects as pests and how they are controlled. You will draw some conclusions about controlling insects. You will have to reason out these answers from the information given in this laboratory exercise and from the observations you make of the insect cultures.

Reports on Insect Orders

Written Reports on Insect Orders

I. Prepare a written report on each of the following insect orders:
- Coleoptera
- Lepidoptera
- Hymenoptera
- Diptera
- Orthoptera

II. Follow these guidelines.
- Each insect order report should be one or two pages in length. (One side of a sheet of paper, typed or hand written, is a page.)
- Begin your report with a description of the order.
  - ❑ Indicate the number of wings.
  - ❑ Indicate the type of mouthparts.
  - ❑ Indicate the type of metamorphosis.
  - ❑ Indicate the type of eyes.
  - ❑ Indicate the special characteristics that set this order apart from the others.
  - ❑ Do not repeat phylum or class characteristics unless they are greatly modified in the particular order.
- Choose two insects as examples of the order and describe them. You may include a description of the following as you describe each example:
  - ❑ Habitat
  - ❑ Life cycle (if interesting or unusual)
  - ❑ Food
  - ❑ Economic and personal relationships to man (pet, pest, or harmful insect; diseases carried by it; competition with man for food)
  - ❑ Social instincts
- *Avoid* repeating material discussed in your text.

R
E
O
Oral Reports on Insect Orders

The class will be divided into small report groups of two or three students. Each group will be assigned an insect order on which to do research and to give a 3- to 5-minute report before the class.

Our group's order is _____.

  I. Following the guidelines given for the written reports, each member of the group should write a report on the insect order assigned for his group's oral report.

 II. Note the following details for an oral report.

- All group members do not need to speak. Each group is allowed only 5 minutes.
- The grade will be the same for each member in the group, no matter which aspect of the report he prepared (e.g., speaking, research, visual aids).
- Prepare together before your presentation is due.
- Each report must have at least one visual aid.
- Present material that would be interesting and valuable to the class, not merely technical information.
- If you read your report, points will be deducted from your grade. You may use notes.
- *Each group must be prepared on its assigned date.* Only the absence of *all* group members will postpone your oral report. If one member of the group is absent, the others must go ahead and present the report. Otherwise, your teacher will impose severe grade penalties.

Insect Metamorphosis and Control

Flour beetles

The flour beetle *(Tribolium sp.)* is found in stored grains and sometimes in packaged foods such as cake mixes. Often it becomes a serious pest.

R
E
O
  I. Observe the living culture of the flour beetle.

- What type of metamorphosis does the flour beetle have? ☐ complete ☐ incomplete
- Name and describe the stages of the beetle's life cycle that you were able to find in

the culture. _____

_____

_____

_____

- From your observation, to what insect order do flour beetles belong?

R
E
O
    _____

- In Area A, draw the various stages of the flour beetle's life cycle that you were able to observe. Draw the stages in proportion and label them.

A

R **E** ●

II. An infestation of flour beetles in a large grain elevator could cause thousands of dollars' worth of damage. How would you control these pests?

- At what stage(s) in its life cycle would the flour beetle probably be easiest to control

  (kill)? ☐ egg ☐ larva ☐ pupa ☐ adult   Why? _____

  _____

- Would it be advisable to put in the flour beetle's medium (grain) a type of chemical insecticide that has to be eaten by the insects to kill them?   ☐ yes   ☐ no

  Why or why not? _____

  _____

  _____

- Some gases (such as carbon dioxide, carbon disulfide, ammonia, and carbon tetrachloride) can be blown through the medium as fumigants to kill flour beetles. Why would fumigants be a more desirable form of control for flour beetles than a liquid spray or

  dust insecticide? (There are several reasons. Give at least two.) _____

  _____

  _____

  _____

●

- Flour beetles can be killed by keeping them at a temperature of 49° C for 2 hours. Which method (fumigation or heat) would be practical for grain storage elevators to

  use? Which would be practical in the home? _____

  _____

  _____

  _____

Fruit Flies and How to Control Them

The fruit fly *(Drosophila sp.)* can be easily seen buzzing around almost any ripe (or more likely, overripe) fruit that is not being refrigerated. These small flies, although more of a nuisance than actual pests, can be a problem for a fruit transporter.

R **E** **O**

I. Observe the living culture of fruit flies.
- What type of metamorphosis does the fruit fly have?   ☐ complete   ☐ incomplete
- Name and describe the stages of the fruit fly's life cycle you found in the culture.

  _____

  _____

  _____

  _____

- From your observation, to what insect order do fruit flies belong? _____
- In Area B, draw the various stages of the fruit fly's life cycle that you were able to observe. Make sure the stages are drawn in proportion and labeled.

R
●

II. Study the control of fruit flies.
- At what stage(s) in its life cycle would the fruit fly probably be easiest to control

  (kill)? ☐ egg ☐ larva ☐ pupa ☐ adult   Why? _____

  _____

B

- Although fruit flies can be killed with heat, the 49° C that kills flour beetles only stops the growth of fruit flies; it does not kill them. What drawbacks does control by increased temperature have? _____

_____

_____

_____

- Lowered temperatures are more advisable than raised temperatures for controlling fruit flies. What drawbacks might lowering the temperature have? _____

_____

_____

_____

- Would a liquid spray or dust insecticide be advisable? (Recall your observation of the insect's life cycle and how the various stages feed.)   ☐ yes   ☐ no

Why or why not? _____

_____

_____

_____

- To prevent mold and other problems, producers transport softer fruits (which are preferred by fruit flies) in open boxes or boxes with air holes. These boxes allow an infestation of fruit flies in one area to spread quickly to another. In this situation, what drawbacks do fumigants have as a control method? _____

_____

_____

_____

- After seeing the drawbacks of the methods most frequently used to control pests in foods, give another possible method of fruit fly control. Describe its advantages and disadvantages. _____

_____

_____

_____

16A–Live Bony Fish

Materials: living fish

Goals:

To observe the motion of fish

To note specialized structures that equip the fish for its environment

To observe the external anatomy of the fish

> Class Osteichthyes, the bony fish, is one of the largest vertebrate classes. From your observation of living fish, you will see how a fish uses its specialized structures in its environment.
>
> Although there is great similarity among most fish, there are some surprising diversities. Delicacy, as well as brute strength, is demonstrated by the members of this class. Their fins often have unusual and intricate forms, and their body shapes take many different forms.

Study of a Living Fish

Observe the movements of fish swimming in an aquarium. Note the different body movements of various fish. Also note the different body and fin structures in each fish. Base your answers for the questions below upon observations of a typical fish (one without major body modifications) found in the aquarium. Remember, you are to observe the natural movements of the fish; so *do not* tap on the glass.

Body Shape

I. Describe the body shape as viewed from the side. _____

_____

II. Describe the body shape as viewed from the front. _____

_____

III. In what ways is the fish's body ideally suited for its aquatic environment? _____

_____

Movements of the Mouth and Opercula

I. Describe the position of the opercula when the mouth is open. _____

II. Describe the position of the opercula when the mouth is closed. _____

III. Why are these movements in the fish important? _____

_____

Eyes and Eyelids

I. Are eyelids present?   ☐ yes   ☐ no

How movable are the eyes in their sockets? _____

II. The pupils are large. Why is this important to the fish? _____

_____

Fins

I. Study the fins closely and determine their number, location, and function. Using information from your text and observations of live fish, fill in the Fish Fins chart below.

Fish Fins			
Name of fin	Number	Location	Function
Pectoral			
Pelvic			
Anterior dorsal			
Posterior dorsal			
Anal			
Caudal			

II. When the fish is not moving, which fins move to keep it in position? _____

_____

_____

_____

III. Observe the fish closely as it rapidly swims forward. Which fin provides the main thrust?
☐ caudal fin   ☐ the pectoral fins   ☐ the pelvic fins   ☐ tail region (behind the anus, anterior to the caudal fin)   ☐ some combination

Explain your answer. _____

_____

_____

_____

Researching Unusual Modifications of the Fish's Body and Fin Structure

I. Body modifications

   After researching, list at least two *unusual* body modifications found in some fish and the purpose they serve. *Do not* use illustrations given in the text or in class.

   1. Body modification: _____

      _____

      Function: _____

      _____

   2. Body modification: _____

      _____

      Function: _____

      _____

II. Fin modifications

   1. Fin modification: _____

      _____

      Function: _____

      _____

   2. Fin modification: _____

      _____

      Function: _____

      _____

Researching the Bony Fish

Read completely the material in your text concerning fish and the yellow perch.
You may wish to read more concerning this subject in a general zoology text.

A Life Process Chart for the Yellow Perch

   I. *Do not* repeat the material covered in the Study of a Living Fish.
   II. *Do* cover the following materials:
   - Scales of the fish.
   - Muscles of the fish.
   - Internal structures of the fish. (Be sure to describe the structure and function of those items italicized in the dissection section of Exercise 16B.)

Preparing a Report

   I. Choose two other fish that interest you, research them, and write a brief report on each one.
   II. These may be salt water, freshwater, or aquarium fish. Choose an exotic fish and tell what makes it unusual.
   III. Each report must be at least one hundred words but not more than two pages.

16B–Dissection of a Bony Fish

Materials: preserved fish (yellow perch), culture dish, hand lens or stereomicroscope, dissection pan, dissection kit, pins, plastic bag

Goal:

To observe the external and internal anatomy of the fish

Observation of a preserved fish will permit you to see many external structures that are not visible on a live specimen. The internal structures of a fish are typical of vertebrates, and fish dissection can be useful in illustrating and learning these structures.

External Structures of a Yellow Perch

Using a preserved specimen of the yellow perch, examine the structures listed below.

I. Mouth
- Describe the teeth. ――――――――――――――――――――――
- Tell why the type and placement of the teeth are important to the feeding habits of the yellow perch. ――――――――――――――――――――

――――――――――――――――――――――――

- Examine the tongue. Describe its texture, location, and attachment to the mouth.

――――――――――――――――――――――――

- Examine the esophageal opening. Insert your probe into it. Explain the need a perch has for a large, elastic esophageal opening. ――――――――――――

――――――――――――――――――――――――

II. Nostrils
- Where are the nostrils located? ――――――――――――――――――
- Describe the structure of the nostrils. ――――――――――――――

――――――――――――――――――――――――

III. Fins
- Raise the dorsal fins by pulling them forward. The dorsal fins of a yellow perch consist of a spiny and a soft portion.
  - To determine whether a structure in a fin is a ray or a spine, put your finger on the very tip of the structure and then push on it. A spine will not bend; a ray bends.
  - How many spines are there on your specimen's dorsal anterior fin? ―――――――
  - Compare the number you counted with the number of spines on other specimens. Is the number the same? ☐ yes ☐ no
    If the answer is *no,* how wide is the variation? ―――――――――
- Tell whether the other fins on the yellow perch are supported by rays or spines or both.

    Pectoral: ☐ rays ☐ spines ☐ both
    Pelvic: ☐ rays ☐ spines ☐ both
    Anal: ☐ rays ☐ spines ☐ both
    Caudal: ☐ rays ☐ spines ☐ both

IV. Body covering
- Locate the lateral line. What function does it serve? ―――――――――――

――――――――――――――――――――――――

- Carefully examine a scale from the yellow perch with a stereomicroscope or with a hand lens. What structures are you able to observe? _____

V. Opercula and gills

- Raise the right operculum, and with a probe carefully separate the layers of gills to examine them. How many layers of gills are there? _____ Is this true of both sides? ☐ yes ☐ no
- Insert your probe through the gills and into the mouth cavity. Note where it enters the mouth. Why is the mouth-gill chamber opening necessary? _____

_____

- With scissors, cut the left operculum away and remove one set of gills by cutting the upper and lower attachments of the *gill arch*.
- Rinse the gills and place them in a culture dish filled with water; examine them closely. Examine the feathery *filaments* and the comblike *rakers*.
- Examine the upper and lower ends of the arch and try to find the blood vessels that enter and leave the gill. Why should the gill be so richly supplied with blood?

_____

_____

_____

- Draw a gill in Area A. Label on your drawing all the parts italicized above.

A

VI. Label on Diagram 16B-1 the external structures of a yellow perch.
- The diagram is an outline. Draw in the external structures not shown.
- Label as many of the external parts as you can.

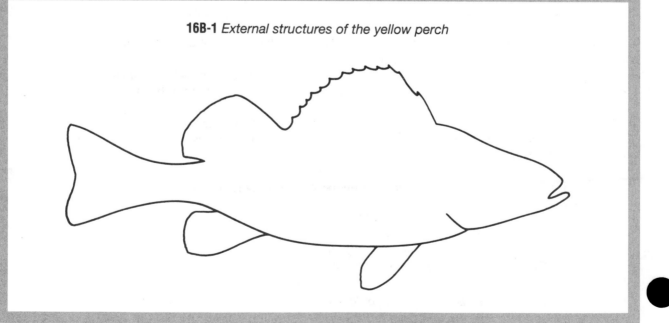

16B-1 *External structures of the yellow perch*

Internal Structures of a Yellow Perch

R
E
0

Read the entire section on dissecting the perch before you begin to cut. Note carefully the diagrams you are to draw. You should include all the following italicized terms in your Life Process Chart of the yellow perch (Exercise 16A). Do the remainder of the exercise in sequence.

I. Open the body cavity.
- Hold your fish with ventral side up, head pointing away from you. Insert your scissors through the body wall in front of (anterior to) the anus and cut along the midline of the body to the area between the gill covers on the lower side of the head.
- Lay your fish on its right side (with the head toward your left). Continue the incision from the point between the gills, around the front of the operculum, to the top of the body cavity. (A good portion of the dorsal side of the fish is a muscle layer. You need cut only to the top of the air bladder.)
- Make another incision close to the anus and cut dorsally to the top of the body cavity.
- With your scalpel, make the remaining incision across the body cavity (just dorsal to the air bladder.)
- Remove the side wall of the body. The removal of the wall will reveal the body cavity with the organs in their normal positions.

II. Locate the internal organs.
- The digestive system
  - ❏ Locate the beige *liver*. It is in the anterior end of the body cavity. Gently raise the lobes of the liver and find the *gall bladder* (which looks like a very tiny, flattened balloon) attached to the lower surface of the liver. Cut the liver free and remove it in one piece, if possible.
  - ❏ Locate the short *esophagus* and *stomach*.
  - ❏ Locate the *intestine* and follow its loops to the *anus*.
  - ❏ Cut the esophagus where it enters the mouth and cut the intestine near the anus.
  - ❏ Remove the digestive system without disturbing the other organs and place it beside the fish in the dissection pan.
  - ❏ Draw in Area B the digestive system as it lies outside the body cavity. Label all the organs italicized above as well as the *pyloric ceca*.
  - ❏ Cut open the stomach. Can you recognize any specific food?   ☐ yes   ☐ no

    If *yes,* what? _____
- The urogenital system
  - ❏ With the alimentary canal removed, you should see the *gonads* and perhaps the *urinary bladder*.
    - ○ The female perch may have a large, yellow-orange *ovary* (called a *roe*) containing many eggs. (If your fish was about to lay eggs, you may have already removed this structure in order to see the other organs.) The ovary could also be a small, beige-colored, drumstick-shaped structure if the fish was not ready to lay eggs.

B

○ The male perch will have small, cream-colored *testes*.

❑ Trace the white threadlike ducts coming from the gonads and the small tube from the urinary bladder to the *urogenital opening*.

❑ Find the *kidneys,* which usually are dark red strands along the spine.

• The air bladder and the circulatory system

❑ Locate the *air bladder* along the top of the body cavity. It may have broken when you removed the body wall.

❑ On the ventral side of the body cavity, near the opercula, locate the *pericardial cavity,* which contains the *heart*.

○ The soft upper chamber of the heart is the *atrium*.

○ Below and anterior to the atrium is the *ventricle*.

○ A purplish, muscular bulb, the *bulbus arteriosus,* gives rise to the *ventral aorta,* which branches to the gills.

❑ Remove the heart and draw it in Area C. Label as many structures as you can.

• The nervous system

❑ Expose the brain of the fish.

○ Hold the fish with its dorsal side up and position its head so that it points away from you. Using your scalpel and scissors, cut away the skin from the skull.

○ Scrape the skull with your scissors to wear away the bone.

○ When the bone becomes thin, pick away the bone with the forceps to expose the brain.

❑ Locate the *olfactory lobes* in front, the larger lobes of the *cerebrum* behind these, and the very large *optic lobes* posterior to the cerebrum. The *cerebellum* is posterior to the optic lobes, and the *medulla oblongata,* an enlargement of the spinal cord, is posterior to the cerebellum and slightly underneath it.

○ Considering the size and function of each brain part, in what function *should* the fish be most adept? _____

Is the fish most adept at this function?   ☐ yes   ☐ no

Explain. _____

○ When you consider the size and function of each brain part, in what function *should* it be least adept? _____

Is the fish least adept at this function?   ☐ yes   ☐ no

Explain. _____

❑ Draw the nervous system in Area D and label the brain regions and the spinal cord as you found them.

C

D

17–Birds and Mammals

Materials: microscope, feathers (contour, including body and flight; down), preserved slides of feathers (contour and down), mammal fur, skeleton of a bird, skeleton of a mammal

Goals:
To learn about the body coverings of birds and mammals
To learn about the physical characteristics that enable birds to fly
To learn about local birds and mammals
To compare the skeletons of a bird and a mammal

The classes Aves and Mammalia contain the "warm-blooded" animals. After man, these organisms are probably the most intelligent of all God's earthly creatures. In this exercise you will observe some of the differences between these two classes; then you will be asked to do research and to prepare reports about birds and mammals native to your area.

The Birds

One of the most significant characteristics of birds is their feathers. After observing these remarkably strong, yet lightweight structures, you will note other structures that equip birds for flight. Then you will be asked to learn about the birds found in your area.

Bird Feathers

I. Obtain a down feather and contour feathers (include flight feathers and body feathers).
- Examine the feather structures described on page 424 of the text.
- What observations can you make regarding the differences between a body feather

and a flight feather? _____

_____

II. Examine a preserved slide of down and contour feathers under a microscope.
- Can you see barbs, barbules, and hooks on the contour feathers? ☐ yes ☐ no
- Can you see all these structures on the down feathers? ☐ yes ☐ no

Explain why all these structures are or are not necessary. _____

_____

_____

*A Bird's Characteristics for Flight

List ten bird characteristics that cause these animals to be ideally suited for flight. (Include

skeletal characteristics and other physical peculiarities.) _____

_____

_____

_____

_____

*Local Birds

I. Prepare a list of ten birds native to your area.
II. Write a description of each bird.
- Each description should be about one page long.

- Include in each description–
  - ❏ Size of bird; coloration; type of beak, wings, legs, and feet.
  - ❏ Food, feeding time, seasonal changes in diet.
  - ❏ Preferred nesting sites, number of young, time of year the young hatch, whether young are altricial or precocial.
  - ❏ If the bird migrates, indicate where it goes and when. If it does not migrate, how does it survive the winter?
  - ❏ Ecological significance, whether the bird helps or harms human interest.
- Obtain illustrations of each bird if possible.

Mammals

Mammals, the animals that have body characteristics and intelligence most like man's, make a fascinating study.

Observing Fur

I. Use a stereomicroscope or a hand lens to examine guard hair and underhair.

[R] [E] [O] II. Compare fur and hair.
- Prepare a wet mount of a guard hair, an underhair, and a hair from your head.
- What differences do you notice among guard hair, underhair, and human scalp hair?

_____

_____

_____

[R] [E] [O] ### *Studying Local Mammals

I. Prepare a list of ten mammals native to your area.
- Be specific. (The term *mouse* is not specific enough. *Field mouse* and *deer mouse* are specific enough for this exercise.)
- Try to list animals from different orders.

II. Write a brief description of each mammal.
- Each description should be about one page long.
- Include in each description–
  - ❏ Type of teeth, food, feeding time, seasonal changes in diet
  - ❏ Preferred home sites, type of home built, number of young, time of year young are born, time it takes young to mature
  - ❏ What the animal does during the various seasons
  - ❏ Ecological significance, whether the mammal helps or harms human interests
- Obtain illustrations of each mammal if possible.

[R] [E] [O] ## A Comparison of Skeletons

I. List at least ten significant differences between a mammal skeleton and a bird skeleton.
- Instead of comparing the skeletons directly, look for differences in structural relationships. In other words, the skeleton of a large bird will, of course, have large bones compared to those of a mouse skeleton. The obvious comparison would be size, but it is better to compare corresponding bones in relation to other bones of the *same* skeleton. For example, it is better to compare the relative lengths of the finger and arm bones in a mammal to the relative lengths of the same bones in a bird.
- Be as specific as possible, using only your textbook for reference.

II. List any additional significant differences.

Name _____

Date _____ Hour _____

18–Succession and Pollution

Materials: sterile (boiled) pond or spring water, dried plant material from a pond, small all-glass aquaria or large jars with lids, microscopes, dropping pipets, slides, coverslips, fertilizer, algae cultures, protozoan cultures, baking soda, vinegar, powdered lime, hydrion (pH) test papers, hydrochloric acid

Goals:

    To observe succession in a microcosm

    To observe the effects of various pollutants upon succession

Succession is the predictable change of a biotic community over a period of time. Succession progresses through a series of stages to the climax stage for that particular area. In this exercise you will set up an ecosystem in a bottle. A small, artificial environment is sometimes called a **microcosm.** A microcosm will progress through various stages and, if permitted to continue long enough, will conclude in a climax. Unless the microcosm is managed by human intervention in the later stages of succession, the artificiality will result in the death (one form of climax) of all the organisms. Lack of space and lack of a wide enough variety of populations in the microcosm prevent the complete cycling of the various substances that exist in natural ecosystems.

Natural succession of an area can, however, be altered by intervention. In the second part of this laboratory exercise, several microcosms will be set up, different factors introduced, and the successions taking place in the microcosms compared.

Setting Up an Aquatic Microcosm

- Clean a 1-gallon glass aquarium or a bottle with a lid. Use salt as a cleansing agent to make sure there is no soap film.
- Fill the container half full of *sterile* (boiled) pond or spring water.
- Place a handful of dried grass, leaves, or other plant material obtained from the edge of a pond into the water.
- Cover the container (a piece of glass placed over the opening is good) and set the jar in a well-lighted area (not in direct sunlight).

Observing Succession in an Aquatic Microcosm

I. After the aquatic microcosm has been set up for 2 or 3 days, make the following observations and record the data you obtain on a classroom chart like the one illustrated on page 149.

- Record statistics about the microcosm.
  - ❑ Do not disturb the microcosm as you make these observations.
  - ❑ Record the temperature (without stirring the microcosm).
  - ❑ Place a drop of the microcosm on a hydrion test paper. Record the pH.
  - ❑ *Turbidity* is the cloudiness of the water. Indicate not only how cloudy the water is but also the color of the water.
- Record statistics about the organisms in the microcosm.
  - ❑ Groups of students will be assigned to make and observe wet mounts from different areas of the microcosm.
    - ○ One group will obtain the material for their wet mount from the surface of the microcosm, another from the middle, and another from the bottom. *Do not* disturb the microcosm.

- Although each group may make and observe several slides, only one entry for each microcosmic area should be made on the chart.
- ❏ Identify as many of the organisms as you can.
  - Use a pictorial key to identify pond organisms or protozoans, if necessary.
  - If you cannot locate the name of an organism you have found, make a reference sketch of it and assign it a number.
  - Record the name or number of the organism on the chart and indicate whether the organism was very abundant, abundant, rare, or very rare in the material on your slide.
- ❏ Do a specimen count.
  - With a microscope focused on the populated area of your slide, count for 15 seconds the organisms you see in your microscope field. Include any that move into the field while you are counting as well as those that were there when you started.
  - Moving the slide slightly each time, repeat the procedure three more times.
  - Average your results and record your 15-second specimen count on the classroom chart.

II. Every other day for 2 or 3 weeks, repeat the observations and record your results on the chart. You should be able to complete this during the first few minutes of class.

[R] [E] [O] *III. Answer the following questions concerning your class's observations.
- • Regarding the number and types of organisms
  - ❏ As the microcosm progresses toward its climax stage, how does its population change?   ☐ increases   ☐ decreases
  - ❏ As the microcosm progresses towards its climax, are there more or fewer *types* of organisms?   ☐ more   ☐ fewer
  - ❏ What progression of the number and type of organisms would you expect in an ecosystem passing through succession? _____

    _____

    _____

    Did your microcosm follow this progression?   ☐ yes   ☐ no
- • Regarding the type of organism
  - ❏ What types of organisms are most abundant in the pioneer stages? _____

    _____

  - ❏ What types of organisms are most abundant as the microcosm approaches climax? _____
  - ❏ Is this progression of organism types what you would expect in an ecosystem passing through succession?   ☐ yes   ☐ no

    Why or why not? _____

    _____

    _____

    _____

- • Conclusions
  - ❏ What can you conclude about the progression of the relative sizes of the individual organisms during succession? _____

    _____

    _____

    _____

  - ❏ What is the effect of the turbidity and pH of the microcosm on its number of organisms and its succession? _____

    _____

Name _____

_____

_____

Microcosm Observations

Date	Temperature	pH	Turbidity	Organisms	Specimen Count
2/14 Day 3	32° C	8	Little turbidity, white material in water.	Top: 1. (small circular algae)— abundant 2. Paramecium—rare 3. Small flagellate—abundant Middle: 4. Paramecium—rare Bottom: 5. Ameba—rare 6. Small flagellate—abundant	Top 5 Middle 2 Bottom 8
2/16 Day 5	33°C	8.3	Little turbidity	Top: 1. (small circular algae)— abundant	Top 8

R E O

Pollution and Succession

In an ecosystem passing through succession, a *pollutant* may be defined as any substance or factor that alters normal succession. In the following exercise you will be asked to add a single pollutant to various microcosms and note how it affects the succession of each microcosm.

  I. Prepare an aquatic microcosm as described in the box on page 147.

 II. When the microcosm is 2 or 3 days old, divide it.
- Thoroughly mix the microcosm to distribute the organisms equally.
- While the culture is mixed, divide it into 4 or 5 equal portions. Each portion will make up one small microcosm.
- Place each portion in a jar large enough to be only half filled.

III. Select and introduce pollutants.
- Organisms are a form of pollutant. Introduce to one of the small microcosms a few of a specific type of organism from an individual laboratory culture of algae, protozoans, or small aquatic organisms (*Daphnia,* for example).
- Another way to pollute the microcosms is to introduce a factor that will alter the physical environment. Consider adding a small quantity of one of these: vinegar (an acid), soluble plant food (nutrients), baking soda (a base), powdered lime, or hydrochloric acid. (You may need to add a little more of the substance every few days.)
- Another pollutant is the abundance of a physical environmental factor. Consider placing one of the small microcosms in direct sunlight, in a dark cabinet, near the heater, or in a cold closet, or adding water to dilute the microcosm by doubling its volume.
- Be sure to keep at least one of the small microcosms as a control and treat it the same way you treated the large microcosm in the previous experiment.

IV. Observe and keep records for each of the small microcosms.

*V. Write a summary of the results.
- Write a summary for each microcosm, telling of its contents and progression.
- Compare the microcosms, pointing out their differences.
- Offer probable explanations for the differences observed in the various microcosms.

_____

_____

_____

_____

_____

_____

_____

_____

_____

_____

_____

_____

_____

_____

_____

_____

_____

_____

_____

_____

_____

_____

_____

_____

_____

_____

_____

_____

19A–Readings on the Human Body Systems

Materials: magazines, 3" × 5" cards (ten to thirty)

Goals:

To permit students to research topics of human anatomy or physiology that interest them

To encourage learning material beyond what is covered in class

To enrich class discussions

For this exercise you will read magazine articles on many aspects of each of the human systems. You will then write a brief report on each of these articles. This activity will help you learn about areas that interest you.

I. Read magazine articles about the human body systems (or parts of the systems), and write a review of each article on a separate 3" × 5" card.
   - Minimum requirements
     - ❑ You must read one article for each of the ten human systems.
     - ❑ The article must be read before the test date for that system. You must bring the 3" × 5" card for that system to class on the test date.
     - ❑ The articles for that system will be considered part of the assigned reading for that test.
   - Extra points
     - ❑ You may read extra articles to earn extra points. Each article above the required number adds one point to your lab grade.
     - ❑ The following grading scale will be used.
       - ○ Ten articles (the required number) earn a C grade.
       - ○ Twenty articles earn a B grade.
       - ○ Thirty articles earn an A grade. You will not get extra points if you read more than thirty articles.
     - ❑ If you choose to read extra articles, you may read a maximum of five articles for any one system.
     - ❑ Although you must read the one required article for each system before the test, extra articles may be read at any time before this laboratory exercise is due.

II. Details of the assignment
   - Writing your reports
     - ❑ Use a separate 3" × 5" card for each article.
     - ❑ Follow the format illustrated in Diagram 19A-1.
     - ❑ You may use *only* one card for each report. Do not use extra cards to make long reports.
   - Length of articles
     - ❑ An article should be about three or four pages long (not including pictures).
     - ❑ If the article is more than eight pages long, you may count it as two articles.
   - Finding articles
     - ❑ You may *not* report on encyclopedia articles. Each article must be from a magazine or must have appeared in a magazine.
     - ❑ If you find a good article, recommend it to classmates. They must read the article themselves in order to write a report on it.
     - ❑ A good place to find articles is the *Reader's Guide to Periodical Literature* available in most libraries. Look under such topics as human anatomy or a particular disease, such as bone cancer or arthritis. Topics such as skeleton or skeletal system are general, and you may not find articles listed under them.
     - ❑ If the article you find is poor (too simple or too difficult), stop reading it and find another.

19A-1 *Sample article card*

- Filling out a 3" × 5" card for an article
  - ❏ Fill out your card with the following information, as shown in the sample in Diagram 19A-1.
  - ❏ To receive credit, you must fill out each card with *all* nine pieces of information in the proper order.
    1. *Title* of article (top line, left side). Indent on the second line if the title is long.
    2. *System* for which you are using this article (top line, right side). Underline it and then write your name underneath the line.
    3. *Name of author(s)* (second line).
    4. *Name of magazine* (third line, left side).
    5. *Date of magazine,* not the date you read it (third line, right side).
    6. *Page numbers* of article. List the page numbers, not how many there were (fourth line, left side).
    7. *Illustrations.* List the number and types (fourth line, right side).
    8. *Material discussed* in the article. Use the remainder of the front side with the first line indented. You may use the back of the card if necessary.
    9. *Evaluation* using this number scale:
       - 1-2 very poor (You learned very little from the article.)
       - 3-4 good
       - 5 excellent

       Write your evaluation in the lower right-hand corner and circle it.
- Although you must bring article cards for certain systems to class on test days, they will not be collected. You will turn in your entire collection of article cards when you turn in your laboratory notebook.
- It would be wise for you to keep a record below of the articles you have read so that you will know at a glance which ones you have to complete.

System	Required	Extra				System	Required	Extra			
Skeletal	☐	☐	☐	☐	☐	Circulatory	☐	☐	☐	☐	☐
Integumentary	☐	☐	☐	☐	☐	Excretory	☐	☐	☐	☐	☐
Muscular	☐	☐	☐	☐	☐	Nervous	☐	☐	☐	☐	☐
Digestive	☐	☐	☐	☐	☐	Endocrine	☐	☐	☐	☐	☐
Respiratory	☐	☐	☐	☐	☐	Reproductive	☐	☐	☐	☐	☐

19B–The Human Body and the Skeletal System

Materials: microscope; preserved slides of dry ground bone, c.s.; human skeleton; skeleton diagrams; colored pencils

Goals:

 To learn the basic terms associated with anatomy

 To observe the typical microstructures and macrostructures of the skeletal
  system

 To learn the names of various bones and joints of the human body

> The human body is an outstanding example of God's intricate design in creation. The more we study it, the more we understand that each of the most minute details has significance. In this laboratory exercise we shall learn the names of some of the obvious parts of the body and look at some details regarding the skeletal system.

Terms of Human Anatomy

Label all of the following terms on one (or both) of the human diagrams below (19B-1).

 I. *Direction* (may be indicated by arrows on the diagrams): anterior, posterior, superior, inferior, medial, lateral, transverse, deep, superficial, proximal, distal

 II. *Cavities:* cranial, buccal, nasal, thoracic, abdominal, pelvic

 III. *Areas:* pectoral, cervical, brachial, lumbar, trunk, thigh, calf, upper extremity, lower extremity, pelvis, buttocks

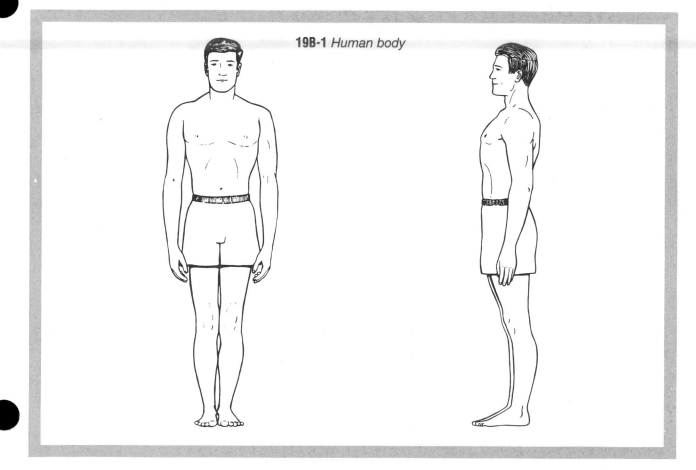

19B-1 *Human body*

The Skeletal System

The primary system of support is the skeleton. The skeleton includes the bones, ligaments, joints, and cartilage of the body. We shall begin with a microscopic study of bone and then proceed to a study of the major structures of the skeleton.

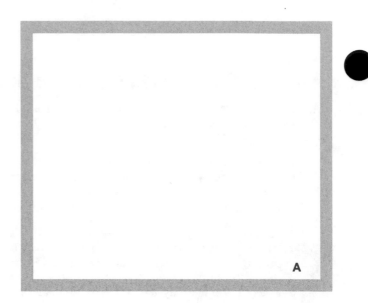

A

R E O **Microstructures**

I. Observe and draw in Area A the preserved slide of dry ground bone, c.s.

II. Label a complete Haversian system. Include the Haversian canal, lamellas, lacunas, canaliculi, and any other structures you can see.

*Macrostructures

R E O I. Learn the bone names and markings indicated on pages 517-18. (Omit those indicated by your instructor.)
- Locate these bones on the skeleton in the laboratory.
- Label them if they are shown on Diagram 19B-2, and below the diagrams, list the bones not shown.

R E O II. Learn about the joints. Fill in the missing information on the Joints of the Human Body chart below.

Joints of the Human Body			
Type	**Name**	**Movement**	**Examples**
Movable	Ball-and-socket	Free movement inside a cone (circumduction)	1. 2.
		Flexion and extension on one plane	1. Elbow (humerus, ulna) 2.
	Pivot	Rotation	1. Humerus and radius 2.
Movable	Gliding		1. Thumb 2. Wrist
Slightly movable	Cartilaginous	Bending, twisting, and slight compression	1. Between vertebrae 2.
Immovable	Suture or fibrous		1. 2.

19B-2 *Human skeleton*

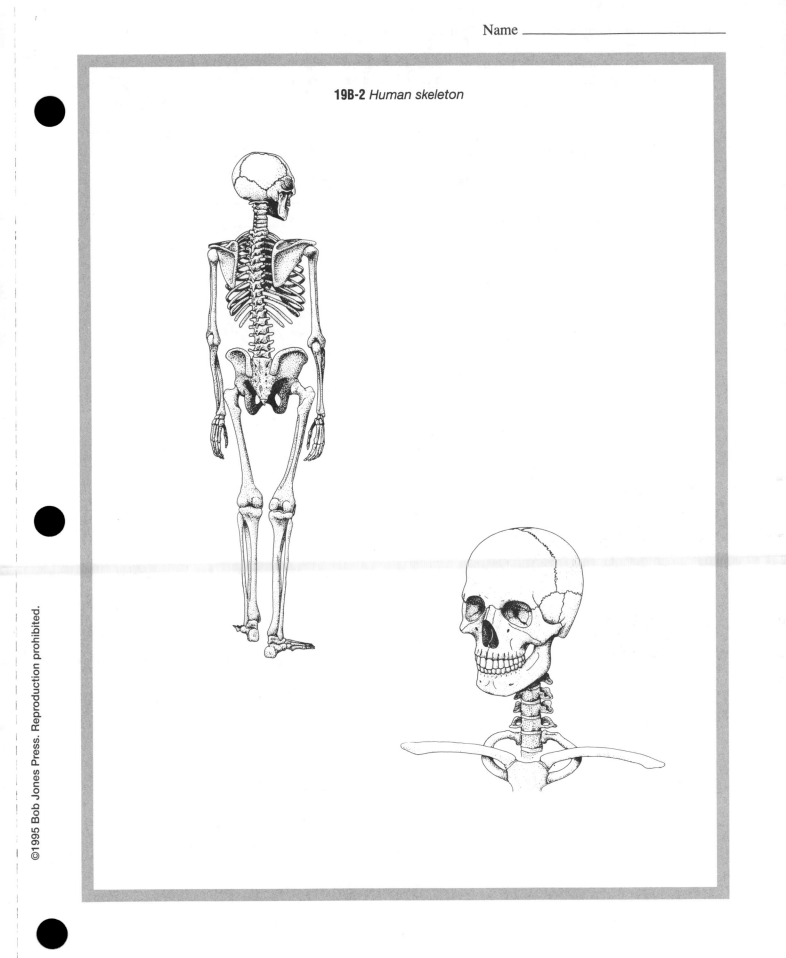

III. Do additional research on sesamoid bones. (*NOTE:* Although they are not always the same thing, sesamoid bones are also called supernumerary bones.)

- What are sesamoid bones? _____

_____

- How do they develop? _____

_____

_____

- List some examples of sesamoid bones. _____

_____

_____

19C–The Human Muscular and Integumentary Systems

Materials: microscope; preserved slides of human skin, c.s., skeletal (striated) muscle, and visceral (smooth) muscle; human muscle diagrams; colored pencils

Goals:

To observe the typical microstructures of the muscular and integumentary systems

To learn the names, origins, insertions, and functions of some of the major human muscles

The human muscular system is a marvel of design. It permits not only movement but also various degrees of strength and extensive flexibility. The human skin is equally marvelous. It is tough enough to block out most substances that would invade our bodies, but soft enough to permit sensation of minute changes in temperature, touch, and pressure–all this while remaining supple enough to bend virtually constantly without breaking. We are truly "wonderfully made."

The Muscular System

The primary system of movement is the muscular system. We shall begin by studying the structures of muscular tissue and then proceed to a study of some of the major muscles of the human body.

Microstructures

I. Observe and draw in Area A a preserved slide of a section of skeletal muscle. Label all the structures you observe.

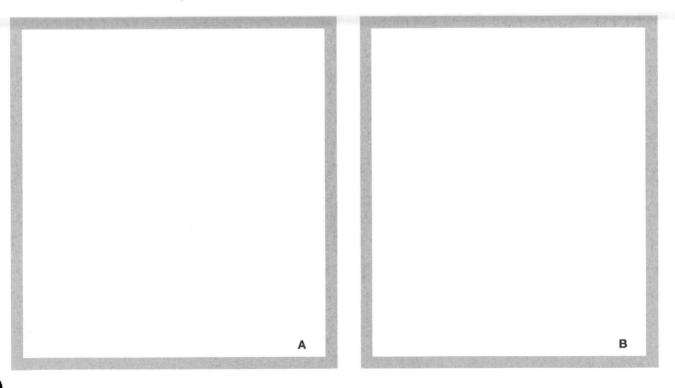

A

B

II. Observe and draw in Area B the preserved slides of visceral and cardiac muscle. Label all the structures you observe.

R
E
O

*III. Fill in the chart below, which deals with the three types of muscles.

The Three Types of Muscles			
Type	Other names	Control	Location (L.) and Function (F.)
Skeletal	1. Striated 2.	□ Conscious □ Subconscious	L. F.
	1. Smooth 2.	□ Conscious □ Subconscious	L. Lining of the internal organs and ducts F.
	Heart	□ Conscious □ Subconscious	L. F.

R
E
O

Macrostructures

I. Study carefully the information on pages 525-27 of your text regarding the attachments and naming of muscles.

II. Answer the following:
- What is the linea alba? _____
- Where is it located? _____
- Where is the Achilles tendon? _____
  _____

III. Learn the name, origin, insertion, and function for each of the human muscles on pages 526-27. Include the diaphragm, which is discussed on pages 439 and 533. Omit those indicated by your instructor.
- Follow these suggestions on how to learn these muscles.
  - On your body, locate each of the muscles you are to know by putting your hand over it and then performing its function. You should be able to feel the muscle working.
  - On your body, locate the origin and insertion while you perform the muscle's function. The function should seem logical when you know the origin and insertion.
  - Consult a human muscle chart to make sure you have located the origin and insertion correctly. Note carefully where the muscle is.
- On the human body outlines (Diagram 19C-1), use colored pencils to sketch and label each of the muscles you are assigned to know. (*NOTE:* One diagram is a dorsal view, and the other is ventral, but both are in anatomical position.)

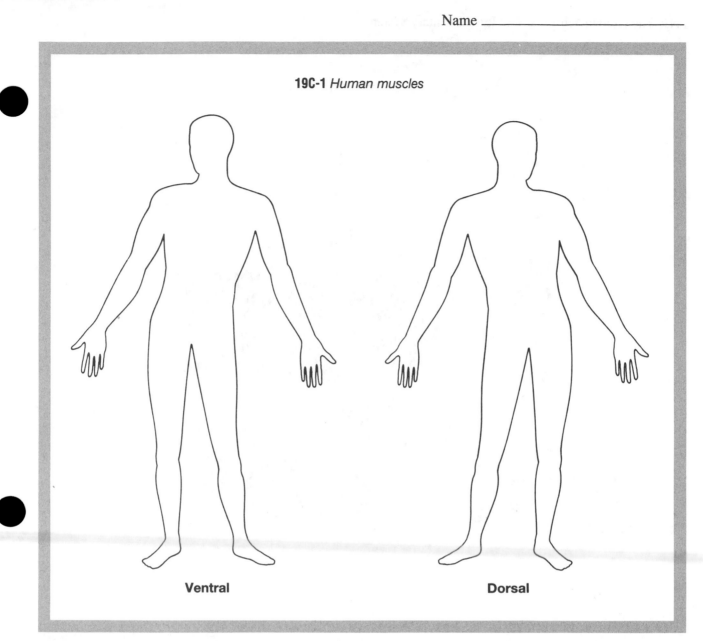

19C-1 *Human muscles*

Ventral

Dorsal

The Integumentary System

The primary function of the integumentary system is protection. Several varied types of skin are found on the body. The thick, tough skin of the palms of the hands and the soles of the feet is considerably different from the thin skin of the face, the arms, and the abdomen.

Observe Human Skin

Observe a preserved slide of human skin. Draw and label the structures you are able to identify in Area C.

C

19C-2 *A section of typical skin*

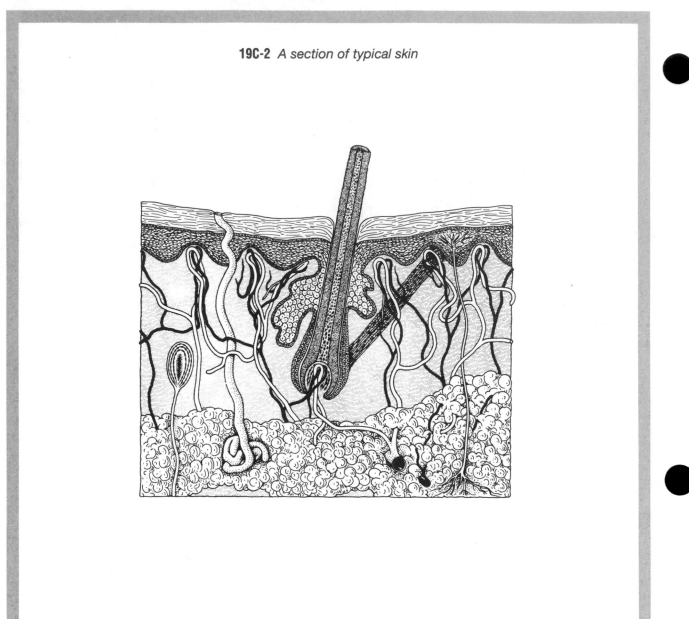

R
E
O
R
E
O

*Label Structures of Human Skin
Identify and label as many structures as possible in Diagram 19C-2.

R
E
O

*Prepare a Report About the Human Skin
I. Read about some skin-related topic or problem.
  • Burns, tans, skin cancer, baldness, warts, moles, birthmarks, oily skin, dry skin, skin transplants, skin wrinkles, aging of the skin, and "face lifts" are possible topics.
  • Consult at least three sources and read at least 5 pages regarding your topic.
II. Prepare a brief report based on your research.
  • Written reports must be at least 100 words long and should be submitted with this lab.
  • Oral reports should be 3-5 minutes long and will be assigned in place of written reports for some students.

20A–The Human Respiratory System

Materials: lung volume bag, rubber band, mouthpiece, paper towels, stethoscope

Goals:

    To measure average lung capacity

    To learn structures of the respiratory system

> The first section of this laboratory exercise will be done as a class demonstration. Various lung volume tests will supply you with data to use in answering the questions. Following the lung volume demonstration are several exercises dealing with the structures of the respiratory system.

Measuring Air Volume

A **spirometer** is a device used to measure the volume of air a person exhales. However, a long plastic bag calibrated in liters may be used instead of the relatively expensive spirometer to measure a person's lung volume. The lung volume bag is not as accurate, but for the purposes of this exercise it will serve well.

How to Use a Lung Volume Bag

  I. Select three students of average size, and select an assistant for each.

  II. Prepare the lung volume bags.

- Insert the mouthpiece partway into the open end of the lung volume bag and secure it with a rubber band. (See Diagram 20A-1.)
- Have the assistant sit down.
- Slide the bag slowly across the assistant's knee while he presses the bag with a paper towel. This will remove all air from the lung volume bag. (See diagram.)

20A-1 *How to empty a lung volume bag*

Measuring Lung Volume

  I. Measure tidal volume.

- Have the person being tested breathe in a normal breath, pinch his nose, put the lung volume bag mouthpiece in his mouth, and breathe out a normal breath.
- The assistant should then take the bag and hold it closed while sliding it across his knee and pressing it with a paper towel in order to force all the air to the bottom.
- The data will be recorded on the chalkboard. In the proper spaces of the Lung Volume chart, copy the data from the chalkboard.
- Empty the lung volume bag, using the procedure described earlier.
- Have each person tested perform this experiment two more times. Record each volume in the proper space of the Lung Volume chart.

  II. Measure expiratory reserve volume.

- Have the person being tested breathe in a normal breath, then breathe out a normal breath, pinch his nose, put the lung volume bag mouthpiece in his mouth, and breathe out as much as possible.
- Using the procedure described in the instructions for measuring tidal volume, measure the air and record the reading for each person in the proper spaces.

Lung Volume

Tidal Volume

Person A	Person B	Person C	Average
1. _____	1. _____	1. _____	_____ l
2. _____	2. _____	2. _____	or
3. _____	3. _____	3. _____	_____ ml

Expiratory Reserve Volume

Person A	Person B	Person C	Average
1. _____	1. _____	1. _____	_____ l
2. _____	2. _____	2. _____	or
3. _____	3. _____	3. _____	_____ ml

Vital Capacity

Person A	Person B	Person C	Average
1. _____	1. _____	1. _____	_____ l
2. _____	2. _____	2. _____	or
3. _____	3. _____	3. _____	_____ ml

- Have each person tested perform this experiment two more times. Record each volume in the proper space of the Lung Volume chart.

III. Measure vital capacity.
  - Have the person being tested breathe in as much as he possibly can, then pinch his nose, put the lung volume bag mouthpiece in his mouth, and breathe out as much as possible.
  - Using the procedure described in the instructions for measuring tidal volume, force the air to the bottom of the bag and record the reading for each person in the proper space.
  - Have each person tested repeat this experiment two more times. Record each volume in the proper space of the Lung Volume chart.

Computing Average Lung Capacities

I. Take all your data and determine averages for the following volumes. (Be careful to use the correct units.)
  - Tidal volume: _____ ml
  - Expiratory reserve volume: _____ml
  - Vital capacity: _____ ml

II. Using these averages, compute the inspiratory reserve volume. _____ ml

III. Assuming a residual volume of 1,000 ml, what would be the average total lung capacity of the people tested? _____ml

IV. According to the information on page 534 of your text, are these lung volume results considered average?   □ yes   □ no   If not, what factors do you think might account for the difference? _____

_____

_____

_____

*Structures of the Respiratory System

I. Label Diagram 20A-2 of the respiratory system as completely as possible.

II. Under each label, indicate what happens to air in that structure. Enclose this information in parentheses.

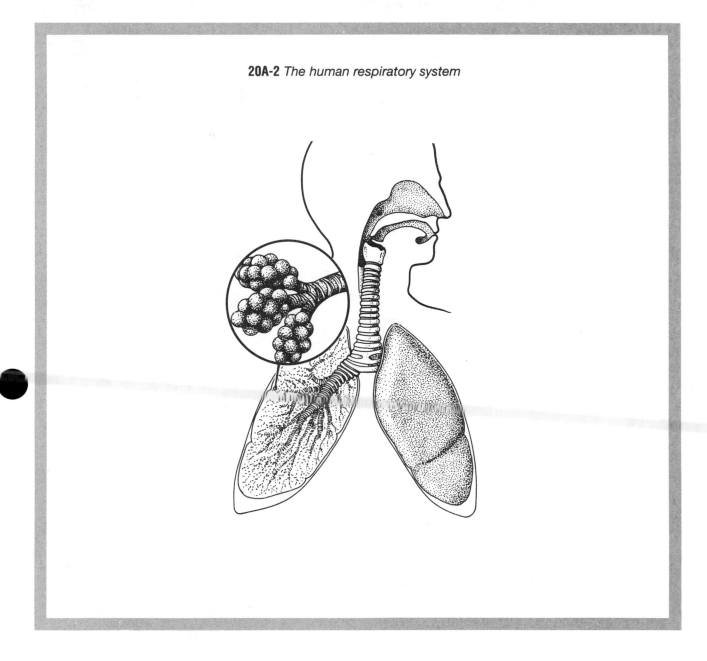

20A-2 *The human respiratory system*

Listening to Your Lungs

Air rushing into and out of healthy respiratory structures makes various sounds. Many respiratory problems cause various abnormal sounds which a physician can hear using a stethoscope. Hopefully you will not hear abnormal respiratory sounds when listening to your lab partner's breathing. It can be interesting, however, to listen to normal sounds of the respiratory system.

I. Listen to the lungs by following these instructions:

- Using a tissue and alcohol, clean the ear plugs of a stethoscope.
- Place the stethoscope in your ears, allowing the tubes to hang freely and being careful not to hit the diaphragm on hard objects. (The noise can be very loud.)

- Place the diaphragm of the stethoscope on your lab partner's back and press lightly while he breathes normally.
- Listen to a normal breath or two in areas A-F as labeled on Diagram 20A-3.

  ❑ Describe the sounds you hear.

  _____

  _____

  _____

  _____

  _____

  _____

  _____

  _____

  _____

20A-3 *Areas to place stethescope*

  ❑ Are the sounds you hear different in different areas? _____

  _____

  _____

  _____

- Listen to a deep breath in the same areas. Do you hear a difference?   ❑ yes   ❑ no

  If so, describe the difference and tell what may account for it. _____

  _____

  _____

  _____

- Listen to areas A and E while the person coughs. Describe what you hear.

  _____

  _____

  _____

- Listen to areas A and E while the person talks. Describe what you hear.

  _____

  _____

  _____

R
E
O

II. Using a stethoscope, listen to a person's throat.
- Listen to your lab partner's breathing in area G.
- Listen to your lab partner's voice in the same area.

- Describe what you heard. _____

  _____

  _____

20B–The Human Digestive System

Materials: none

Goals:

To learn about the structures of the digestive system and the process of digestion in the human body

To learn about calories and weight gain or loss

The first part of this laboratory exercise involves identifying and labeling structures of the human digestive system and completing a chart dealing with human digestion. The last part of the exercise may reveal some information about calories, weight gain, and weight loss.

Structures of the Digestive System

R
E
O

*I. Label Diagram 20B-1.

- Label as many structures as you can. You should have at least eleven structures labeled.
- Under each label indicate what activity of *physical digestion* happens in that structure. If the structure is not involved in physical digestion, give a brief statement of its function. Enclose this information in parentheses.

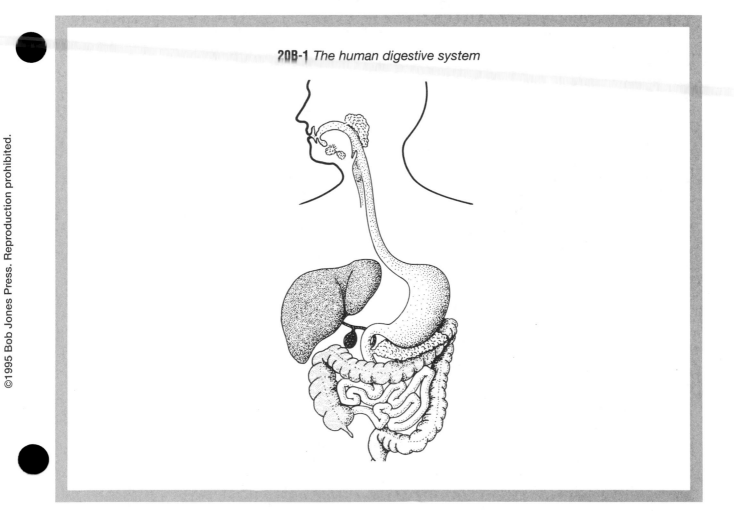

20B-1 *The human digestive system*

*II. Fill in the Chemical Digestion chart. If certain foods undergo no chemical digestion in a particular area, draw a line through that space.

Chemical Digestion		Starches	Fats	Proteins
Mouth	†Enzymes			
	‡Beginning substances			
	§Ending substances			
Stomach	†Enzymes			
	‡Beginning substances			
	§Ending substances			
Small Intestine	†Enzymes			
	‡Beginning substances			
	§Ending substances			

† List all the enzymes involved in chemical digestion in the proper spaces, regardless of the sequence in which they work.
‡ List all the substances acted on by any of the enzymes listed.
§ List the substances that result after all the enzymes act on the beginning substances you listed.

Calories and Pounds

Some people think that calories and pounds are different names for the same thing. This is not true. *Calories* are units of heat energy; *pounds* are units of weight. In the human body, however, calories and pounds are converted from one to the other. It is good to understand the relative proportions of calories contained in food to pounds of body weight.

There are many factors that could alter the numbers given in the charts below. For example, a person who is in poor physical condition or is overweight will use more calories doing a particular physical activity. Certain apples contain more sugar than others and thus would have more calories.

*I. Listed below are some activities and the calories they burn per hour. Use these figures to answer the following questions.

Calories Used for Selected Activities

Activity	Calories per Hour	Activity	Calories per Hour
Watching TV, Reading	25	Walking ($2\frac{1}{2}$ mph)	210
Driving car	50	Golfing, Lawn mowing	250
Eating	50	Bowling	270
Sewing	50	Swimming ($\frac{1}{4}$ mph)	300
Typing	50	Volleyball, Roller skating	350
Washing dishes	75	Table tennis	360
Playing piano	75	Hiking	400
Brushing teeth or hair	100	Tennis	420
Dusting furniture	150	Shoveling	500
Mopping floors	200	Skiing	600
Bicycling ($5\frac{1}{2}$ mph)	210	Running (10 mph)	900

- How many hours would one have to watch TV to lose a pound of body weight?

  _____

- How many hours would one have to wash dishes to lose a pound of body weight?

  _____

- How many hours would one have to walk at 2.5 mph to lose a pound of body weight?

  _____

- How many hours would one have to play volleyball to lose a pound of body weight?

  _____

- How many hours would one have to run at 10 mph to lose a pound of body weight?

  _____

*II. Listed below are some foods and their caloric content. Use these figures to answer the following questions.

Selected Foods and Calorie Values

Fruits		**Chicken, fried** ($\frac{1}{2}$ breast, $3\frac{1}{3}$ oz.)	154
Apple (1 large)	70	Egg (1)	80
Banana (1 large)	85	Frankfurter (1)	155
Cantaloupe ($\frac{1}{2}$)	40	Hamburger, on bun ($\frac{1}{4}$ lb.)	416
Orange (1 large)	70	Ocean perch, fried (3 oz.)	195
Raisins (1 cup)	460		
Strawberries (1 cup)	55	**Seeds and Nuts**	
Watermelon (2 lb. slice)	120	Almonds, shelled (1 cup)	850
		Peanut butter (1 T.)	90
Vegetables		Peanuts, shelled (1 cup)	840
Broccoli (1 cup)	60		
Carrots, cooked (1 cup)	45	**Breads and Cakes**	
Celery stalk (8 in.)	5	Bread, white (1 slice)	62
Sweet corn (5-in. ear)	65	Cake, angel food (2-in. section)	110
Cucumber (1-in. slice)	5	Cheesecake (4 oz.)	215
Onions (1-in. slice)	80	Doughnut, sugar (1.8 oz.)	233
Green peas (1 cup)	110	Pancake (4-in. diameter)	60
Pepper, green (1 raw)	15	Pie, Boston cream (3.3 oz.)	329
Potato, baked (5 oz.)	90	Pie, pumpkin (4-in. section)	265
Potatoes, French-fried (2 oz.)	200		
		Miscellaneous	
Dairy Products		Cola (6 oz.)	73
Butter or margarine (1 T.)	100	Fudge (1 oz.)	115
Cottage cheese (1 oz.)	30	Honey (1 T.)	60
Ice cream (1 cup)	295	Ketchup (1 T.)	15
Milk, whole (1 cup)	165	Mayonnaise (1 T.)	110
Yogurt (1 cup)	120	Pickle, dill (1 large)	15
		Salad dressing, French (1 T.)	90
Meats		Soup, chicken (1 cup)	75
Beef, roast (3 oz.)	265	Sugar (1 T.)	50
Beef stew (1 cup)	250		

- How many apples would one have to eat to gain a pound of body weight?

  _____

- How many pats of butter (a pat is 1 T. [tablespoon]) would one have to eat to gain a pound of body weight? _____

- How many cups of ice cream would one have to eat to gain a pound of body weight?

  _____

- How many cups of peanuts would one have to eat to gain a pound of body weight?

  _____

R
E
O

*III. Although many factors are involved in weight gain and loss, working the following problems will help you to see the relationship between the two. (Indicate whether there is a gain or a loss of weight and how many pounds are involved.)

- One day at breakfast, Tom read that the quantity of cereal he was consuming gave him a breakfast of 300 calories. He decided that two boiled eggs, two slices of toast with a quarter tablespoon of butter on each, and an orange would be a better breakfast. If Tom kept his other meals the same and did not change his amount of activity, what would be his weight change in one year?

  _____

- Mary had not grown taller, but last year's dresses did not fit around the middle. She decided that for the thirteen weeks of summer vacation, she would invest the two hours a day she normally spent doing her school assignments in physical exercise. Mary decided that six days a week she would spend one hour walking, a half hour in the pool swimming, and a half hour bicycling to and from the pool. If she did not change her food intake, how much weight change could she expect?

  _____

- Harry enjoyed his summer job at the bank, but he noticed that he always gained about 20 pounds in thirteen weeks. He knew that he would do better in soccer if he could keep that weight off. Normally he had two sugar doughnuts at his morning break and another two at the afternoon break. He decided to substitute a cup of yogurt for each of these snacks. If all other factors remained the same, would the amount of weight Harry usually gained change?   ☐ yes   ☐ no

  Explain. _____

  _____

  _____

  _____

21A–Blood

Materials: fresh blood, glass slides, Tallquist-Adams hemoglobin scale test book-let, anti-A and anti-B human blood sera, capillary tubes, toothpicks, preserved slides of human blood, cotton swabs

Goals:

To observe some of the clinically important characteristics of human blood

To observe human blood cells

> The circulatory system is one of the first to react to diseases and disorders in the body. The composition of the blood, the action of the heart, and the pressure of the blood in the blood vessels give the physician a good idea of the physical well-being of his patient. Although most of the procedures followed in this and the next lab are a bit "crude" by modern clinical standards, they are the basis for most of the refined techniques used today to detect specific illnesses and conditions.
>
> To prevent infection, the teacher will supply the blood necessary for sections of this laboratory exercise and will do a number of the procedures as demonstrations.

Blood Types

Before a transfusion can be given, the blood must be accurately typed. If the wrong type is transfused, the recipient's blood may agglutinate, causing death. Blood is usually typed by testing it with sera. Blood-typing serum is made from blood *plasma*; therefore, it contains only antibodies. Anti-A serum, then, contains anti-A antibodies and, thus, causes blood containing A antigens to agglutinate. (See pp. 554-55 of your text.)

R E O

*I. Answer the following questions regarding blood-typing sera, antigens, and antibodies.

- What antigens would be found in anti-B serum? _____

  What antibodies would be found in anti-B serum? _____
- If the red blood cells agglutinate when anti-A serum is placed on the blood, what

  type(s) of blood may the person have? _____
- If the red blood cells agglutinate when anti-A serum is placed on the blood and also when anti-B serum is placed on the blood, what type(s) of blood may the person

  have? _____
- If the red blood cells do not agglutinate when anti-A or anti-B serum is placed on the

  blood, what type(s) of blood does the person have? _____

R E O

II. Your teacher will type a blood sample by following these procedures.

- Place two separate drops of blood from one person on either end of a clean, dry glass slide and lay the slide on a piece of paper that has the letter *A* marked near one end of the slide and the letter *B* marked near the other end.
- Without touching the pipet to the blood, place a drop of anti-A serum on the drop of blood closest to the letter *A*. Stir the drop of blood with a toothpick. Does the blood agglutinate?   ☐ yes   ☐ no
- Repeat the above operation, using anti-B serum on the blood closest to the letter *B* and a fresh toothpick. Does the blood agglutinate?   ☐ yes   ☐ no

- What type of blood was tested? _____
  - ☐ What types of blood could safely receive the blood you tested? _____

  - ☐ What types of blood could safely be given to the person you tested? _____

R E O Hemoglobin Count

The amount of hemoglobin found in the blood determines its oxygen-carrying capacity. Because hemoglobin is a pigment, the amount of it in a quantity of blood can be measured by the color of the specimen. Although the Tallquist-Adams method has been replaced by more accurate methods of measuring hemoglobin, we will use it as a simple test.

I. Test a blood sample using the Tallquist-Adams hemoglobin count method. Follow these instructions.
- Place one drop of blood on half a section of a test paper from a Tallquist-Adams test booklet.
- Fold back the unused portion so that it absorbs the excess blood from the underside of the test paper.
- When the gloss of moisture has disappeared, match the color of the dry blood by moving it up and down behind the scale found in the test booklet. This comparison should be done in direct sunlight if possible.

21A-1 *Method of preparing a Tallquist-Adams test paper*

II. Answer the following questions regarding the blood you tested.
- What per cent category does the blood match most closely? _____
- According to the information in the test booklet, what is the significance of this category? _____

_____

*• What would this test quickly tell a physician concerning a patient? _____

_____

_____

R
E
O

Observing Blood Cells

I. Observe a preserved slide of blood.
- Be sure to observe a section of the slide where the blood is one cell layer thick. Such an area usually appears to have nothing on it when you look at it with the naked eye.
- Observe red blood cells.
  - ❑ Do you see any atypical shapes?   ❑ yes   ❑ no
  - ❑ What might account for them? _____
  _____
- Scan the slide until you find at least three white blood cells. How can you distinguish them from the red blood cells? _____
  _____

II. Draw blood cells in Area A.
- Draw three or four red blood cells and at least two white blood cells.
- Label all the features of white blood cells you can identify.

A

R E O Blood-Clotting Time

The time it takes for blood to clot is significant in surgery and other clinical procedures. If a patient's blood clots too slowly or too quickly, the physician will have difficulty in performing necessary operations during surgery. The following simple test can be used to determine blood-clotting time. You will need a large drop of very fresh, uncontaminated blood.

I. Fill a capillary tube with blood.
- Use a drop of blood about the size of a small pea that has formed on the person's finger in less than 10 seconds.
- Holding the capillary tube almost parallel to the floor, touch one end of the tube to the drop of blood.
- The blood will flow into the capillary tube. It should flow almost completely to the opposite end, without air bubbles in the tube. If it does not, either you had an obstruction in your capillary tube or the blood was not fresh. Wipe the finger with sterile cotton and try again.

II. Time the clotting.
- As soon as the tube is filled, begin timing the clotting, using either a stopwatch or the second hand on a clock.
- Wait one minute.
- Break off a short section of the capillary tube, being careful not to get broken glass in your finger.
- As you pull the broken piece away from the larger piece, look for a "holding together" of the blood within the tube. This "holding together" would be a blood clot.
- Wait 30 seconds and break off another piece, looking for the "holding together."
- Break off another piece every thirty seconds until you see the "holding together."
- Normal clotting time is from two to six minutes.

III. Answer the following questions.
- How long did it take the blood to begin clotting? _____

*• Why would some blood have a shorter clotting time than others? _____

20A-2 *Blood-clotting time*

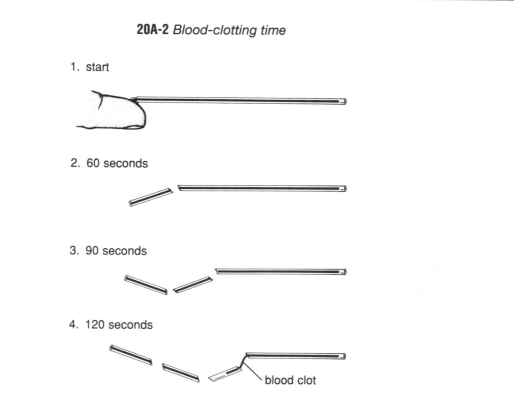

1. start

2. 60 seconds

3. 90 seconds

4. 120 seconds

blood clot

21B–**Human Circulation**

Materials: sphygmomanometer, stethoscope, stopwatch (clock with second hand)

Goals:

To learn to take a pulse
To listen to the heart
To learn how blood pressure is measured
To compare changes in the pulse rate and the breathing rate

During almost every physical exam your pulse will be taken and your blood pressure will be measured. Many different diseases or disorders will affect a person's pulse rate and blood pressure. By knowing these statistics a physician can begin to form his diagnosis of his patient's condition.

Also in this laboratory exercise you will listen to the sounds of a person's heart. Many conditions of the heart can be determined by listening to the sounds of the closing of its valves.

Counting Your Pulse and Listening to Your Heart

An irregular heartbeat is an indication of disease, disorder, or emotional trauma. One of the first things a doctor wants to know about a patient is his pulse rate. Another part of almost every physical examination is listening to sounds of the heart. In this exercise you will count your partner's pulse rate, and he will count his own heart rate while he engages in various activities. Afterwards you will compare the different rates.

Where to Find Your Pulse

Use one of the two methods described below to find your pulse. Your radial pulse can be monitored by someone else. The carotid pulse is the usual method a person uses to find his own pulse rate. (It is recommended that you learn to take a pulse using both methods.)

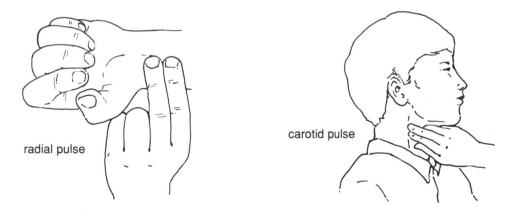

radial pulse

carotid pulse

The Radial Pulse

• Have your partner sit quietly for about 4 minutes. (Work on other sections of the lab.)
• While he is seated, find his radial pulse by placing your fingertips (not your thumb) over the place where the radial artery passes over the radius of the wrist.

The Carotid Pulse

• Sit quietly for about 4 minutes. (Work on other sections of the lab.)
• Hold your head so that your jaw is horizontal or tilted up slightly.
• Place the anterior (palm) side of your index and middle finger on the side of your neck below the jaw, under the ear, in the area of the carotid artery. Press lightly.

The Pulse and Heart Rate

R E O *I. Take a pulse.
- Determine your pulse by using a stopwatch or a clock with a second hand.
  - ❑ Count the number of pulses that take place in 15 seconds.
  - ❑ Record the number on scrap paper. Multiply by 4 to get the rate per minute.
  - ❑ Repeat the procedure two more times.
  - ❑ Average the results.
- What is your pulse rate while you are seated? _____ beats per minute

R E O II. Listen to your heart.
- While you are seated, listen to your own heart, following these instructions.
  - ❑ Using a tissue and alcohol, clean the earplugs of a stethoscope.
  - ❑ Place the stethoscope in your ears, allowing the tubes to hang freely.
  - ❑ Place the diaphragm of the stethoscope just below your third rib, slightly to the left of the sternum.
- Using a stopwatch or a clock with a second hand, count the number of beats that take place in 15 seconds.
  - ❑ A "lubb-dubb" sound counts for one beat, not two.
  - ❑ Record this number on scrap paper. Multiply by 4 to get the rate per minute.
  - ❑ Repeat the procedure two more times.

  - ❑ What is your seated heart rate? _____ beats per minute

R E O III. Compare your pulse rate and your heart rate.
- Should your pulse rate and your heart rate be the same?   ☐ yes   ☐ no

  Explain your answer. _____
  _____

- Is your pulse rate and your heart rate the same?   ☐ yes   ☐ no   If your answer
  is no, offer an explanation of why it is not the same. _____
  _____
  _____

R E O Pulse and Breathing Rates During Activity

I. The following should be completed by one member of a laboratory group. The data of this one person should be used by everyone to make his own graph (II) and answer the questions (III).
- Seated
  - ❑ You already have your subject's seated pulse rate; transfer that information to the box on the next page.
  - ❑ After having him sit quietly for 4 minutes (working on his lab), count your subject's breathing rate for 30 seconds, and multiply this number by 2. Record this information in the box on the next page.
- Standing
  - ❑ Have your subject stand quietly (while working on his lab) for 3 minutes.
  - ❑ Count his breathing for 30 seconds. Multiply the number by 2 and record the information.
  - ❑ At the same time, have him take his pulse for 15 seconds. Multiply the number by 4 and record the information.
- Walking
  - ❑ Have your subject walk the distance prescribed by your instructor. As soon as he returns, do the following:
  - ❑ Count his breathing for 30 seconds. Multiply the number by 2 and record the information.
  - ❑ At the same time, have him take his pulse for 15 seconds. Multiply the number by 4 and record the information.
- Running
  - ❑ Have your subject run the distance prescribed by your instructor. As soon as he returns, do the following:

❑ Count his breathing for 30 seconds. Multiply the number by 2 and record the information.

❑ At the same time, have him take his pulse for 15 seconds. Multiply the number by 4 and record the information.

	Seated	Standing	Walking	Running
Pulse Rate	_____	_____	_____	_____
Breathing Rate	_____	_____	_____	_____

II. Plot the preceding information on the graph below, using one color for the pulse rate and another for the breathing rate.

Pulse and Breathing Rates

	Seated	Standing	Walking	Running

200
195
190
185
180
175
170
165
160
155
150
145
140
135
130
125
120
115
110
105
100
95
90
85
80
75
70
65
60
55
50
45
40
35
30
25
20
15
10

III. Answer the following questions.
  • Between which two adjacent activities is there the largest increase in the pulse rate?

  _____   What explanation can you offer

  for this being the largest increase? _____

  _____

  • Between which two adjacent activities is there the largest increase in breathing rate?

  _____

  What explanation can you offer for this being the largest increase? _____

  _____

  _____

  • Would you expect the largest increase in pulse rate and breathing rate to be between

  the same two activities?   ☐ yes   ☐ no   Why or why not? _____

  _____

  _____

  • Based on your data, is the largest increase in pulse rate and breathing rate between the
  same two activities?   ☐ yes   ☐ no   If this is not in keeping with what you said

  you expected (in the previous question), account for the difference. _____

  _____

  _____

Measuring Your Systolic Blood Pressure

Blood pressure is the pressure of the blood against the walls of the arteries. Carefully read the section on blood pressure in your text (p. 564). Although professionals take blood pressure readings quickly and easily, the process is not as easy as it looks. Nurses in training often spend long hours learning the proper techniques. For this laboratory exercise we will deal with the systolic pressure, which is easy to determine. (Instructions for finding the diastolic blood pressure are also given for those who would like to try.)

Taking a Person's Systolic Blood Pressure
  I. Set up the sphygmomanometer.
   • Place the cuff tightly around your lab partner's arm in the area of the belly of the biceps brachii.
   • Turn the thumbscrew near the squeeze bulb until the valve is closed.
   • Have your lab partner bend his arm and place it palm up on the table.
   • Place the stethoscope earpieces in your ears. Be careful not to hit the diaphragm against any object.
   • Find your partner's radial pulse with your fingers.
  II. Take the systolic blood pressure of your partner.
   • While feeling your partner's radial pulse, squeeze the bulb repeatedly until you can no longer feel a pulse in the radial artery.

Warning! The remainder of the exercise must be done in 30 seconds. If you are unable to complete it in 30 seconds, you *must* release the pressure on the arm and permit the blood to flow freely into the arm for a minute before you try again. ***Do not cut off the circulation in the arm for more than 30 seconds.*** Also, do not flex the arm muscles while the cuff is tight. Such movements cause the mercury to rise and can destroy the sphygmomanometer.

      ❑ Keep your eye on the mercury column. The pulse should stop near 140 mm Hg.
      ❑ As soon as the pulse cuts off and you have let the mercury rise about twenty points higher on the scale, stop squeezing the bulb.
- Place the diaphragm of the stethoscope in the cubital fossa (pit in the bend of the arm).
- Partially release the thumbscrew. You will hear the air hiss out and see the column of mercury drop.
      ❑ Listen for the sound of the first spurt of blood as it passes through the partially closed artery.
      ❑ When you first hear the sound, note what number the mercury is on. (The mercury should take a quick little jump as the sound starts.)
- Immediately release the thumbscrew completely.
  Note: If you must repeat the procedure more than three times in order to do it right, switch the cuff to the other arm.

III. Answer the following questions.
- What was the person's systolic blood pressure? _____
*• Normal systolic blood pressure for adults is about 120 mm Hg; for young people it is

  slightly lower. What would you know about a person whose pressure is higher than

  that? (List three possible explanations.) _____

  _____

  _____

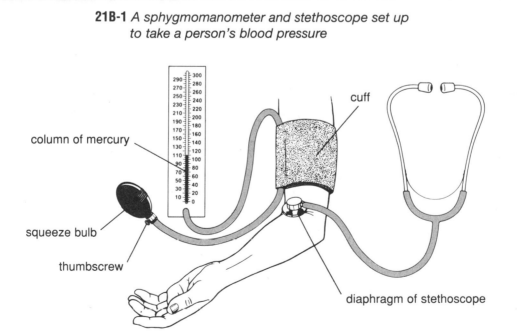

21B-1 *A sphygmomanometer and stethoscope set up to take a person's blood pressure*

column of mercury

cuff

squeeze bulb

thumbscrew

diaphragm of stethoscope

R
E
O

Taking a Person's Diastolic Blood Pressure

I. Procedure
- After taking the systolic blood pressure, instead of releasing the thumbscrew rapidly, allow the air to escape slowly.
- Continue listening to the sounds.
  - ❑ At one point the sounds will become softer and muffled.
  - ❑ At this point the level of the mercury column indicates the diastolic blood pressure.

II. Answer the following questions.
- What is your partner's diastolic blood pressure? _____

- How would that blood pressure (BP) normally be written? _____

- Is your partner's blood pressure normal for his age?   ☐ yes   ☐ no

  If not, what may account for the irregularity? _____

  _____

  _____

22A–**Human Reflexes**

Materials: reflex mallet, penlight

Goals:
>To perform some simple tests on various structures of the nervous system
>To note the clinical value of such tests to a physician

>A reflex is considered the lowest level of human behavior because it involves responses that do not involve a conscious level. In other words, your body performs reflexes without your having to think about them. As you study the reflex arc and various human reflexes, you should come to understand why they are important and how they operate.

The Reflex Arc

Reflexes originate at **receptors** found in the skin, tendons, muscles, and other body structures. When stimulated, these receptors send impulses over **sensory neurons** (*afferent neurons*) to the **central nervous system.** In the CNS, connections are often made through **interneurons** (*association neurons*) to **motor neurons** (*efferent neurons*). As impulses travel over these motor neurons, they cause **effectors** to contract, producing the reflex action. These innate (inborn) behaviors are unlearned, nearly instantaneous reactions to a single, simple stimulus.

R **Demonstrating the Knee-Jerk (Patellar) Reflex**
  I. Sit comfortably in a chair and cross your legs above the knees, or sit on a high surface so that your feet do not touch the floor. Keep the thigh of your leg relaxed.
 II. Have your lab partner tap your patellar tendon just below the patella with the reflex mallet.
   • Do not watch as the tendon is struck.

   • What is the reaction? _____
   _____
   _____
   _____

III. Try variations of the patellar reflex. Try to stiffen your bent leg so that the reflex will not work. Is it possible to tense the leg so much that the reflex will not work?   ☐ yes   ☐ no
   • Try the patellar reflex with the leg at different degrees of straightness (with the knee at different angles).
     ❑ Does this affect the strength of the reflex?   ☐ yes   ☐ no
     ❑ Does the reflex get weaker or stronger as the knee is straightened?
        ☐ weaker   ☐ stronger

R **Studying a Reflex Arc**
E
O
  I. Label on Diagram 22A-1 all the following terms: receptor, sensory neuron, axon of sensory neuron, dendrites of sensory neuron, central nervous system, interneurons, motor neuron, axon of motor neuron, dendrite of motor neuron, effector.
 II. A doctor tests reflexes for several reasons. List at least two. _____
   _____
   _____
   _____

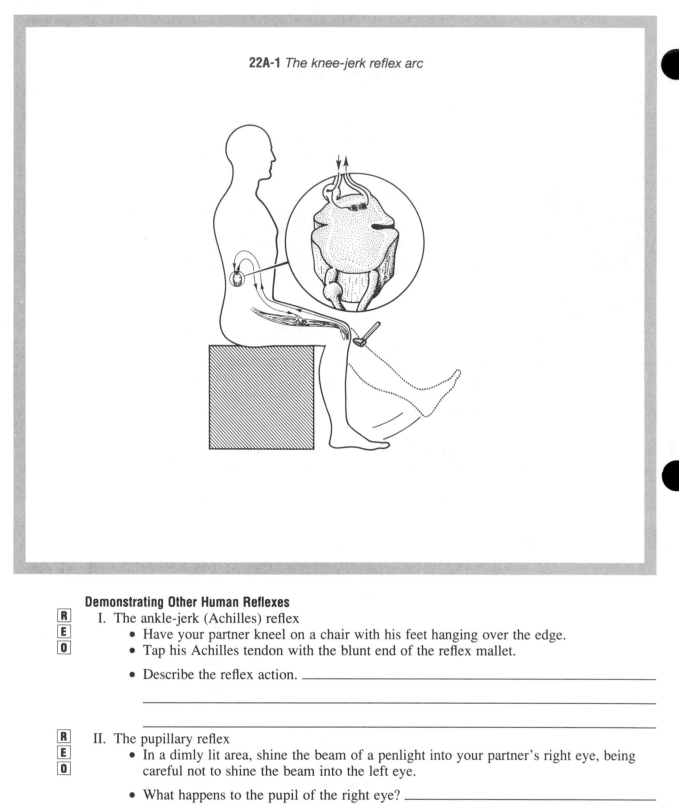

22A-1 *The knee-jerk reflex arc*

Demonstrating Other Human Reflexes

R
E
O

I. The ankle-jerk (Achilles) reflex
- Have your partner kneel on a chair with his feet hanging over the edge.
- Tap his Achilles tendon with the blunt end of the reflex mallet.

- Describe the reflex action. _____
  _____
  _____

R
E
O

II. The pupillary reflex
- In a dimly lit area, shine the beam of a penlight into your partner's right eye, being careful not to shine the beam into the left eye.

- What happens to the pupil of the right eye? _____

- What happens to the pupil of the left eye? _____
- Try the experiment again, shining the beam into the left eye this time. Are the results

  the same?   ☐ yes   ☐ no   If not, why not? _____
  _____
  _____

Name _____

Date _____   Hour _____

22B–**Minor Senses**

Materials: metal or glass rods, hot water, ice water, beakers, washable ink pen, sugar cubes, vanilla extract, cotton swabs, ruler

Goal:

To perform some simple tests on various minor senses of the human body

> Although called the minor senses–taste, smell, balance, and touch (including pressure, pain, and temperature sensation)–are all important to a person's well being. Because these senses are often not as dramatic as sight and hearing, they are often taken for granted. But if one of these senses is not working properly, a person is handicapped. In this exercise you will test some of these not-so-minor senses.

The Senses of Taste and Smell

Two closely allied senses are the senses of taste and smell. Having a cold shows you that many of the tastes you enjoy are actually smells. Try these experiments to determine some of the relationships between taste and smell.

R E O **The Taste and Smell of Sugar**

   I. Smell a sugar cube.

      • Describe the smell. _____

      • Based on the smell, what would you expect sugar to taste like? _____

      _____

   II. The taste of sugar

      • Rinse your mouth with clean water.

      • Stick your tongue out of your mouth and dry it with a paper towel.

      • Place a sugar cube on the center of your dry tongue. Do not pull your tongue back into your mouth.

      • Record the time it takes for you to taste the sugar. _____ seconds

      • Remove the sugar cube as soon as you taste it.

      • Rinse your mouth with clean water.

      • Stick your tongue out of your mouth and wet it with clean water. Do not pull it back into your mouth.

      • Place the opposite side of the *same* sugar cube on the same area of your tongue.

      • Record the time it takes to taste the sugar. _____ seconds

      • Explain the difference in the amounts of time it took to taste the sugar.

      _____

      _____

R E O **The Taste and Smell of Vanilla**

   I. Smell the vanilla extract and then describe the smell. _____

   II. Dip a cotton swab into some vanilla extract and touch the swab to your tongue. (You may

      need to touch it to several areas of the tongue.) Describe the taste. _____

      • Does vanilla extract taste the way it smells?   ☐ yes   ☐ no

      • Which sense do you think accounts for the taste we normally call vanilla (such as in

      vanilla ice cream and vanilla pudding)? _____

Sensation of Heat and Cold on the Skin

Your skin receives numerous sensations. Your sense of touch (see Laboratory Exercise 1A) involves only one set of nerves. Pain, temperature, and pressure (and possibly other sensations) are perceived by other nerve endings in the skin. In this exercise you are asked to determine whether or not heat and cold are different sensations of the same nerve or are the sensations of two different nerves.

R E O **Sensing Hot and Cold**

I. Obtain a beaker of hot water and place a blunt metal or glass rod in it. Make sure that the water is not hot enough to burn the skin. Also obtain a beaker of ice water and place a similar rod in it.

II. Test your partner's sense of hot or cold.
  - With a washable ink, place six small dots on the back of your partner's hand. On paper, diagram the hand, draw in the dots, and give each dot a letter.
  - Blindfold your partner.
  - Randomly place either the hot or cold rod on each of the six dots until every dot has been tested twice for hot and twice for cold.
    - ❏ Quickly dry the rod before you place it on the dot.
    - ❏ Touch the rods with the same pressure to the skin.
    - ❏ Leave the rods in contact with the skin for three seconds, after which your partner must tell if it was hot or cold.
    - ❏ Return the rods to the proper beaker between testings to keep them at the proper temperature.
    - ❏ Record the number of correct and incorrect responses for both hot and cold for each dot.

III. Answer the following questions.
  - Was your partner more often correct sensing hot or cold?   ☐ hot   ☐ cold
  - Were each of the dots equally sensitive to hot and cold or were some dots more prone to be correct about one temperature or the other? _____
  _____
  _____
    - ❏ If different areas were sensitive to different temperatures, what would this result suggest? _____
    _____
    - ❏ If all areas were equally sensitive to different temperatures, what would this result suggest? _____
    _____

R E O **Plotting the Sensation of Heat and Cold**

I. With washable ink, mark an area 1-inch square on the back of your partner's hand and then draw a grid in the square, dividing each side into sixths. (See the boxes below.)

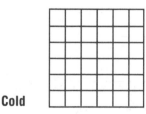
Cold

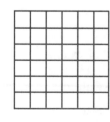
Heat

II. Using hot and cold rods as described above
  - Locate and mark on the diagram all the areas within the square that are sensitive to the cold probe.
  - Locate and mark on the diagram all the areas within the square that are sensitive to the hot probe.

III. According to your experiment, are heat and cold receptors in identical locations on the hand?   □ yes   □ no

From this fact, what can you conclude about temperature receptors? _____

_____

_____

_____

The Sense of Balance

R
E
O

Your inner ear contains the delicate structures responsible for your sense of balance. These structures are dependent upon the properties of fluids. Moving fluids are used to send the information necessary for your brain to know your position and movements. Your sense of balance is usually quite accurate, but the inner ear fluids can send impulses to your brain which do not reflect reality.

I. Test normal visual and motor coordination.
   • Have your partner sit cross-legged in a swivel chair.
   • Place your extended index finger about 20 inches in front of his chest and test his ability to touch your finger.
      ❏ Have him raise his arm above his head.
      ❏ Have him extend his index finger and quickly drop his arm until his finger comes into contact with yours. Did his finger make contact on the first try?
        □ yes   □ no
      ❏ Repeat this experiment eight times. Record the number correct. _____
   • Have your partner repeat the experiment with his eyes closed.
      ❏ Did his finger make contact?   □ yes   □ no   If not, by how much did he miss? _____
      ❏ Repeat this experiment eight times. Record the number correct. _____

II. Test visual and motor coordination after movement.
   • Quickly twirl him in the chair for 15 seconds with his eyes open.
      ❏ Stop him abruptly and try the finger-touching experiment with his eyes open.
      ❏ How many tries did it take for him to make contact as well as he did with his eyes open before twirling? _____
   • When he is no longer dizzy, have him close his eyes and repeat the twirling-chair test.
      ❏ He should then open his eyes, note where your finger is, close his eyes, raise his hand above his head, and try to make contact.
      ❏ How many tries did it take for him to make contact as well as he did with his eyes closed before twirling? _____
   • When he is no longer dizzy, repeat the twirling-chair test with his eyes closed.
      ❏ This time have him keep his eyes open as he tries to touch your finger.
      ❏ How many tries did it take him to make contact? _____

III. Answer the following questions. (Some may require careful reasoning.)
   • When did he perform better?   □ before being twirled   □ after being twirled

   Account for this, and tell what structures are responsible. _____

   _____

   _____

   _____

   _____

- How difficult was performing the following experiments compared to performing the experiment "without twirling, eyes open"?
  - ❏ Without twirling and with eyes closed while he tries to make contact

  _____

  - ❏ With eyes open while he twirls and with eyes open while he tries to make

  contact _____

  - ❏ With eyes closed while he twirls and with eyes closed while he tries to make

  contact _____

  - ❏ With eyes closed while he twirls and with eyes open while he tries to make

  contact _____

- What would account for these differences in difficulty? _____

  _____

  _____

  _____

22C–The Eye and the Ear

Materials: Snellen eye chart, swivel chair, penlight, red and green cellophane, white paper, Holmgren color vision test, tuning forks of assorted frequencies (including 128 and 256 cps)

Goals:

To perform some simple vision and hearing tests

To note the clinical value of such tests to a physician

Often, a minor shortcoming of an individual's vision or hearing may go unnoticed for years. For example, an astigmatism in one eye may be compensated for by the other eye so that a person may not be aware that he has blurred vision. Some people who have red-green color blindness (one of the most common forms of color blindness) do not realize it until they are adults. In this laboratory exercise you will perform some simple tests on your eyes and ears.

The Eye and Sight

Vision is one of the senses on which humans rely most. It is also more prone to minor disorders than are other senses. In the following exercises, you will perform some simple tests on your vision (or your lab partner's vision).

*Structures of the Eye

I. Examine your partner's eye (or your own eye in a mirror) and identify the following structures. Give definitions where required.
   - Lids: flaps of tissue which cover the eyes
   - Conjunctiva: _____
   - Openings of nasolacrimal ducts: openings of the tubes (ducts) that carry tears from the eyes into the nose
   - Cornea: _____
   - Sclera: _____
   - Pupil: _____
   - Iris: _____

II. Label as many structures of the eye as possible on Diagram 22C-1 on the next page.

Snellen Test for Visual Acuity

A person's visual acuity (visual sharpness) can be tested with a Snellen eye chart, which consists of rows of black letters of different sizes printed on a white card. Beside each line of letters is printed the distance from which those letters can be read by the normal eye.

Check your visual acuity
   - Remove glasses. (If it is convenient, remove contact lenses.)
   - Stand 20 feet from the chart and cover your left eye with your hand.
   - Have your lab partner point out the line of letters that is marked "20 feet." Read the lines as your partner checks to see if you are correct. If you can read most of the letters on this line correctly, you have 20/20 vision for that eye.
       - If you are able to read the line marked "20," try the next smaller line. Continue until you can no longer read most of the letters accurately.

22C-1 *The eye*

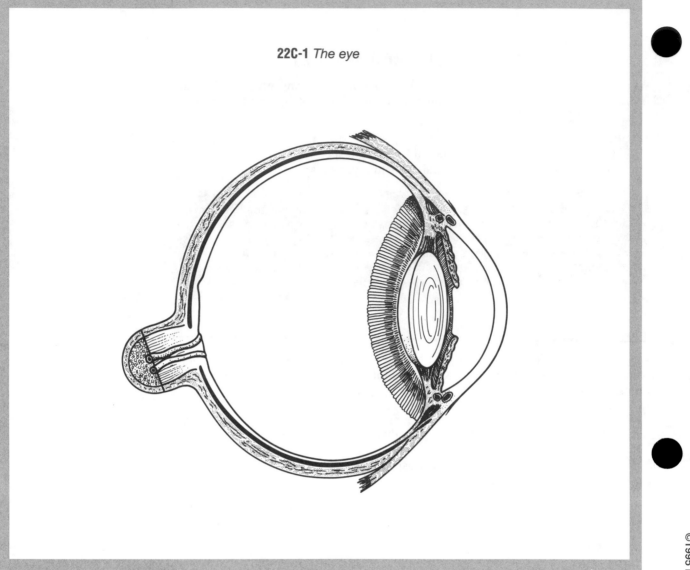

□ If you cannot read the line marked "20," have your partner point to the line with the next larger size of type, and so on, until you can read accurately most of the letters on the line that he indicates. (Your partner should point out the letters of the line at random so that you do not memorize the order of the letters.)

□ Check the reading recorded for your right eye's vision: □ 20/15   □ 20/20   □ 20/25   □ 20/30   □ 20/40   □ 20/50   □ 20/70   □ 20/100   □ 20/200

• Repeat this test, covering your right eye to test your left eye's vision. Check the reading recorded for your left eye's vision: □ 20/15   □ 20/20   □ 20/25   □ 20/30   □ 20/40   □ 20/50   □ 20/70   □ 20/100   □ 20/200

[R]
[E] **Testing for Astigmatism**
[O]
*I. Define astigmatism. _____

_____

II. Check yourself for astigmatism.
• Cover your left eye and hold the diagram for testing astigmatism (Diagram 22C-2) about 6 inches in front of your right eye.
• Look directly into the center of the empty circle of the diagram. Be sure your pupil is directly over the central white area.
• If any of the lines appear blurred, you probably have an astigmatism in the corresponding area of your right eye.

- Do you have an astigmatism in your right eye?   ☐ yes   ☐ no   If so, in which areas (indicated by numbers at ends of lines)? _____
- Repeat the procedure, covering the right eye and observing with the left eye.
- Do you have an astigmatism in your left eye?   ☐ yes   ☐ no   If so, in which areas? _____

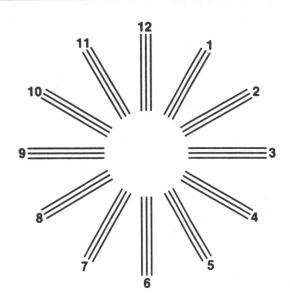

22C-2 *Test for astigmatism*

[R] **Demonstration of the Blind Spot**
  I. Read about the blind spot on pages 594-95 of your text.
  II. Find your blind spot by using Diagram 22C-3.
    - Position the diagram so that the dot is to the right of the plus sign (+).
    - Hold the diagram about 18 inches from your eye, with the plus sign *directly* in front of your right eye. Cover your left eye.
    - Move the diagram slowly toward you as you stare at the plus sign. At a certain point the dot will disappear. The dot is then in your blind spot.
    - Have your partner measure the distance from your eye to the paper. What is the distance? _____
    - Repeat for your left eye. With the dot to the left, place the plus sign directly in front of your left eye and cover your right eye. What is the distance? _____
  III. What effect would the blind spot have on a person who has only one eye? Should such a person be allowed to drive?   ☐ yes   ☐ no   Why or why not? _____
_____
_____
_____

22C-3 *Blind spot test*

Visual Accommodation

*I. Read about visual accommodation on page 595 in your text.

II. Demonstrate visual accommodation.
- Have your partner look at an object across the room while you hold a pencil about 18 inches in front of his nose. Then ask him to look at the pencil.
- What was the change in the size of the pupils? _____
- Did his eyes move in any other way?   □ yes   □ no   If so, how?

_____

III. Demonstrate near-point accommodation.
- Another important part of accommodation is *near-point accommodation*. The near point is the closest distance at which sharp focus is attained.
- Determine the near point of your eyes by covering your left eye and focusing with your right eye on the *D* at the beginning of this sentence.
  - ❏ Move this page toward your right eye until the letter no longer appears sharp and clear.
  - ❏ Move the page away until the letter is clear again.
  - ❏ Have your partner measure the distance from the page to your eye.
- Repeat the process for the left eye.
- Record your near-point accommodation distance:

  Left eye: _____   Right eye: _____

- The near-point accommodation distance increases with age because the lens of the eye loses its elasticity.
  - ❏ Is your near-point accommodation distance normal for your age?   □ yes   □ no
  - ❏ When a person can no longer focus on the print of a book at a ''comfortable'' distance (about 20 inches), he needs reading glasses. Based on your present near-point accommodation distance, at about what age should you expect to need reading glasses?

    _____ years old

Average Near-Point Accommodation Distance by Age
10-20 years–3 $\frac{1}{2}$ inches
20-30 years–4 $\frac{1}{2}$ inches
30-40 years–6 $\frac{3}{4}$ inches
40-50 years–20 $\frac{1}{2}$ inches
50-60 years–33 inches

Afterimages

I. An *afterimage* is the image that a person sees after he stops looking at an object. Such images are most common after looking at an object which is in sharp contrast to its background.
- A *positive afterimage* is one that is the same color as the object observed.
- A *negative afterimage* is the complementary color. Negative afterimages are caused by ''bleaching'' (fatigue of visual pigments).

II. Observe afterimages.
- Sit in a darkened area.
- Flash a penlight into one eye for not more than one second. Then close your eyes. Is the afterimage positive or negative?   □ positive   □ negative
- Holding a piece of red cellophane between the light and the eye, flash a penlight into one eye for not more than one second. Then close your eyes. Is the afterimage positive or negative?   □ positive   □ negative
- Repeat this test, using a piece of green cellophane. Is the afterimage positive or negative?   □ positive   □ negative
- Shine a penlight steadily into one eye for about 20 seconds and then quickly look at a piece of white paper. (Blinking your eyes will help the appearance of the afterimage.) Is the afterimage positive or negative?   □ positive   □ negative
- Holding a piece of red cellophane between the light and your eye, repeat this test. Is the afterimage positive or negative?   □ positive   □ negative
- Repeat this test, using a piece of green cellophane. Is the afterimage positive or negative?   □ positive   □ negative

Testing for Colorblindness

I. The Holmgren color vision test consists of a set of colored wool strands that matches a set of mounted wool strands.

> *NOTE:* More specific and more accurate tests must be taken to determine colorblindness accurately. The Holmgren test merely indicates that other tests may be necessary. Even a very poor performance on the Holmgren test may not mean that a person is colorblind.

II. Ask your partner to match the loose strands with the mounted ones as rapidly as possible.
- As you administer the test, note any of the following reactions in your partner:
  - ❑ Hesitation before placing a colored strand by the one it matches
  - ❑ Comparisons (laying a strand beside various mounted threads to determine which one it matches)
  - ❑ Mistakes (whether or not they are corrected)
- If your partner shows any of these reactions, note which colors caused the problems.
- Did you show colorblindness tendency?   ❑ yes   ❑ no

  If so, in what color range? _____

Hearing

You depend greatly on your sense of hearing. The ear plays a vital role in sound perception. Your ears tell you more than just the kind and volume of sound, as some of these experiments will demonstrate.

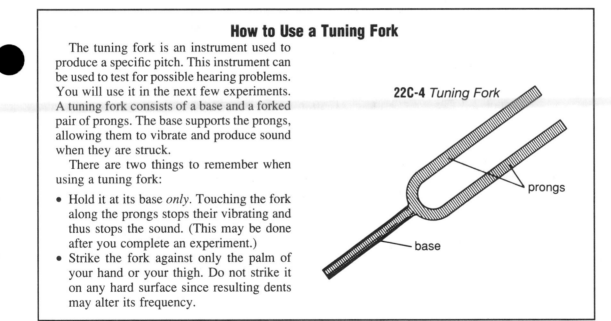

How to Use a Tuning Fork

The tuning fork is an instrument used to produce a specific pitch. This instrument can be used to test for possible hearing problems. You will use it in the next few experiments. A tuning fork consists of a base and a forked pair of prongs. The base supports the prongs, allowing them to vibrate and produce sound when they are struck.

There are two things to remember when using a tuning fork:

- Hold it at its base *only*. Touching the fork along the prongs stops their vibrating and thus stops the sound. (This may be done after you complete an experiment.)
- Strike the fork against only the palm of your hand or your thigh. Do not strike it on any hard surface since resulting dents may alter its frequency.

22C-4 Tuning Fork

prongs

base

[R]
[E]
[O] **Testing Your Hearing**

I. Localizing sound

- Sit quietly with your eyes closed.
- Your partner will strike the fork on his hand and hold it 8 to 10 inches away from the sides, top, and then back of your head.
- As he moves the fork to different positions around your head, *point* to the direction from which the sound is coming. (Talking drowns out the sounds made by the tuning fork; the room where you do this should be quiet.)
- Your partner may need to strike the tuning fork each time he moves it.
- Were you able to locate sound near the sides of your head?   □ yes   □ no
  Back of your head?   □ yes   □ no   Top of your head?   □ yes   □ no
- Place your index finger over the opening of one of your ears and repeat the experiment.
  - Was there any change in the results?   □ yes   □ no
  - Why or why not? _____

[R]
[E]
[O] II. Bone conduction

- Conduction of sound through the skull
  - Sit quietly and plug both ears with your fingers.
  - Your partner will strike the tuning fork and rest the base of the fork on the top of your head without touching the prongs.
  - Signal by a slight movement of your head when you hear the fork.
  - Your partner will remove the fork. Can you still hear the sound?   □ yes   □ no
  - Your partner will immediately replace the tuning fork on your head. Can you hear the sound?   □ yes   □ no
- Conduction of sound through the teeth
  - Your partner will rinse and dry both the tuning fork and his hands. He will strike the fork and place its base (not the vibrating prongs) between your teeth while you plug your ears. Only the teeth should come into contact with the tuning fork. (Your lips should not touch it.) Can you hear the sound?   □ yes   □ no
  - Remove the fork and wipe it dry.
  - Is there any difference between the sounds heard in these bone conduction experiments?   □ yes   □ no   If so, how did the sounds differ?

    _____

- Conduction of sound through the temple
  - Sit quietly and plug both ears with your fingers.
  - Your partner will strike the tuning fork and place its base against your right temple. Do you hear the sound?   □ yes   □ no
  - Now repeat the test on the left temple. Do you hear the sound?   □ yes   □ no
  - Was there any major difference between what you heard when the right temple was tested and what you heard when the left was tested?   □ yes   □ no

    Give the probable reason for your answer. _____

    _____

Testing for Deafness

Deafness can result when structures malfunction in any of three different areas: within the parts of the ear that conduct the sound waves (eardrum, ossicles, and other structures), within the nerves and sensory cells of the inner ear, or within the central nervous system. In class, we will perform tests for the first two types of deafness.

Often sound-conduction deafness affects only one ear. This *unilateral* (one-sided) *sound-conduction deafness* is caused by a blockage of sound waves. A person is said to have *acoustic nerve deafness* if he cannot hear because of problems in his inner ear.

I. Test for unilateral sound-conduction deafness.
- While you sit quietly, your partner will strike a 128 or 256 cps tuning fork and carefully place the base of the fork on the center of your forehead.
- Where does the sound seem loudest? ☐ right ☐ center ☐ left
- If you hear the sound better in the left ear or the right ear, you may have sound-conduction deafness. This type of deafness eliminates the background noise that a normal ear hears. Because there is less surrounding noise to distract a sound-conduction-deaf ear, the sound heard from the tuning fork on the skull registers more volume in that ear.
    - Is there a tendency toward sound-conduction deafness in your right ear?
      ☐ yes ☐ no
    - Is there a tendency toward sound-conduction deafness in your left ear?
      ☐ yes ☐ no
- What can correct unilateral sound-conduction deafness? _____
  _____

II. Test for acoustic nerve deafness
- While you are sitting quietly, your partner will strike a 128 or 256 cps tuning fork and carefully place the base of the fork on the center of your forehead.
- Plug your right ear. In which ear is the sound heard loudest?
  ☐ right ☐ left ☐ no difference
- Repeat the experiment, this time plugging the left ear. In which ear is the sound heard loudest? ☐ right ☐ left ☐ no difference
- If the right ear is plugged and the sound is heard better in the left ear, there may be nerve deafness on the right side. Sound conducted through the skull is naturally transmitted better (louder) to a plugged ear than to an open ear. If the sound is heard louder in the *unplugged* ear, some difficulty other than conduction must be causing the problem.
    - Is there any tendency toward acoustic nerve deafness in your right ear?
      ☐ yes ☐ no
    - Is there any tendency toward acoustic nerve deafness in your left ear?
      ☐ yes ☐ no
- What can be done for acoustic nerve deafness? _____
  _____
  _____

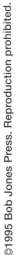

23–Drugs in Our Culture

Materials: library

Goals:

To learn about the physical effects of various psychotropic drugs

To learn about the effects of psychotropic drugs in our culture

According to many people, psychotropic drugs are one of the major problems faced by our culture. Drugs begin with mental effects, but soon they physically affect the one who takes them. In many cases these drugs cause mental, emotional, and physical scars that may trouble the drug user for the rest of his life. The drug abuse also affects his family and his friends in different, often serious, and always harmful ways.

The economic effect on our society involves not only the money exchanged on the black market but also the millions spent on law enforcement and public and private rehabilitation. It is estimated that the yearly cost of the productivity lost to drugs in the work place is in the hundreds of millions of dollars.

In this exercise you (or a group of students, if your class does this exercise as a group project) will select or be assigned a drug to research. Only when one knows about the psychotropic drugs and their effects can one make intelligent decisions about drug-related concerns in our complex society. It may be easy for you to decide not to be involved with drugs. But since drugs pervade our society, you will need to make decisions regarding everything from the spending of public money to counseling friends regarding their position on drugs and related issues. This project is designed to help you to be ready for these problems.

Drugs and Their Effects

I. Select a drug (or a group of drugs) and research the effects of the drug.

- Use a library's catalogue to locate books that contain information about the drug. Read those parts that contain pertinent information.
- Consult the *Reader's Guide to Periodical Literature* for the past several years to find articles containing information about the drug. Read those that contain pertinent information.
- Information regarding drugs and their use is frequently available from physicians, hospitals, pharmacists, law enforcement authorities, drug rehabilitation centers, and government agencies responsible for drug education. Consult these or other similar sources regarding material about the drug.
- Try to find the following information about the drug. Be more specific than the information found in the text.
    - ❏ Briefly describe the history of the drug. Who first used it? Where? When was it introduced to the modern drug culture?
    - ❏ List the physical symptoms caused by the drug. Distinguish between long-term and short-term effects and between those experienced by "casual users" and "heavy users."
    - ❏ List the drug's mental/emotional effects that cause people to want to take it. Describe these effects on both "casual users" and "heavy users."
    - ❏ How is the drug taken? What problems does a person who uses this drug encounter because of the way it is taken?
    - ❏ What is the source of the drug (synthetic, a foreign country, etc.)? How difficult is it to produce/refine?
    - ❏ Are there international difficulties (problems between governments) because of the illegal trade of this drug? How extensive are they?

□ How much is spent by government agencies (federal, state, local) to control the supply of this drug? How effective is the control? Is there a "short supply" of the drug because of these control efforts?

□ What kinds (groups) of people use this drug? (level of education, age, economic group, etc.) How often and how much of this drug do the different groups use?

□ What kinds of drug education programs are aimed at people not using this drug? What kind of drug education programs are aimed at people using this drug? Are the drug education programs considered effective?

□ Approximately how many people use (or are addicted to) the drug in the U.S., in your state, in a nearby major city?

□ How much does the drug cost ("street price") for a single dose? to support a "casual" or mild habit? to support a major addiction?

□ What kind of drug rehabilitation is offered for abusers of this drug? How much does this rehabilitation of one individual cost? How effective is it? Who pays for this rehabilitation?

□ Does this drug have legitimate medical uses? What are they? What measures do physicians take to make sure their patients do not abuse this drug?

II. Prepare a report about the information you find.

- Written reports
  □ Write a 3- to 5-page report on the drug you researched.
    ○ The introduction and conclusion of your report should be in paragraph form.
    ○ The main part of your report can be in paragraph form or it can be in the form of a list of statements dealing with the answers to the questions asked above.
  □ Include a complete bibliography of the sources from which you obtained information.

- Oral report
  □ Prepare a 4- to 7-minute oral report on the drug you researched.
  □ The oral report should cover as many of the questions presented above as possible.
  □ Be sure to include references to any source other than printed sources from which you obtained information. (In other words, you do not need to tell about library research sources, but if you talked to someone about this material, you should mention him as part of your report.)
  □ Details for an oral report
    ○ Visual aids are not required but may improve the group's grade.
    ○ Present material that would be interesting and valuable to the class.
    ○ If you read your report, points will be deducted from your grade. You may use notes.
    ○ If done by a group:
      ◆ All group members do not need to speak.
      ◆ The grade will be the same for each member of the group, no matter which aspect of the report he prepared.
      ◆ Prepare your presentation together before it is due.
      ◆ *Each group must be prepared on its assigned date.* Only the absence of all group members will postpone your oral report. If one member of a group is absent, the others must go ahead and present the report. Otherwise, your teacher will impose severe grade penalties.
    ○ Creativity in your presentation is encouraged. If you (or members of your group) feel that the proposed presentation may not be acceptable, check the proposal with your teacher.

24–Chicken Embryology

Materials: fertilized chicken eggs, incubator, scissors, dropping pipet, shallow dishes (finger bowls or large culture dishes), forceps, physiological saline, scalpel

Goals:

To observe chicken embryos at different levels of development
To compare the embryonic growth rate of different structures
To learn about various embryonic structures

> Embryology is the study of the process through which a single cell grows, divides, and gives rise to thousands of individual cells of many different types. In a relatively short time, these individual cells are able to work together to sustain life. Although embryology is a fascinating study, little is known about the process by which cells with identical genetic make-up can become so diverse as to form bone, muscle, liver, thyroid gland, and cartilage. Equally little is known about how cells develop in the right places so that they all fit together in a workable, complete organism. Other than descriptive statements, such as "Cells in this area form a lump that becomes the so-and-so," very little can be said. The embryo is too tiny for general observation, and any experimentation greatly affects it. Those intricate chemical messengers that turn genes on and off to cause cell differentiation elude man's clumsy methods of study, at least at this time.
>
> In this laboratory exercise we will look at several stages of the embryological growth of a chicken egg in an attempt to observe some of these marvels.

Incubating Chicken Eggs

Fresh, fertilized eggs can be kept at a cool room temperature without incubation for several days. This lowered temperature temporarily stops the embryo's development. Then, when the eggs are placed in an incubator set at 38° C (100° F), embryonic growth starts again. If incubated for 26 days, normal, fertilized chicken eggs will hatch.

Before the laboratory period begins, eggs should be placed in an incubator at intervals so that on the appointed day the egg will have been incubated the proper amount of time. For this exercise, about 4 different embryonic stages are recommended. Eggs incubated 4, 9, 12, and 14 days would be ideal. For large classes, however, eggs incubated 3, 6, 9, 12, 15, and 18 days could be used.

Several eggs should be incubated for each time period desired so that if one is infertile or if an accident should happen, there are still other eggs to observe. With a pencil, mark on each egg the date and time that its incubation began. Twice a day during the incubation period the eggs should be turned over so that the chick embryos do not become attached to their shell. A shallow pan of water should be kept in the incubator so that the eggs do not dehydrate.

The class should be divided into groups, with each group responsible for opening an egg of a different age. Once the eggs have been opened, each student should observe all the eggs and record his observation in the proper spaces on page 198.

Opening a Chicken Egg

Eggs Incubated 3 to 9 Days

I. Without rolling the egg, take it from the incubator. The embryo should be on top of the yolk. If you cut and remove the top part of the shell, you should be able to find the embryo without having to rotate the yolk.

II. With the egg lying on its side, draw an oval on the egg as illustrated in Diagram 24-1.

III. Carefully insert the point of a pair of scissors a short distance through the shell and cut *cautiously* around the oval.

IV. Using forceps, remove the loose piece of shell and locate the embryo.
- If the embryo is not visible, use forceps to grasp the chalaza (see the diagram on p. 434 of your text) and rotate the yolk.
- With a dropping pipet, remove some albumen in order to see the embryo more easily.
- With eggs incubated 4 to 9 days, you will need to cut the amnion to see the embryo clearly. Be sure the other students see these membranes before you cut them.

24-1 *Opening an egg incubated less than 10 days*

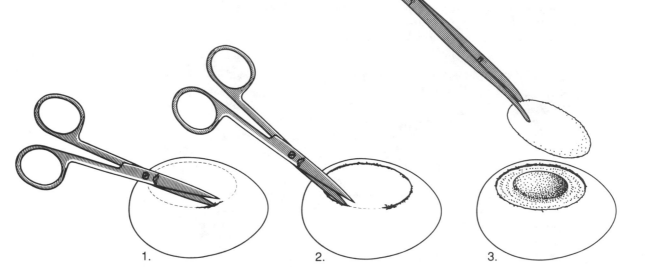

1.   2.   3.

Eggs Incubated More Than 10 Days

I. Obtain the eggs from the incubator.
II. Tap the large end of the egg with the handle of a pair of scissors or a scalpel to crack the shell. (See Diagram 24-2.)
III. Using forceps, pick away the shell, being careful not to break the shell membrane.
- After a portion of the shell has been removed, place the egg in a shallow dish of physiological saline.
- Continue picking off the shell until it is completely removed.
IV. After observations have been made with the shell membrane intact, break the shell membrane and observe the structures inside.
V. Various membranes will need to be cut before the embryo is clearly visible. Be sure the other students in the class see the membranes before you cut them.

24-2 *Opening an egg incubated more than 10 days*

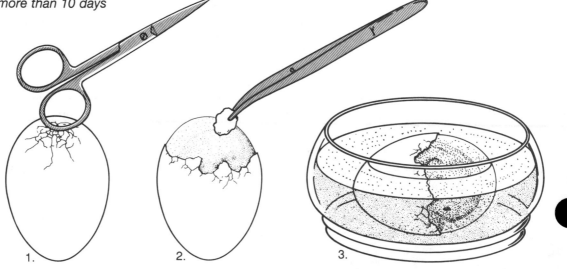

1.   2.   3.

Observing a Chicken Embryo

I. Look for these structures as you observe:

- **Yolk and yolk sac:** The yolk is the stored food for the embryo. Blood vessels formed by the embryo grow to encircle the yolk sac. As the yolk is used, the yolk sac decreases in size.
- **Shell membrane:** The shell membrane is just inside the eggshell and surrounds the albumen (egg white).
- **Amnion and amniotic fluid:** See page 416 of the text.
- **Allantois:** See page 416 of the text.
- **Somites:** Somites are lumps of tissue along the back of the young embryo. These structures develop into the vertebrae, ribs, and muscles of the chicken's body. The column of somites extends beyond the area of the arm and leg buds. But as the body grows, the arm and leg buds appear to move to their proper positions.
- **Blood, heart, and blood vessels:** Blood is one of the first obvious tissues formed by the embryo. The heart is one of the first organs formed. It begins as a pumping tube, which then twists back on itself and becomes a four-chambered pumping organ. At first it is outside the body, but later it is enclosed in the body cavity. Visible blood vessels go to various egg structures to accomplish different functions.
- **Brain and spinal cord:** The heads of embryos are generally large in comparison to their bodies. The spinal cord is one of the first organs to be recognizable.
- **Limbs:** Starting as bumps on the sides of the body, the limbs slowly take form. Feathers, claws, and scales form before the chick hatches.
- **Eyes and ears:** The eyes form early in embryonic development. They are complex organs that must be able to function when the chick is hatched. Eyelids form after the eyes do and then grow closed over the eyes. The ear openings can be found along the neck.
- **Mouth and beak:** The mouth begins as an opening to a hollow tube. The tube becomes the alimentary canal. In time, the opening of the tube becomes a mouth and then develops a beak and an egg tooth. The egg tooth is a structure that the chick uses to break the shell when it hatches.

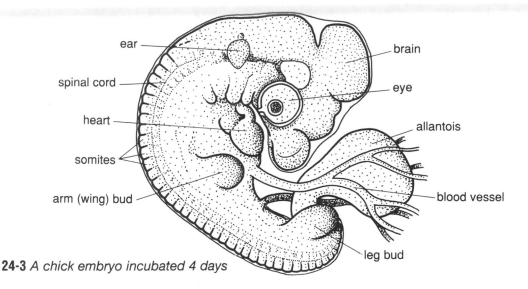

24-3 *A chick embryo incubated 4 days*

II. Record your observations on the Embryo Development chart.

- Read the summary (p. 198) to find out what types of observations you need to make.
- Be sure that you observe all the eggs when they are first opened, and record any observations you may have at that time.
- Observe the embryos when they have been removed from their protective membranes.
- In the spaces provided on the Embryo Development chart, describe extensively the development of each of the structures listed.

Chicken Embryo Development

Structures	Time	Days	Days	Days	Days	Days	Days
Yolk and yolk sac							
Amnion and amniotic fluid							
Allantois							
Somites							
Blood, heart, and blood vessels							
Brain and spinal cord							
Limbs							
Eyes							
Ears							
Mouth and beak							

Summary

R E O
I. Prepare a report (1-2 pages) discussing the changes in the yolk, yolk sac, amnion, amniotic fluid, and allantois of the chicken eggs you observed. Keeping in mind the functions of these structures, give probable reasons for the changes you observed.

R E O
II. Prepare a report (1-2 pages) discussing the development of the heart, blood, blood vessels, brain, spinal cord, and somites of the chicken embryos you observed. Describe their changes as the embryo becomes larger. Keeping in mind the function of each of these structures in the adult chicken, give probable reasons for the different rates of growth you observed.

R E O
III. Prepare a report (1-2 pages) discussing the relative developments of the front and back limbs, eyes, ears, mouth, and beak of the chicken embryos you observed. Keeping in mind what a chick has to do as soon as it is hatched, explain why the sequence of development in each of these structures is logical or not logical.

Laboratory Final Examination
The Frog

Materials: preserved frog, dissection pan, dissection kit, pins, reference materials, mounted frog skeleton, plastic bag

Goals:
   To demonstrate, as a final exam project, the level of your laboratory skills
   To review the subphylum Vertebrata, class Amphibia, as well as human anatomy and physiology
   To learn about the frog

The "Frog Lab" (as this laboratory final examination will be called) will serve as a final test of your laboratory skills. The value of this lab will be 120 points. These points will be earned through written quizzes and the demonstration of laboratory skills. This laboratory exercise has no blanks to fill in, no drawings to make, and no illustrations to label. Instead, you are asked to know the answers to the questions and to know the material presented. Whether or not you have learned this material will be indicated by how well you do on the quizzes.

You will have your own specimen for dissection and will be graded individually on all parts of the Frog Lab. Your ability to follow directions and your skills in performing laboratory procedures can then be judged by the quality of your work. You must do your own work. You may consult your classmates or your instructor about information sources or directions, but you must do the dissection yourself. You are encouraged to study with other students, quizzing one another over the material, to prepare for the quizzes.

Contents

Preparation for the Frog Lab

   I. Preliminary procedures
      • Read the *entire* Frog Lab before you come to class.
      • Read completely Chapter 16 in your text.
      • Plan to read and consult other texts as you work on the Frog Lab. **You will not find in your text all the information you need to know to complete the dissections and the quizzes successfully.** The books listed on page 200 are recommended; your instructor may suggest others.

Suggested References for the Frog Lab

Boolootian, Richard A., and Stiles, Karl A. *College Zoology.* 9th ed. New York: Macmillan Publishing Company, Inc., 1976.

Gilbert, Stephen G. *Pictorial Anatomy of the Frog.* Seattle: University of Washington Press, 1965.

Hickman, Cleveland P. et. al. *Integrated Principles of Zoology.* 6th ed. St. Louis: C. V. Mosby Company, 1979.

Storer, Tracy I., and Usinger, Robert L. *General Zoology.* 5th ed. New York: McGraw-Hill Company, 1972.

Underhill, Raymond A. *Laboratory Anatomy of the Frog.* 4th ed. Dubuque, Iowa: Wm. C. Brown Publishers, 1980.

Wells, T. A. G. *The Frog: A Practical Guide.* New York: Dover Publications, 1964.

II. Order of work
- This lab *must* be done in the order presented in the table of contents.
- The Muscle, Bone, and Skin Quiz; the Systems-Functions Quiz; and the Frog Master Quiz are your primary opportunities to earn points.
- While you are taking the Muscle, Bone, and Skin Quiz and the Systems-Functions Quiz, the quality of your dissection skill will be judged, and points will be awarded for your dissection work.
- You may take the quizzes at any time during the time allotted for the Frog Lab.
  - You may study your dissected frog for as long as you wish before coming to take a quiz.
  - You must take the quiz before you go on to the next section of the lab.
  - Allow yourself enough time to complete the quiz. Once you begin a quiz, it *counts,* whether you finish it or not.
- Plan ahead for the lab times.
  - You will work on the Frog Lab in class from _____ to _____.
  - Your instructor may announce additional times that the laboratory will be open

    for work on the Frog Lab. They include _____

    _____.
  - The entire Frog Lab must be finished and the Score Sheet handed in by

    _____ P.M. on _____.

III. Special notes
- *Scores and time planning*
  On the Score Sheet are listed the values of the various sections of the Frog Lab. Occasionally a student will spend days skinning the frog. Removing the skin in one piece is valued at only five points. To spend so much time skinning the frog, therefore, is unwise. After reading the Frog Lab, make a schedule to help you budget your time.
- *Frogs like moist habitats*
  As you work on your frog, keep it moist. As it is exposed to the air, it dries out and becomes brittle, breaking easily and costing valuable points.
- *Frogs for the night*
  When storing your frog overnight, place its internal structures in its body cavity and then wrap the entire organism in a *very wet* paper towel. Place this in a plastic bag. Remove as much air as possible, close the bag tightly, and tie it shut. Write your name on the bag with a pen or marker.
- *A souvenir of your biology days*
  You may keep your dissected frog after the dissection if you wish. Place it in a small jar of alcohol, and it will keep for years. Otherwise, when you are finished with a portion of it *and your work has been graded,* you may wrap it in a paper towel and throw it away.

©1995 Bob Jones Press. Reproduction prohibited.

External Structures of the Frog

I. You should know the external structures of a frog well enough to do the following:
- Identify on your specimen each of the structures listed below. Know how each structure operates and what its functions are. Know the system to which each structure belongs.
  1. Nostrils
  2. Nictitating membrane
  3. Tympanic membrane
  4. Forelimb
  5. Hind limb
  6. Anus
  7. Mouth (Buccal cavity)
     a. Maxillary teeth
     b. Vomerine teeth
     c. Internal nares (nostril openings)
     d. Tongue
     e. Opening of Eustachian tube
     f. Opening to vocal sac
     g. Glottis
     h. Opening to esophagus
  8. Skin
- Be able to answer the following questions about the frog's external structures:
  - ❏ Do the nostrils connect with the buccal cavity? If so, of what importance is this connection?
  - ❏ How do frogs make noise (croak)?
  - ❏ How do frogs breath (take in and force out air)?
  - ❏ How many toes does a frog have on its forelimbs? on its hind limbs? What are the toes like? What is the ratio of their extended length to the length of the leg? Compare toes on the hind limb and forelimb.
  - ❏ What causes the skin of the frog to have color? to change color?
  - ❏ Frogs are said to have thin, moist skin. Explain what keeps the skin moist and why it is thin.
  - ❏ What is important about the thumbs of a frog?

II. Tips for study
- You should make several quick diagrams of these external structures.
- As you do your research, jot down notes about pertinent facts you discover and list any questions you have.
- Use these diagrams and notes as a study guide when preparing for the quizzes.

Skinning the Frog

I. Removing the skin of the frog
- Make a cut on the ventral side of your frog from the lower abdomen to the lip (Diagram FL-1, from point A to point D).
- From this cut (line AD) make extensions toward the ends of the extremities of the limbs (lines BF and CE, both right and left sides).

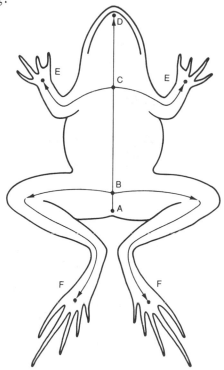

FL-1 *Removing frog skin*

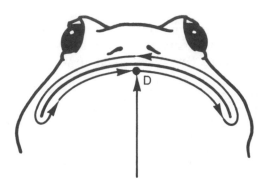

FL-2 *Cutting around the lips*

- Starting at the previous cut to the lip (point D), cut the skin around the lips (Diagram FL-2).
- Remove the frog's skin.
  - ❏ Be careful around the eyes, tympanic membranes, and anus, where additional cuts may be necessary.
  - ❏ Mesenteries (connective tissues) and blood vessels hold the skin of the frog to its body. Most of these will pull apart easily. A few will need to be cut.
  - ❏ The skin of the front and hind feet will come off like gloves. Do not leave skin on the toes.
  - ❏ The skin of the frog should come off in *one* piece.

II. Saving and getting credit for the skin of the frog
- Wrap all of the frog skin in a wet paper towel and save it until you are ready to take the Muscle, Bone, and Skin Quiz.
- As you take the Muscle, Bone, and Skin Quiz, your instructor will grade your frog skin. He will be looking for the following:
  - ❏ Directions followed accurately
  - ❏ Neatness
  - ❏ The skin taken off in one piece without being torn

Bones and Muscles

I. Bones
- Learn the bones of the frog.
  - ❏ Study carefully Diagram FL-3.
  - ❏ Study carefully the mounted frog skeleton in the classroom.
- Note these facts about the frog skeleton.
  - ❏ Know the structures in Diagram FL-3. The structures you are asked to learn are basically the same structures you learned for humans.
  - ❏ There are several differences between human skeletons and frog skeletons, all of which you should recognize. Note the differences in the areas listed below:
    1. Ribs
    2. Number of vertebrae
    3. Ilium
    4. Radius and ulna; tibia and fibula
    5. Carpals and tarsals
    6. Sternum
    7. Clavicle and scapula (suprascapula)

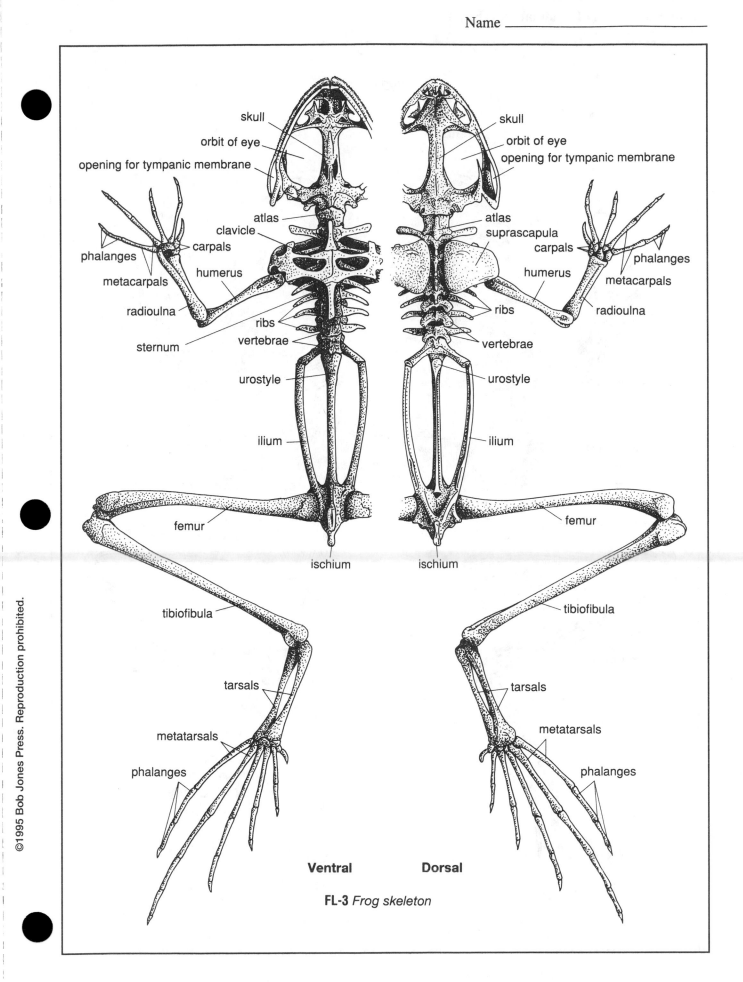

skull

orbit of eye

opening for tympanic membrane

skull

orbit of eye

opening for tympanic membrane

atlas

clavicle

carpals

phalanges

metacarpals

humerus

radioulna

sternum

atlas

suprascapula

carpals

phalanges

metacarpals

humerus

radioulna

ribs

vertebrae

urostyle

ribs

vertebrae

urostyle

ilium

ilium

femur

femur

ischium

ischium

tibiofibula

tibiofibula

tarsals

tarsals

metatarsals

metatarsals

phalanges

phalanges

Ventral

Dorsal

FL-3 *Frog skeleton*

FL-4 *Frog muscles*

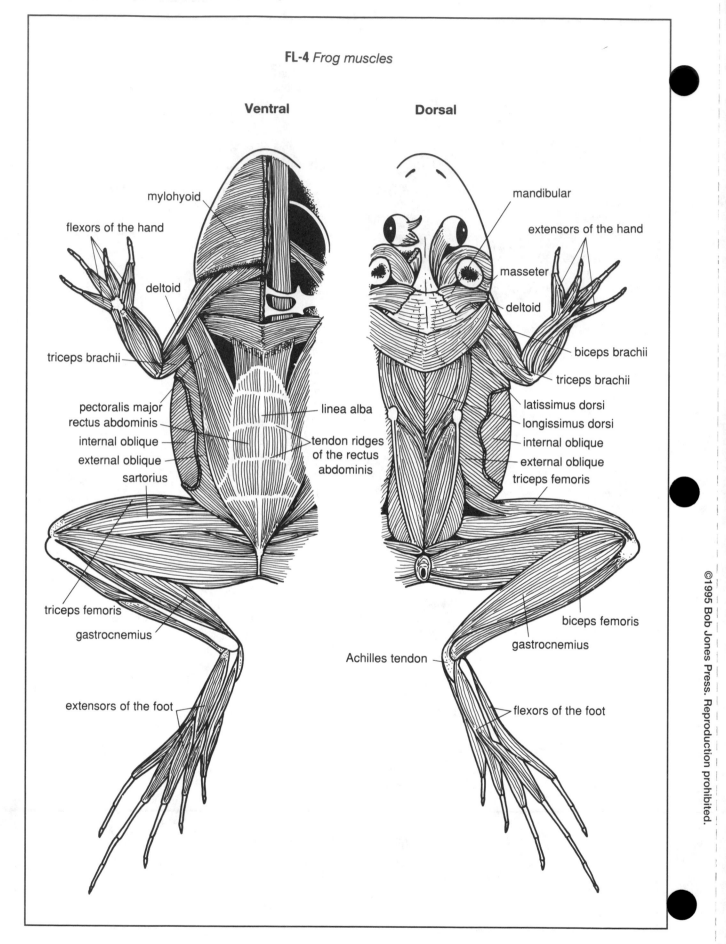

Ventral

- mylohyoid
- flexors of the hand
- deltoid
- triceps brachii
- pectoralis major
- rectus abdominis
- internal oblique
- external oblique
- sartorius
- triceps femoris
- gastrocnemius
- extensors of the foot
- linea alba
- tendon ridges of the rectus abdominis

Dorsal

- mandibular
- extensors of the hand
- masseter
- deltoid
- biceps brachii
- triceps brachii
- latissimus dorsi
- longissimus dorsi
- internal oblique
- external oblique
- triceps femoris
- biceps femoris
- gastrocnemius
- Achilles tendon
- flexors of the foot

Muscles of the Frog

Name	Origin	Insertion	Function
Biceps brachii *(flexor antibrachii)**	Proximal humerus	Proximal radioulna	Flexes forearm
Biceps femoris *(iliofibularis)*	Ilium	Tibiofibula	Extends thigh and flexes leg
Deltoid	Scapula, clavicle	Humerus	Abducts arm
External oblique	Scapula, vertebrae	Sternum, linea alba	Compresses abdomen
Gastrocnemius	Distal femur	Achilles tendon to metatarsals	Flexes leg and extends foot
Internal oblique *(transversus)*	Ilium, vertebrae	Sternum, linea alba	Compresses abdomen
Latissimus dorsi	Dorsal skin, vertebrae	Humerus	Extends arm posteriorly; rotates arm
Longissimus dorsi	Urostyle	Skull, vertebrae	Elevates head; extends back
Mandibular	Skull (near tympanic membrane)	Mandible	Lowers mandible
Masseter	Zygomatic process	Mandible	Raises mandible
Mylohyoid	Margin of mandible	Central tendon of mylohyoid	Raises floor of the mouth (breathing)
Pectoralis major	Sternum, rectus abdominis	Upper humerus	Adducts shoulder forward
Rectus abdominis	Pubic symphysis (of pelvic bone)	Sternum	Compresses abdomen; flexes trunk
Sartorius	Pubis	Tibiofibula	Flexes thigh at hip; flexes leg
Triceps brachii *(anconeus)*	Scapula	Radioulna	Extends forearm
Triceps femoris (includes the rectus femoris)	Ilium	Tibiofibula	Extends leg; flexes thigh
Extensors of the hand	Radioulna (dorsal)	Carpals and metacarpals (dorsal)	Extend hand
Extensors of the foot	Tibiofibula (ventral)	Tarsals and metatarsals (ventral)	Extend foot
Flexors of the hand	Radioulna (ventral)	Carpals and metacarpals (ventral)	Flex hand
Flexors of the foot	Tibiofibula (dorsal)	Tarsals and metatarsals (dorsal)	Flex foot

*Muscle names in italics are used in some books and are included here for reference.

II. Muscles
- Learn the muscles of the frog.
  - ❑ Be able to identify the muscles listed in the chart on page 205 and illustrated in Diagram FL-4 when they are pointed out.
  - ❑ Be able to list the origin and insertion of each muscle.
  - ❑ Be able to demonstrate the function of each muscle.
- Observe these notes about frog muscles.
  - ❑ The muscles and structures you are asked to know are basically the same as the ones you learned for humans.
  - ❑ Muscle functions in the frog are often different from those in the human because of the difference between the body positions. The origins and insertions, however, are generally the same.
  - ❑ You will need to make no further cuts on your frog to be able to see all of the muscles indicated, with the exception of the internal oblique.
  - ❑ The masseter may have been torn as you opened the mouth of the frog to see the structures inside.
  - ❑ You may use your probe to locate and slightly separate the muscles.

III. Review: You and your classmates can study these structures by pointing them out for each other and asking questions (about function, modification, origin, and so forth) until you have mastered the material.

Muscle, Bone, and Skin Quiz

I. About the quiz
- The Muscle, Bone, and Skin Quiz is a written 15-point quiz that includes specimens with numbered labels.
- You may take the quiz anytime you wish, and you may spend as much time on it as you need. (Average time is about 15 minutes. Check the clock before you begin to make sure you have adequate time to complete the quiz.)

II. Taking the quiz
- When you come to obtain your copy of the quiz from the instructor, bring the following:
  - ❑ Your dissection pan, containing the skinned frog and the frog skin
  - ❑ Your Score Sheet
- While you take the quiz, your frog skin will be graded and your score entered on the Score Sheet.
- When you have finished the quiz, hand it in and pick up your dissection pan and Score Sheet.

III. After the quiz
- ***Do not discuss the content of the Muscle, Bone, and Skin Quiz with anyone.***
- Your score on the quiz will be given to you as soon as it is graded, and you will have a chance to review it at that time.
- You will have no further need of your frog skin and may discard it if you wish.

Opening the Frog's Body Cavity

I. Words of warning
- Be careful not to cut the internal organs as you make the incisions described below.
- *Do not* cut off limbs or any other structures unless you are instructed to do so.
- There are many ways to open the body cavity (coelom) of a frog. The method described below is recommended. It usually results in fewer damaged organs.

II. Making the incisions
- Cut along the linea alba from the lower part of the rectus abdominis (Diagram FL-5, point A) to the lip (point D).
  - ❑ You will need to cut around the sternum (point B to point C).
    - ○ You will need to cut through bone in this area.
    - ○ Be careful not to cut so deeply that you damage the heart.

❑ When cutting in the area of the mylohyoid, be careful not to damage other structures in the mouth.

- Carefully cut from above the sternum to just above the shoulders on both sides (point C to point E).
- Carefully cut laterally from just above the origin of the rectus abdominis (point F) to the dorsal surface of the sides (point G).
- The forelimbs of the frog should be bent dorsally, breaking the sternum and opening the flaps of the body wall to reveal the internal organs.

FL-5 *Opening the frog's body cavity*

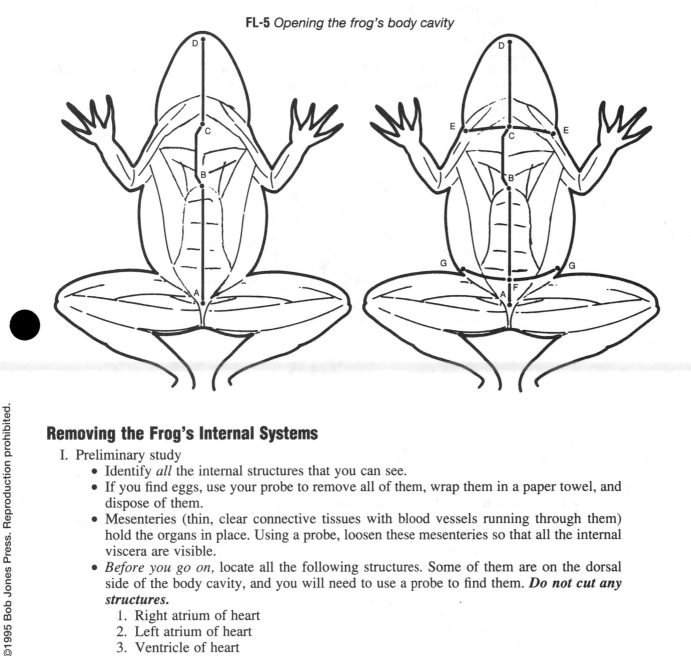

Removing the Frog's Internal Systems

I. Preliminary study
- Identify *all* the internal structures that you can see.
- If you find eggs, use your probe to remove all of them, wrap them in a paper towel, and dispose of them.
- Mesenteries (thin, clear connective tissues with blood vessels running through them) hold the organs in place. Using a probe, loosen these mesenteries so that all the internal viscera are visible.
- *Before you go on,* locate all the following structures. Some of them are on the dorsal side of the body cavity, and you will need to use a probe to find them. ***Do not cut any structures.***
  1. Right atrium of heart
  2. Left atrium of heart
  3. Ventricle of heart
  4. Venae cavae
  5. Artery leading from heart
  6. Liver
  7. Stomach
  8. Small intestine
  9. Colon (large intestine)
  10. Spleen

11. Mesenteries
12. Trachea
13. Lungs
14. Pulmocutaneous artery and pulmonary vein
15. Gall bladder
16. Bile duct
17. Hepatic portal vein
18. Kidneys
19. Fat bodies
20. Adrenal glands
21. Ovaries or testes (Ovaries may have been removed with the eggs.)
22. Urinary bladder
23. Spinal cord

- As you begin your dissection of the various systems, remember that *each part must be entire and connected with the rest of the system* if you are to receive full credit for the dissection.

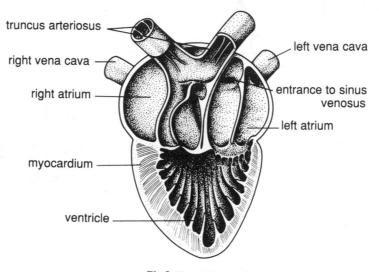

FL-6 *Frog heart, l.s.*

II. Removing the circulatory system
- It is easy to remove the heart. But identifying its structures *after* it has been removed from the body cavity can be difficult. *While it is in its natural position,* identify each of the following:
    1. Truncus arteriosus
    2. Right and left atria
    3. Ventricle
    4. Right and left anterior venae cavae
    5. Posterior vena cava
    6. Sinus venosus
    7. Pulmonary vein
- Be able to trace the blood flow through the frog's heart and to tell the oxygen content of the blood at all the various stages of the cardiac cycle of the frog.
- Remove the heart with as much of each blood vessel as possible (approximately $\frac{1}{2}$ inch).
- Wrap the circulatory system structures in a wet paper towel, and set them aside for further study and evaluation.

III. Removing the respiratory system
- Identify the structures of the respiratory system.
  - ❏ Locate the lungs, found dorsal to the digestive system.
  - ❏ The trachea is very short and connects the lungs. It is sometimes helpful to put a probe down the proper opening of the mouth in order to find the trachea.

NOTE: Some students find it better to remove the digestive and respiratory systems together (see the instructions below on how to remove the digestive system) and then to separate the systems when they are both out of the body cavity. This may be advisable, especially with smaller frogs.

- Cut the trachea as near the buccal cavity as possible.
  - ❏ Do *not* cut the alimentary canal or damage the spine or spinal nerves.
    - ○ The alimentary canal will be removed in another section.
    - ○ If you cut into the back, the nerves will be damaged.
  - ❏ If the trachea is cut properly, the lungs will come out attached to each other.
  - ❏ Mesenteries holding the trachea and the alimentary canal together should be removed.
- Study carefully the method the frog uses to breathe.
  - ❏ Are the lungs large enough to obtain oxygen for the frog's entire body?
  - ❏ Without a diaphragm and a rib cage, how does the frog force air into and out of its lungs?
  - ❏ How do frogs make the "croaking" sound?
- Wrap the respiratory system in a wet paper towel and save it for future study and evaluation.

IV. Removing the digestive system
- Carefully cut the lining of the mouth as close to the lips as possible. This will permit the mouth *with the tongue attached* to be removed as part of the alimentary canal. (See Diagram FL-7.)

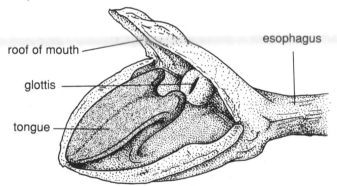

roof of mouth

esophagus

glottis

tongue

FL-7 *Frog mouth as removed for Frog Lab*

- Cut the large intestine just *above* the place where the urinary bladder joins the alimentary canal. Be careful *not* to cut the urinary bladder or any other structure.
  NOTE: Students sometimes ruin kidneys, fat bodies, and other structures of the urogenital system or nervous system by carelessly removing them with the digestive system.
- Carefully separate any mesenteries connecting digestive organs to parts of the urogenital system and the vertebrae.
- The entire digestive system–with the liver, gall bladder, spleen, and pancreas intact– should now come out of the body cavity. (*Note:* Diagram 16C-6 on p. 408 of your text does not show the mouth with the digestive system, *but your specimen should.*)

- Slowly tease the mesenteries with your probe so that the alimentary canal can be straightened.
    - Be careful not to cut the bile duct or pancreatic duct. The liver and the pancreas should be attached to the alimentary canal at the proper place (the duodenum).
    - The spleen is attached to the digestive system only by mesenteries. Leave it attached.
- Know all the structures of the digestive system (Diagram 16C-6, p. 408 of the text) and their functions. The functions are the same as in humans.
- Be able to answer the following questions:
    - How long is the alimentary canal?
    - How long is it in relation to the length of the frog?
    - Is this proportional to the relationship between human height and the length of the human alimentary canal?

V. Removing the urogenital system
- The excretory system and the reproductive system (along with parts of the endocrine, digestive, and other systems) will count as one system, the urogenital system.
- Carefully locate the following structures, which will be considered part of the urogenital system:
    1. Fat bodies
    2. Dorsal aorta and vena cava
    3. Renal arteries and veins
    4. Testes or ovaries (If eggs have been removed, ovaries have usually been destroyed.)
    5. Kidneys
    6. Adrenal glands (difficult to see)
    7. Ureters
    8. Vasa efferentia (difficult to see)
    9. Oviducts or seminal vesicles (Oviducts may have been destroyed when the eggs were removed.)
    10. Urinary bladder
    11. Cloaca
    12. Anal opening
- Cut the mesenteries connecting these structures to the body wall.
    - Be careful not to cut the ureters, the oviducts, the vasa efferentia, or the renal arteries and veins.
    - Carefully lift the urogenital system from the body wall.
    - *Do not* disturb the spinal nerves, which are directly under these organs.
- Cut the cloaca below the place where the urinary bladder attaches to it. Be careful not to cut any nerves.
- Cut the dorsal aorta and the vena cava just anterior to the top of the kidneys. Be careful not to cut any nerves.
- Remove the urogenital system as a unit.
- Know all the structures of the urogenital system listed above and their functions. They are basically the same as those of humans.
- Wrap the urogenital system in a wet paper towel and save it for future study and evaluation.

VI. Removing the nervous system
- Observe the nerves as they appear in the dorsal area of the body cavity.
    - Compare them with Diagram 16A-3 on page 391 and 16C-8 on page 410 of the text and Diagram FL-8. Be sure you know the labeled structures.
    - Note the color and texture of the nerves.
- Follow the spinal nerves as they branch down the limbs.
    - Cut away the muscles and the bones of the limbs. Muscles and bones may be discarded. If possible, trace the nerves to the toes.
    - Keep the structures moist.

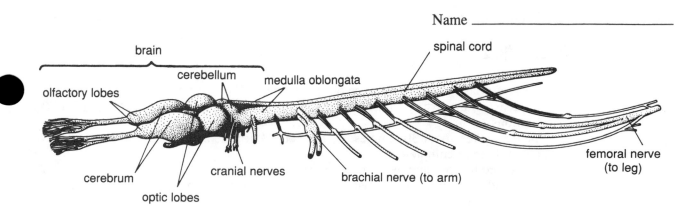

FL-8 *Nervous system of the frog*

- Remove enough of the skull to reveal the brain.
  - ❏ Removing the dorsal side of the skull is recommended; however, you can also reveal the ventral side of the brain.
  - ❏ A good way to get to the brain is by cracking the skull with the handle end of the scalpel and then carefully removing the pieces of the skull. *Be careful;* the brain is easily damaged.
  - ❏ All the brain lobes should be visible.
- Cut away the tissue around the anterior end of the frog so that only the muscle-covered skull and vertebral column (with nerves coming out of it) remain.
- Cut away one or two of the vertebrae on the dorsal side to reveal the spinal cord.
- Know all the structures and functions of the nervous system in Diagram 16C-8 on page 410 of your text. They are basically the same as the structures and functions in humans. Include olfactory nerves, nasal sac, and spinal nerves (not labeled in text).
- Note the eyes and tympanic membranes of the frog and know their structures and functions.
- Wrap the nervous system in a wet paper towel and save it for future study and evaluation.

Systems-Functions Quiz

I. The quiz
   - The Systems-Functions Quiz is a written 15-point quiz involving labeled specimens.
   - Follow the instructions for taking the Muscle, Bone, and Skin Quiz (p. 206), but this time present the dissected frog systems in your dissection pan, as illustrated in Diagram FL-9.

II. After the quiz
   - *Do not discuss the content of the Systems-Functions Quiz with anyone.*
   - You will have no further need of your frog, and you may discard it or put it in a jar to keep. Frog parts should be put *in the trash,* not down the drain.

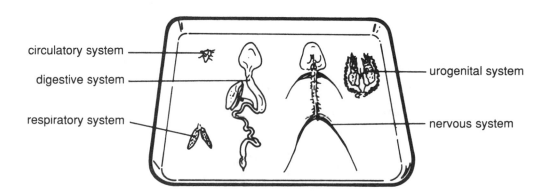

FL-9 *Dissected frog (all systems dorsal side up)*

Frog Master Quiz

I. The quiz
- The Frog Master Quiz is a written 60-point quiz (half of the total value of the Frog Lab) that does not involve specimens but does have drawings, objective questions, and essay questions.
- The quiz takes about 30 minutes. Before you ask for the quiz, make sure that you have enough time to complete it.
- To prepare for the quiz, be sure to do the following:
  - ❑ Read the supplemental materials suggested in the Frog Lab and know what you have read.
  - ❑ Know the structures mentioned in the Frog Lab and their functions.
  - ❑ Know the answers to all questions asked in the Frog Lab.

II. Taking the quiz
- When you are ready, ask your instructor for the quiz. You will need a blank sheet of paper on which to write your essay answers.
- When you hand in the Frog Master Quiz, attach your Score Sheet to it. You are now finished with the Frog Lab.
- *Do not discuss the content of the Frog Master Quiz with anyone.*

Laboratory Final Examination
Score Sheet

I. Grading of dissection and taking quizzes
   - Present this Score Sheet to your instructor when you come to take your Muscle, Bone, and Skin Quiz and when you come to take your Systems-Functions Quiz.
   - Leave the Score Sheet with your dissected frog so that scores for your laboratory skills can be recorded.
   - After you have taken the quiz and it has been graded, take the score sheet with your quiz score on it and *keep it in a safe place*. (You will lose points if you lose this sheet.)

II. Taking the Frog Master Quiz
   - You must turn in this Score Sheet attached to the Frog Master Quiz.
   - You must turn it in by _____ on _____ to receive any credit for your Frog Lab.
   - You need to turn in only this sheet with the Frog Master Quiz. You should not turn in the rest of the Frog Lab or any dissected frog parts.

Scores

Quizzes	Points Possible	Points Missed
• Muscle, Bone, and Skin Quiz	15	_____
• Systems-Functions Quiz	15	_____
• Frog Master Quiz	60	_____

Skills	Points Possible	Points Missed
• Skin	5	_____
• Circulatory System	4	_____
• Digestive System	5	_____
• Respiratory System	3	_____
• Urogenital System	4	_____
• Nervous System	5	_____
• General Skill	4	_____
Total	120	_____
Grade		_____

Life Process Chart

Organism _____

Phylum _____ Class _____ Genus _____

Structure   **Notes**

Movement *(structures responsible for movement, types of movement)*

Body Covering *(what covers the body, how it protects the animal)*

Support *(structures responsible for support, what they are made of)*

Nutrition *(structures of digestion, methods of ingestion, types of food, assimilation)*

Respiration *(structures used in gas exchange for respiration)*

Structure	Notes

Circulation *(structures responsible for internal movement of substances)*

Excretion *(structures for the collection and elimination of soluble wastes)*

Responses *(structures for receiving stimuli and for responses, level of responses)*

Reproduction–Asexual *(structures for and types of asexual reproduction)*

Reproduction–Sexual *(structures for sexual reproduction)*

Other Notes *(habitat, size range, unusual examples, etc.)*

Life Process Chart

Organism _____

Phylum _____ Class _____ Genus _____

Structure   **Notes**

Movement *(structures responsible for movement, types of movement)*

Body Covering *(what covers the body, how it protects the animal)*

Support *(structures responsible for support, what they are made of)*

Nutrition *(structures of digestion, methods of ingestion, types of food, assimilation)*

Respiration *(structures used in gas exchange for respiration)*

Structure	Notes

Circulation (*structures responsible for internal movement of substances*)

Excretion (*structures for the collection and elimination of soluble wastes*)

Responses (*structures for receiving stimuli and for responses, level of responses*)

Reproduction–Asexual (*structures for and types of asexual reproduction*)

Reproduction–Sexual (*structures for sexual reproduction*)

Other Notes (*habitat, size range, unusual examples, etc.*)

Name _____

Life Process Chart

Organism _____

Phylum _____ Class _____ Genus _____

Structure   **Notes**

Movement *(structures responsible for movement, types of movement)*

Body Covering *(what covers the body, how it protects the animal)*

Support *(structures responsible for support, what they are made of)*

Nutrition *(structures of digestion, methods of ingestion, types of food, assimilation)*

Respiration *(structures used in gas exchange for respiration)*

Structure	Notes

Circulation *(structures responsible for internal movement of substances)*

Excretion *(structures for the collection and elimination of soluble wastes)*

Responses *(structures for receiving stimuli and for responses, level of responses)*

Reproduction–Asexual *(structures for and types of asexual reproduction)*

Reproduction–Sexual *(structures for sexual reproduction)*

Other Notes *(habitat, size range, unusual examples, etc.)*

Life Process Chart

Organism _____

Phylum _____ Class _____ Genus _____

Structure   **Notes**

Movement *(structures responsible for movement, types of movement)*

Body Covering *(what covers the body, how it protects the animal)*

Support *(structures responsible for support, what they are made of)*

Nutrition *(structures of digestion, methods of ingestion, types of food, assimilation)*

Respiration *(structures used in gas exchange for respiration)*

Structure	Notes

Circulation *(structures responsible for internal movement of substances)*

Excretion *(structures for the collection and elimination of soluble wastes)*

Responses *(structures for receiving stimuli and for responses, level of responses)*

Reproduction–Asexual *(structures for and types of asexual reproduction)*

Reproduction–Sexual *(structures for sexual reproduction)*

Other Notes *(habitat, size range, unusual examples, etc.)*

Life Process Chart

Organism _____

Phylum _____ Class _____ Genus _____

Structure   **Notes**

Movement *(structures responsible for movement, types of movement)*

Body Covering *(what covers the body, how it protects the animal)*

Support *(structures responsible for support, what they are made of)*

Nutrition *(structures of digestion, methods of ingestion, types of food, assimilation)*

Respiration *(structures used in gas exchange for respiration)*

Structure	Notes

Circulation (*structures responsible for internal movement of substances*)

Excretion (*structures for the collection and elimination of soluble wastes*)

Responses (*structures for receiving stimuli and for responses, level of responses*)

Reproduction–Asexual (*structures for and types of asexual reproduction*)

Reproduction–Sexual (*structures for sexual reproduction*)

Other Notes (*habitat, size range, unusual examples, etc.*)

Life Process Chart

Organism _____

Phylum _____ Class _____ Genus _____

Structure   **Notes**

Movement *(structures responsible for movement, types of movement)*

Body Covering *(what covers the body, how it protects the animal)*

Support *(structures responsible for support, what they are made of)*

Nutrition *(structures of digestion, methods of ingestion, types of food, assimilation)*

Respiration *(structures used in gas exchange for respiration)*

Structure	Notes

Circulation *(structures responsible for internal movement of substances)*

Excretion *(structures for the collection and elimination of soluble wastes)*

Responses *(structures for receiving stimuli and for responses, level of responses)*

Reproduction–Asexual *(structures for and types of asexual reproduction)*

Reproduction–Sexual *(structures for sexual reproduction)*

Other Notes *(habitat, size range, unusual examples, etc.)*

Name _____

Life Process Chart

Organism _____

Phylum _____ Class _____ Genus _____

Structure   **Notes**

Movement *(structures responsible for movement, types of movement)*

Body Covering *(what covers the body, how it protects the animal)*

Support *(structures responsible for support, what they are made of)*

Nutrition *(structures of digestion, methods of ingestion, types of food, assimilation)*

Respiration *(structures used in gas exchange for respiration)*

Structure	Notes

Circulation (*structures responsible for internal movement of substances*)

Excretion (*structures for the collection and elimination of soluble wastes*)

Responses (*structures for receiving stimuli and for responses, level of responses*)

Reproduction–Asexual (*structures for and types of asexual reproduction*)

Reproduction–Sexual (*structures for sexual reproduction*)

Other Notes (*habitat, size range, unusual examples, etc.*)

Name _____

Life Process Chart

Organism _____

Phylum _____   Class _____   Genus _____

Structure   **Notes**

Movement *(structures responsible for movement, types of movement)*

Body Covering *(what covers the body, how it protects the animal)*

Support *(structures responsible for support, what they are made of)*

Nutrition *(structures of digestion, methods of ingestion, types of food, assimilation)*

Respiration *(structures used in gas exchange for respiration)*

Structure	**Notes**

Circulation *(structures responsible for internal movement of substances)*

Excretion *(structures for the collection and elimination of soluble wastes)*

Responses *(structures for receiving stimuli and for responses, level of responses)*

Reproduction–Asexual *(structures for and types of asexual reproduction)*

Reproduction–Sexual *(structures for sexual reproduction)*

Other Notes *(habitat, size range, unusual examples, etc.)*